guide to the

PYRAMIDS
OF EGYPT

ALBERTO SILIOTTI
Preface by ZAHI HAWASS

To Jean-Philippe Lauer, who dedicated
his life to the study and reconstruction
of the archaeological site at Saqqara

THE AMERICAN UNIVERSITY IN CAIRO PRESS

CONTENTS

Texts and photographs
Alberto Siliotti
(Translation by A.B.A., Milan)

Preface and comments by
Zahi Hawass

Editorial coordination
Valeria Manferto De Fabianis
Laura Accomazzo

Graphic design
Patrizia Balocco Lovisetti
Deborah Michelon

1 The pyramids of Giza in a 17th century engraving.

2-3 The pyramids of Giza, shown here from the south, were built during the Fourth Dynasty on a limestone plain in the desert. In the foreground is the pyramid of Menkaure, preceded by three small satellite pyramids, while farther north are the great pyramids of Kafre and Khufu. The Giza plateau was one of the necropolises of Memphis, the capital of Egypt during the Old Kingdom. Today UNESCO has added the entire archeological area of Giza to its World Heritage list.

4 The great Sphinx of Giza has become a monument to and symbol of Egyptian civilization. Its mysterious appearance and the absence of any inscriptions have led to fanciful theories on its real origins and true age.

5 Among the masterpieces of the Old Kingdom are the so-called Triads of Menkaure, five groups of statues found in 1908 during excavations made in the lower temple area of the pyramid of Mycerinus. In each group the pharaoh is represented with the goddess Hathor (on his right), and a deity which personifies a nomo, *an administrative province of ancient Egypt.*
On the backgroung can be observed the pyramid of Kafre.

First published in Egypt in 1997 by
The American University in Cairo Press
113 Kasr el Aini Street
Cairo, Egypt

This edition published by arrangement with
White Star S.r.l. - Vercelli, Italy

Dar el Kutub No 5207/97
ISBN 977 424 446 X

Printed in Italy

PREFACE

by Zahi Hawass

*T*here are many people who believe that a great civilization predates the current chronology for ancient Egyptian Dynasties. But no single piece of material culture, not a single object nor piece of an object, has been found at Giza that can be interpreted as coming from a lost civilization. Instead we find an abundance of tombs, bodies, ancient boats, hieroglyphic inscriptions, pottery, bakeries and so on, from the Egyptian culture of the Fourth Dynasty, about 2500 BC. In archaeology we have no evidence for an advanced civilization prior to about 3200 BC. Theories and speculations about a lost civilization seem to excite people more than the discovery of the culture that we actually find at Giza and elsewhere in Egypt, the culture of Egyptians of whose existence we are certain. It was a great culture. Why do people need to look for another? As scientists we keep an open mind, but we have to base our ideas about the past on archaeological evidence.

6 top The face of Khafre in the great diorite statue which Mariette found in the pyramid's lower temple, expresses the calm majesty typical of sculptures from the Old Kingdom. (Cairo Museum)

6 bottom Menkaure, here shown in one of the famous stelae known as the Triads, succeeded Khafre. He is responsible for building the so-called third pyramid of Giza. (Cairo Museum)

6-7 Standing out against the horizon, the three massive pyramids seem to emerge from the limestone rocks of the Giza plateau.

INTRODUCTION

Unique among the seven wonders of the ancient world in having survived the ravages of time, the great pyramids of Giza continue to dazzle and inspire the countless stunned visitors who tour these immense masses of stone, grandiose testimony to the extraordinary civilization that flourished in the Nile Valley between the fourth and the third millennia.

Herodotus travelled through Egypt in the fifth century BC and was fascinated by the pyramids. He can be considered as the first western historian to study the Nile civilization, and wrote at length about these monuments and the pharaohs who built them in the second book of his *Histories*. In fact he recounted numerous falsehoods that have become firmly rooted in the collective conscience: the tens of thousands of slaves who laboured under the whips of the slave-drivers are, in fact, the fruit of his occasionally vivid imagination.

Napoleon, on the eve of the celebrated Battle of the Pyramids, was also enchanted by the pyramids and, rallying his troops, pronounced the famous phrase, 'Men, up there forty centuries are watching you'. Meanwhile the scholars who travelled with his expedition incredulously recorded that the three pyramids of Giza were so huge that the material used in their construction would be sufficient to build a wall around the whole of France.

It is difficult to explain the mysterious power that undoubtedly emanates from the pyramids of Giza and which has been responsible for rivers of ink from those who have constructed fantastic hypotheses about their function: treasure chests of lost knowledge, books of stone concealing obscure mathematical, astronomical or esoterical messages, receivers of cosmic energy ...

A veil of mystery still lies over the pyramids as, despite all the research and studies carried out to date, we still do not know with any certainty how they were really constructed: strangely the ancient Egyptians left us no records of their techniques, and hypotheses are all we can safely put forward. Recent excavations and research have, on the other hand, thrown new light on the life that went on around the pyramids – on the lives of the workers who built them, and those of the dignitaries who lived at court and were worthy of a last resting place alongside their king. Although the pyramids of Giza are the most famous in Egypt, the symbol and glory of the Fourth Dynasty, there are others that are actually older and no less grandiose. At Saqqara in the Third Dynasty, the legendary and later deified architect Imhotep constructed for the pharaoh Djoser a prototype stepped pyramid that was later perfected and developed by his successor Snefru at Meidum and at Dashur, the latter a site only opened to the public in late 1996.

This guide presents, for the first time, a comprehensive and exhaustive description of all the principal pyramids and the great Memphite necropolises of the Old Kingdom in the light of the most recent excavations and research. Thanks to an abundant collection of maps, plans and reconstructions, readers can explore the civilization that developed on the banks of the Nile between the fourth and third millennia BC.

D

EGYPT IN THE OLD KINGDOM

BEFORE THE PYRAMIDS
(3200–2635 BC)

Around the end of the period of Naqada II, the long process of development which had begun during the fourth millennium BC culminated with the creation of a monarchy, a state, an architecture and the first signs of writing. As it created a king and a centralized government, Egypt left the prehistoric period and entered a period usually known as the **predynastic** period, Thinite period or period of Naqada III.

The formation of increasingly large proto-urban centers had become necessary due to a growing aridity that required inhabitants of the area to find sites better adapted to neolithic settlements and life. This led to the strengthening of central power and the development of a leader who became a king, responsible for organizing, regulating and protecting his city. His power was expressed through emblems and legitimized through his relationship to a superior entity, the god.

This set the foundations for the future pharaonic civilization, where the king was the leader of a centralized system, the cornerstone of which was the royal palace, a concept so important that eventually sovereign and his palace (in Egyptian designated by the word *per-aa*, 'the great house') were considered one and the same, giving rise to the word *pharaoh*. The architecture and religion that would become, and remain, a state religion – a group of devotional acts that would legitimate the power of the king as a mediator between the divine and human, sky and earth – were thus born.

A class of officials aided the king in governing both the country and its economy, and a head of this oligarchy soon arose, known by the end of the Second Dynasty as the *tjaty* or vizier.

The period which precedes the formation of these first so-called Thinite dynasties (from Thinis, where according to the historian Manetho the first kings originated), is still obscure: it is known that there were numerous sovereigns and that Egypt was divided into two realms, one in the South and one in the North, which developed naturally from the distribution of settlements during the period of Naqada I.

In the North the role of the king had taken shape in the city of *Buto* (now Tell el-Fara'un) on the Nile Delta, while in the South the monarchy was installed at ancient *Nekhen* (near the current site of Kom el-Ahmar), which is better known by its Greek name, Hierakonpolis, the great proto-urban

10 left The names of the kings of the first three dynasties were written within a graphic element, later called a serekh, *which represented a royal palace surmounted by an image of the god Horus in the form of a hawk. At the beginning of the reign of Huni, the last pharaoh of the Third Dynasty, the* serekh *was replaced by the cartouche. The photo shows the* serekh *of Djet, the Serpent King, the third sovereign of the First Dynasty, depicted on the funerary stele found in Abydos. (Paris, Louvre Museum)*

centered on the power unifying Upper and Lower Egypt, connected by the figure of the king.

Of the little information we have on the reign of Menes, it may be assumed that he waged war against the Nubians and Libyans in the lands bordering Egypt, and that at that time there was regular trade with the closest regions of the Middle East. He was buried in Abydos, where all the kings of the First Dynasty and two sovereigns of the Second Dynasty were later buried.

Menes was succeeded by Horus Djet (also known as the Serpent King, from the pictogram used to indicate his name) and other sovereigns. Qa'a was the last king of the First Dynasty.

A very dark period with serious internal disorder probably followed until the Second Dynasty began with Hotepsekhemwy; its representatives were probably native to the Delta. The first two sovereigns of the Second Dynasty were not buried at Abydos, but rather at Saqqara, where there were already large and complex tombs for some high officials of the First Dynasty, such as that of Hemaka.

Unlike the kings of the First Dynasty, those of the Second Dynasty never succeeded in maintaining the unity of the country, and this period saw the return of a monarchy with two sovereigns, one for the North and the other for the South, until Khasekhem, assuming the name of Khasekhemwy, came to the throne of Hierakonpolis and reunited the country. The Second Dynasty ended with this king.

It is considered probable that the wife of Khasekhemwy was the mother of Djoser, the second sovereign of the Third Dynasty. This would explain the smooth transition between the two dynasties. Under Djoser, who reestablished the capital at Memphis, Egypt left the early dynastic period and entered the period known as the **Old Kingdom**: the period of the great pyramids had begun.

center founded on the left bank of the Nile. The kings of Buto chose a red crown as their symbol, with the cobra-goddess Wadjet as their protecting deity; the kings of Hierakonpolis a white crown, with the vulture-goddess Nekhbet as theirs. The first of these kings is known as Scorpion, from the pictogram inscribed on a ceremonial baton found in Hierakonpolis that depicts this creature.

During this period, about which little is known, the names of two other kings, Ra and Sechen, appear, followed by Narmer, who unified the country (or rather, conquered the North) and was the last king of the predynastic period. Narmer's successor, Horus Aha, who probably came to power under the name of Menes, was the founder of the First Dynasty.

The First Dynasty lasted over two centuries, from the beginning of the third millennium to 2635 BC. During Menes's reign a second capital was founded in the North, enabling this territory to be effectively controlled – impossible to do from Hierakonpolis, which was over 600 km away. Thus the city known as *Ineb-hedj*, 'the White Wall,' was founded, which later took the name of Memphis, the first large capital of Egypt.

In order to maintain cohesion between the two parts of a strongly dichotomous country, the coronation rituals were celebrated at Memphis. They soon became quite complex and

THE AGE OF THE PYRAMIDS
(2635–1780 BC)

There was a new development with the advent of the Third Dynasty, not so much in the social structure as in the philosophical and religious area.

While in the early dynastic period the royal tomb was closely connected with an affirmation of earthly power, of which, like the palace, it was an outer expression, with the Third Dynasty the tomb also became a symbol of the divinity of the pharaoh, of his survival in the afterlife, of his celestial power that went beyond death and could be used to benefit the entire country.

In order to express these new ideas, Imhotep, the high chancellor and architect of King Netcherykhet (better known as Djoser, as he was called by the beginning of the New Kingdom), designed a mastaba for the king, which he later decided to elevate with a series of superimposed mastabas: thus was born the step pyramid of Saqqara, which symbolized a stairway reaching up toward heaven or thrown

down from heaven to earth, to permit the heavenly ascent of the pharaoh. This was an idea which was expressed at various times in the Pyramid Texts, the collection of formulas and invocations carved into the pyramids, starting in the Fifth Dynasty and developing into the Coffin Texts and *The Book of the Dead*.

It is not known whether Djoser was truly the first king of the Third Dynasty, but it is certain that he was the first to use the step pyramid to express the new concept of royalty, thus initiating the age of the pyramids. Due to the lack of written sources, little is actually known of the details of the rituals celebrated at the

*12 above left
The step pyramid of Djoser at Saqqara, designed by the famous architect Imhotep during the Third Dynasty, can be considered the first pyramid built in Egypt. The monument, which* *symbolized a ladder to heaven to facilitate the union of the king's soul with his divine father Ra, is the result of a series of superimpositions and extensions of what was originally a mastaba.*

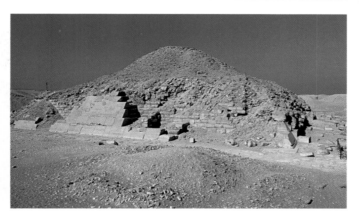

12 above right The pyramid of Meidum, attributed to Huni (the last king of the Third Dynasty) and to Sneferu (the first king of the Fourth Dynasty), who enlarged it by transforming it from a step pyramid to a true pyramid, is considered the transition point between the two forms. In reality, recent studies have come to the conclusion that the pyramid of Meidum was never completed and that the mass of rubble that surrounds it is the remains of the ramps used in its construction.

12 below left The pyramid of Khufu is the largest monument left from Egyptian civilization, and attests to the incredible technological level reached by the middle of the third millennium BC. The pyramid was originally 146 m high, but today reaches only 138 m. Its original volume was over 2,500,000 cu m.

12 below right The remains of the solar temple of Niuserre are located at Abusir. The solar temple, a religious structure which made its first appearance during the Fifth Dynasty, consisted of a pyramid-shaped foundation on which a non-monolithic obelisk was erected.

12-13 Sneferu's south pyramid at Dahshur, also known as the Bent Pyramid, owes its name to the change in inclination of its sides; the angle was reduced, thus decreasing the size of the monument itself. Probably this decision was dictated by signs of structural collapse within the pyramid.

13 above The pharaohs of the Fifth Dynasty - Sahure, Niuserre, Neferikare and Neferefre - built their pyramids at Abusir. The pyramids from this period, which reflect a development in religious concept and a change in the economic conditions of the country, are smaller in size, with poorly cut blocks used for the central portion.

13 center In El-Kula, a village in Upper Egypt, there is a small step pyramid dating from the Third Dynasty. There are six other similar pyramids known in Egypt. The significance of these monuments is not yet completely understood, but they may mark the capitals of the first administrative provinces.

13 below The pyramid which Unas, the last king of the Fifth Dynasty, erected at Saqqara, is the first to contain hieroglyphic texts carved into the walls of its inner chambers. These are known as the Pyramid Texts, a series of invocations and magical formulae connected to the funerary ritual.

time of the Third Dynasty. It appears clear, nevertheless, that within the framework of the new concept of royalty expressed during this period, the pyramid and its annexes were in harmony with the rites which had recently begun, including the celebratory ceremony known as the *Heb-sed* (*Sed* festival) with its ritual runs which regenerated the forces of the king, ensuring that his power, and thus the unity of the country, would be maintained.

Two innovations introduced during this period were the construction of the funerary temple where the cult of the divine pharaoh was practiced; and the *serdab*, a completely sealed room which contained a large statue of the pharaoh and was connected to the outside only through a small fissure. This statue was the equivalent of the king himself and permitted the dead

pharaoh to be present, allowing him to communicate with the outside world through the holes in the walls and thus benefit from sacrifices, offerings and fumigations.

The four successors to Djoser also adopted the concept of the pyramid tomb, and seven more smaller pyramids were constructed during the Third Dynasty in addition to these royal pyramids. Located in Middle and Upper Egypt, near large predynastic and early dynastic sites, the function of these structures is unknown. In the provinces, however, they could be symbolic representations of royal power in the provinces.

Under the reign of Sneferu, the first pharaoh of the Fourth Dynasty, the pyramid took on its final form as an expression of the increasingly great importance given to the solar cult associated with the cult of the

pharaoh, a concept which would continue to develop and would lead to the construction of sun temples during the Fifth Dynasty. As religious thought developed, it was no longer considered necessary to have a celestial stairway, for the steep sides of the pyramid, a materialization of the rays of the sun in the stone, also permitted the pharaoh to make his heavenly ascent.

Sneferu modified the step pyramid that Huni, the last king of the Third Dynasty, had built in Meidum, about 60 km south of Cairo, and covered it with a new outer layer. In Dahshur, some 50 km north of Meidum, he also had a pyramid built for himself, the so-called South Pyramid or Bent Pyramid, in which there is a curious change in the inclination of its faces, which decreases by over 10° starting at about the upper third of the pyramid. It is not known why the architects of Sneferu made this change, but it may be surmised that following signs of structural collapse it was decided to reduce the weight of its structures.

Starting in the period of Sneferu, pyramids also acquired other annexes which would be perfected during the later pyramids of the Fourth Dynasty: the satellite pyramid (for the queen), together with the valley temple, and the processional ramp that connected the pyramid to a funerary temple.

At the end of the Third Dynasty, the great changes both in philosophy and religion and in the architecture of the pyramids had consolidated, and construction techniques had been refined: the foundations had been laid for the construction of the great pyramids of Giza.

The pyramids of the pharaohs of the Fourth Dynasty reached a level of perfection in architectural style which was never equaled thereafter. They were distinguished by gigantic forms, the use of enormous blocks of carefully cut rock, and completely developed adjoining structures: the funerary temple, satellite pyramids, the processional ramp and the valley temple.

Around the end of the Fourth Dynasty, during the period of Menkaure, pyramids began to grow smaller. This tendency became increasingly evident during the Fifth Dynasty due not only to changes in religious concepts, but also, and perhaps primarily, to political and economic changes, which probably included a weakening of royal power and the need for a decrease in public spending. The pyramids of the Fifth Dynasty are in fact not as large and are built of smaller, hastily cut blocks and inexpensive materials such as local limestone, all of which factors contributed to the relatively short life span of these structures.

At the end of the Fifth Dynasty, under King Unas, an important innovation took place that would also characterize the pyramids of the Sixth Dynasty. Although the architectural style did not change and the size remained modest, the so-called Pyramid Texts begin to appear on the walls of the funerary chambers.

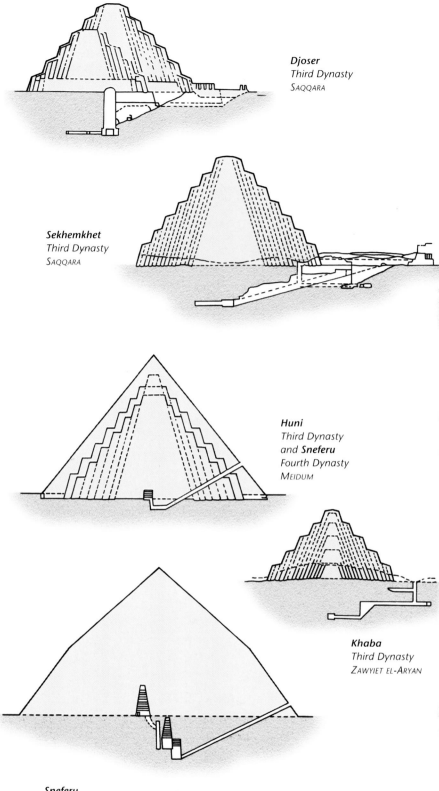

Djoser
Third Dynasty
SAQQARA

Sekhemkhet
Third Dynasty
SAQQARA

Huni
Third Dynasty
and **Sneferu**
Fourth Dynasty
MEIDUM

Khaba
Third Dynasty
ZAWYIET EL-ARYAN

Sneferu
(north pyramid or
bent pyramid)
Fourth Dynasty
DAHSHUR

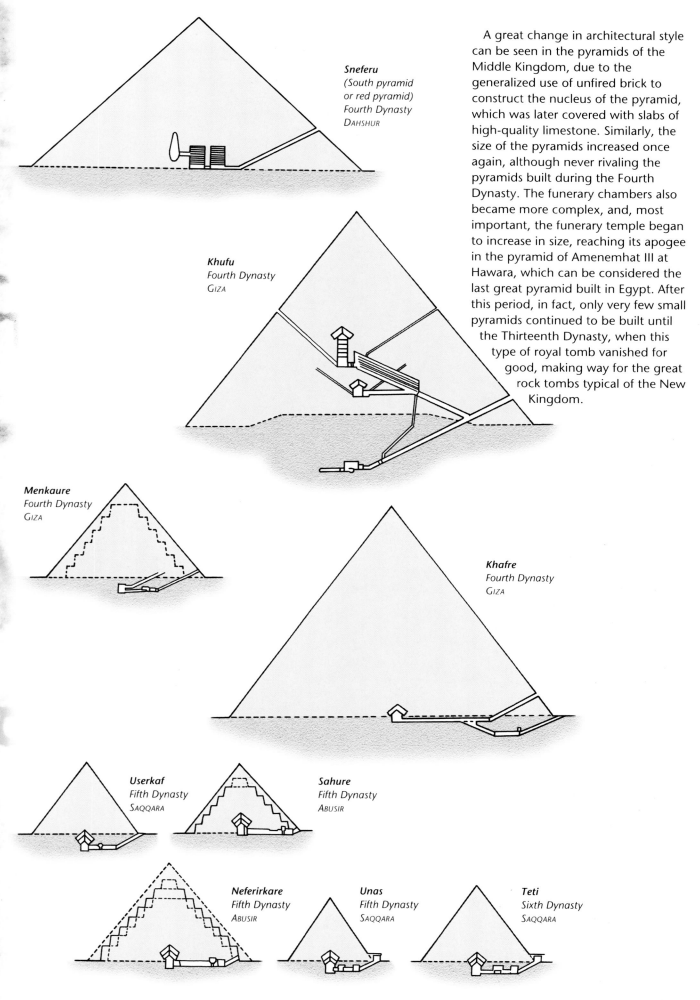

Sneferu
*(South pyramid
or red pyramid)
Fourth Dynasty*
DAHSHUR

Khufu
Fourth Dynasty
GIZA

Menkaure
Fourth Dynasty
GIZA

Khafre
Fourth Dynasty
GIZA

Userkaf
Fifth Dynasty
SAQQARA

Sahure
Fifth Dynasty
ABUSIR

Neferirkare
Fifth Dynasty
ABUSIR

Unas
Fifth Dynasty
SAQQARA

Teti
Sixth Dynasty
SAQQARA

A great change in architectural style can be seen in the pyramids of the Middle Kingdom, due to the generalized use of unfired brick to construct the nucleus of the pyramid, which was later covered with slabs of high-quality limestone. Similarly, the size of the pyramids increased once again, although never rivaling the pyramids built during the Fourth Dynasty. The funerary chambers also became more complex, and, most important, the funerary temple began to increase in size, reaching its apogee in the pyramid of Amenemhat III at Hawara, which can be considered the last great pyramid built in Egypt. After this period, in fact, only very few small pyramids continued to be built until the Thirteenth Dynasty, when this type of royal tomb vanished for good, making way for the great rock tombs typical of the New Kingdom.

CHRONOLOGICAL TABLE
All dates are approximate

PREDYNASTIC – 3200–2920 BC

EARLY DYNASTIC – 2920–2635 BC

Dynasty 0
Scorpion King
Narmer

First Dynasty – 2920–2780 BC
Horus Aha
Djer
Djet
Den
Anedjib
Semerkhet
Qa'a

Second Dynasty – 2780–2635 BC
Hotepsekhemwy
Raneb
Nynetjer
Seth-Peribsen
Khasekhemwy*

OLD KINGDOM – 2635–2140 BC

Third Dynasty – 2635–2561 BC
Sanakhte
Horus Netcherykhet (Djoser)
Horus Sekhemkhet
Khaba
Huni

Fourth Dynasty – 2561–2450 BC
Sneferu
Khufu (Cheops)
Djedefre
Khafre (Chephren)
Menkaure (Mycerinus)
Shepsekaf

Fifth Dynasty – 2450–2321 BC
Userkaf
Sahure
Neferirkare
Shepseskare
Neferefre
Niuserre
Menkhauhor
Djedkare Isesi
Unas

Sixth Dynasty – 2321–2140 BC
Teti
Pepy I
Merenre
Pepy II

FIRST INTERMEDIATE PERIOD – 2140–2100 BC

Seventh, Eighth, Ninth and Tenth Dynasties

MIDDLE KINGDOM – 2100–1750 BC

Eleventh Dynasty (Theban Dynasty)

Twelfth Dynasty
Amenemhat I
Sesostris I
Amenemhat II
Sesostris II
Sesostris III
Amenemhat III
Amenemhat IV
Queen Sobekneferu

SECOND INTERMEDIATE PERIOD – 1750–1550 BC

NEW KINGDOM – 550–1076 BC

THIRD INTERMEDIATE PERIOD – 1076–712 BC

LATE PERIOD – 712–332 BC

GRECO-ROMAN PERIOD – 332 BC– AD **395**

*Recent studies affirm that Khasekhemwy was the direct predecessor of Djoser

16 above The List of Kings is found in the temple of Sethos I in Abydos. The List contains the cartouches of the 76 kings of Egypt who preceded Sethos I. This epigraphic document, along with the Stone of Palermo, the Royal List of Karnak, *the* Royal List of Saqqara *and* the Royal Canon of Turin, *provides the basis for the chronology of ancient Egypt.*

16 below The so-called Stone of Palermo *is the principal fragment of a larger and more complete table dating from the mid-Fifth Dynasty, which reports a chronicle of the years the sovereigns of the first five dynasties* reigned, and is the most important document currently known for the chronology of the Old Kingdom. Other fragments of the original tablet are conserved at the Cairo Museum and the Petrie Museum of London.

jedefre **ABU RAWASH**
                  IV *Dyn.*

CAIRO

N

ZA   ▲ *Khufu*
Dyn.   ▲ *Khafre*
          ▲ *Menkaure*
                      ▭▭ *Khaba*
ZAWYET   III *Dyn.*
EL-ARYAN

BU GHURAB   *Niuserre* ▮
          V *Dyn.*   *Userkaf* ▮
                      ▲ *Sahure*
ABUSIR   ▲ *Niuserre*
          V *Dyn.*   ▲ *Neferirkare*
                  ▲ *Neferefre*

                  ▲ *Teti* VI *Dyn.*
                  ▲ *Userkaf* V *Dyn.*
                  ▰▰ *Djoser* III *Dyn.*
SAQQARA   ▲ *Unas* V *Dyn.*
                  ▭▭ ▲ *Pepy I* VI *Dyn.*
Sekhemkhet   ▲ *Merenre* VI *Dyn.*
   III *Dyn.*   *Djedkare Isesi* ▲ V *Dyn.*
          Pepy II VI *Dyn.* ▲ *Mastaba El- Fara'un*
                      ▱ (*Shepseskaf*) IV *Dyn.*

                  ▲ *Userkara-Khenger* XIII *Dyn.*
          anonym ▲ XIII *Dyn.*
                  ▲ *Sesostris III* XII *Dyn.*

          Sneferu ▲ IV *Dyn.*
          Amenemhat II ▲ XII *Dyn.*
              Sneferu ▲ IX *Dyn.*
DAHSHUR   *Amenemhat III* ▲ XII *Dyn.*

              Pyramids of ▲
              Mazghunah   XII *Dyn.* ?
                         ▲

EL-LISHT *Amenemhat I* ▲ XII *Dyn.*

          Sesostris I ▲ XII *Dyn.*

MEIDUM *Huni + Sneferu* ▲
          III *Dyn.*   IV *Dyn.*

HAWARA *Amenemhat III* ▲ XII *Dyn.*

EL-LAHUN *Sesostris II* ▲ XII *Dyn.*

Pyramid

**Step
Pyramid**

Mastaba   ▱

Sun Temple   ▮

**Incomplete
buildings** △

THE EXPLORATION OF THE PYRAMIDS

The pyramids of Giza, the only one of the Seven Wonders of the Ancient World which has survived to this day, never fails to amaze and fascinate travelers fortunate enough to see them with their own eyes. Herodotus, the famous Greek historian who visited Egypt in the fifth century BC, dwells at great length on the pyramids and their history in Book II of his *Histories*. Indeed, his works are the source of numerous inaccuracies and clichés which are still commonly believed today. For example, Herodotus' image of thousands of slaves forced to work under the whips of cruel overseers to erect the pyramids for the eternal glory of the pharaoh

(Herodotus, II, 124–7), is in fact a myth, though everyone hears it from childhood on.

Diodorus Siculus, who traveled to Egypt some centuries later, gives a less fanciful account, but still picks up some statements from Herodotus. For example, he recounts that, in order to build the pyramid of Khufu, '360,000 men were employed and the pyramid was completed in twenty years', while Menkaure, 'outraged by the cruelty of his predecessors, aspiring to live a more honorable life, and desiring the well-being of his subjects', settled for a smaller pyramid (Diodorus, I, 63–54).

Even the geographer Strabo, who

18-19 *This engraving from the 19th century illustrates a possible interpretation of the passage in Herodotus' Histories (II, 125), in which the Greek historian explains the technique the ancient Egyptians utilized to raise the limestone blocks of the pyramids, using machines equipped 'with short rods'.*

traveled to Egypt and sailed the Nile to the first cataract, devoted a few pages to the pyramids of Giza. With respect to the largest, he wrote: 'There was a rock which could be removed,' and a little later he quite accurately noted that the pyramids had been constructed using a rock full of inclusions that resembled lentils (Strabo, *Geographica*, 17, 1, 33–4), referring to those small, coin-shaped fossils called *nummuliti* which made up the limestone blocks.

During the extremely long period from the high Middle Ages to the eighteenth century when the great works of pharaonic Egypt were forgotten by everyone but the quarrymen who used them as an inexhaustible source of construction materials, the pyramids of Giza were the only monuments Europeans knew of and visited.

Although Middle and Upper Egypt had become impenetrable for Europeans, Alexandria remained the meeting point for the two most important trading routes in the then-known world: the road that ran from India and the Far East across the Red Sea and the Nile, and the Mediterranean route followed by the great Venetian merchants who controlled trade with the Orient. Faithful to its centuries-old role as a great trading center, Alexandria also became a popular stopping-off point for numerous pilgrims on their way to the Holy Land, who could not travel into the interior of the country but could easily go from Alexandria to Cairo by sailing down the Nile.

19 above The summit of the Great Pyramid was depicted like this in a lithograph by the painter Luigi Mayer. Even in the earliest representations of this monument, the lack of the pyramidion, the monolithic block which was placed on the apex of the pyramid, can be noted. Travelers and early tourists left a great deal of graffiti on the limestone blocks that constitute the small platform on the summit of the Great Pyramid.

Arab geographers and writers of the Middle Ages were also interested in the pyramids: their often fanciful accounts refer to amulets and talismans, hidden treasures and statues of precious stones. For example, according to Ibrahim Ibn Wasif Shah, who lived in the twelfth century, 'In the western pyramid [Khafre], 30 granite storehouses were built and filled with every sort of riches...' while the historian al-Massudi, closely interweaving fact and fantasy, states that around 820 AD the caliph al-Mamun made a large breach in the pyramid of Khufu, within which he found a small treasure whose value corresponded exactly with the sum he had invested in order to retrieve it, and an emerald receptacle which he 'ordered brought to his treasury and which was one of the most extraordinary marvels ever made in Egypt'.

The Venetian noble Gabriele Capodilista, who traveled to Egypt in 1458 during his pilgrimage to the Holy Land, gives us one of the first descriptions of the pyramids of Giza, which he describes as 'the granaries of the pharaoh, which are made of square blocks of bare rock like the tomb of Romulus, but much higher than a common tower.' Like many pilgrims of the period, obsessed with biblical references, he believed the pyramids had been built by Joseph, the son of Jacob, to accumulate grain in years of abundance and thus overcome the years of famine that he had prophesied to the pharaoh.

In the famous 1459 planisphere of Brother Mauro Camaldolese, the pyramids are the only pharaonic monument present in the depiction of Egypt, and the accompanying comment seems to accept the biblical interpretation: 'It is said that these pyramids were the granaries of the pharaoh.' Of course, many other medieval travelers, such as Benjamin of Tudela, who was in Egypt in 1173, and the doctor Jean de Mandeville, shared similar opinions.

In his *Treatise on the Holy Land*, published in 1524, Francesco Suriano describes the pyramid of Khufu as 'made in the shape of a diamond, like Noah's arc, all covered with bare

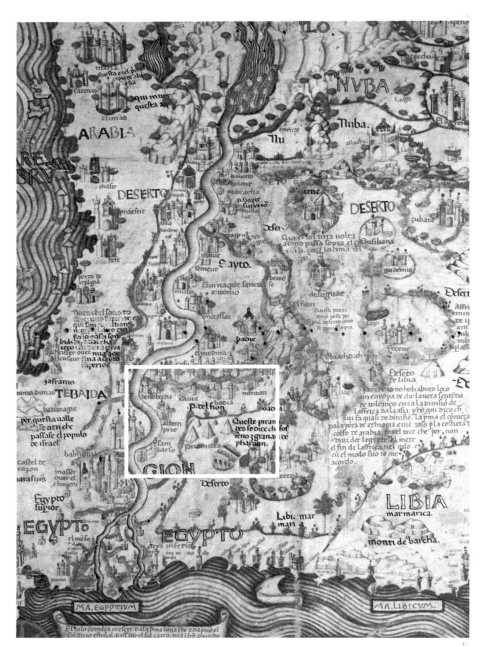

20 In his famous Map of the World of 1459, Fra' Mauro Camaldolese includes one of the oldest representations of Egypt and the course of the Nile. The picture below shows a detail of Fra' Mauro's Map of the World,

depicting the pyramids of Giza next to a comment supporting the Biblical tradition: 'Those pyramids which it is said were the granaries of the pharaohs'. (Venice, Biblioteca Marciana).

21 above left St Mark's basilica in Venice contains one of the oldest representations of the pyramids, which at the time were considered ancient granaries of the pharaohs, as dictated by Biblical tradition.

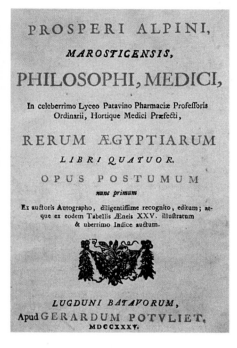

rock using marvelous artistry and no mortar', and he admired the Great Sphinx, which he described as 'a head of fine marble, so large as to amaze those who gaze upon it: 60 ells [about 69 m] in length, with the ear 5 ells in length, where eagles make their nest; the nose is 10 ells in length'.

In 1582 the Venetian consul Giorgio Emo traveled to Egypt with the Belluno physician and naturalist Prospero Alpino, who upon his return to Europe published his essential work *Rerum Aegyptiorum Libri Quatuor.* Alpino devoted himself to all types of scientific observations, many of which concerned the pyramids at Giza, and he performed one of the first scientific studies of the pyramid of Khufu, the height and perimeter of which he measured. He also climbed to the top of the monument and reported the deterioration of the blocks located on the north side. The Sphinx, which he imagined to be hollow, also interested him, as did the pyramids of Khafre and Menkaure, which he correctly identified as ancient tombs of kings.

21 above right The photo shows the frontispiece of Rerum Aegyptiarum Libri Quattuor, *published in 1735, one of the most important medical and naturalistic works by the famous Belluno botanist and physician, Prospero Alpini.*

21 below Prospero Alpino visited Egypt in 1582 in the company of the Venetian consul Giorgio Emo, and undertook his first scientific studies of the flora and fauna of the country. In Giza Alpini studied and measured the pyramid of Khufu, and also examined the other pyramids on the site, and the Sphinx.

View of the Pyramids *of* DASHOUR, & *of the* Great Pyramid.

22 and 23 above Some of the first portrayals of the pyramids of Dahshur and the Great Pyramid of Giza, for which a rather accurate cross-section is provided, include those which were used to illustrate A Description of the East and Some Other Countries, *by the Revd Richard Pococke, who visited Egypt between 1737 and 1738.*

23 below Frederik Norden, a captain in the Danish navy, visited Egypt in 1738, at almost the same time as Pococke. Norden, along with Pococke, should be considered as one of the most important travelers of the 18th century, and he too published an extremely interesting book accompanied by numerous drawings and plans.

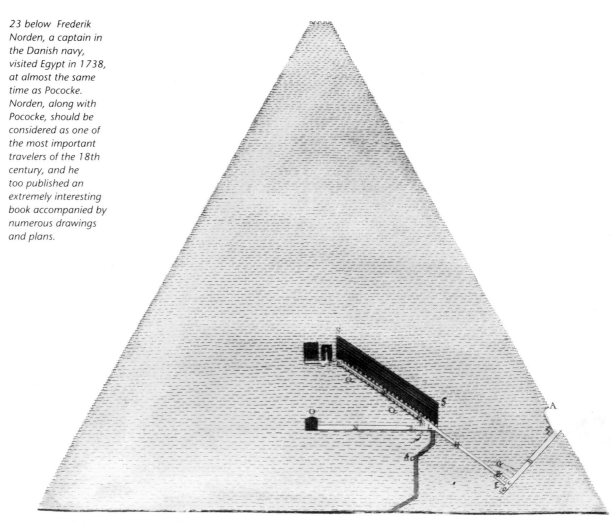

In 1638 John Greaves, an English astronomer, visited the pyramids of Giza, making the first accurate measurements of the monuments, which he published in his *Pyramidographia*. In 1735 Benoît de Maillet, in his *Description de l'Égypte, contenant plusiers remarques curieuses sur la géographie ancienne*, which contains a long, detailed description of Egypt, accurately drew the first section of the pyramid of Khufu.

In 1738 Frederik Ludwig Norden, a Navy officer in the service of Christian VI, the king of Denmark, was invited to Egypt in order to prepare an exhaustive report on the country. He carefully explored the pyramid of Khufu, and described not only the archeological area of Giza but also the pyramids of Saqqara and Dahshur and that of Meidum, which, he says, 'the Arabs call the "false pyramid"'.

The Revd Richard Pococke, Bishop of Meathe, who visited Egypt between 1737 and 1738, also described the pyramids with great accuracy and correctly identified the site of ancient Memphis, although, in a rather fanciful theory, he asserted that the Egyptians built the pyramids by covering small hills with rock. Pococke also visited the pyramids of Saqqara, Meidum and Dahshur, making quite accurate drawings of each of them.

24 above The pyramid of Meidum is accurately depicted in this drawing by Dominique Vivant Denon, who participated in the Napoleonic expedition and on his return published the famous work Voyage dans la Haute et la Basse Egypte.

24-5 This view of the Abusir and Saqqara pyramids (to the left) and those at Giza (to the right) was drawn by Denon during a flood of the Nile, when the waters of the river reached the foot of the limestone plateau of Giza, as they had in ancient times.

*24 below
The architectural perfection of the Great Gallery that leads to the sepulchral chamber of the pyramid of Khufu elicited great wonder in 19th century travelers.*

Nevertheless, the experts who came with the 1798 Egyptian expedition of Napoleon Bonaparte, including the celebrated Dominique Vivant Denon, were the first to study the monuments of pharaonic Egypt methodically and scientifically. They devoted ample time to the pyramids, all parts of which were measured with great precision, with a calculation of heights and angles. Napoleon himself made calculations, and his figures were confirmed by the mathematician Gaspare Monge, who estimated that the blocks with which the three pyramids of Giza were built could be used to raise a wall 3.7 m high and 30 cm thick all around France.

25 above This drawing by Vivant Denon shows the main entry to the pyramid of Khufu. Until 1819 this was the only one of the three pyramids at Giza which could be entered. At present the entrance to the pyramid is through a passageway located about 15 m lower, dug by the first tomb robbers.

25 below The scientists who accompanied the Napoleonic expedition, shown here by Denon as they measure the Sphinx, were the first to draw and describe the monuments of ancient Egypt with scientifically accurate detail. The fruit of their immense labor was published in the colossal Description de l'Egypte, which includes nine volumes of text and eleven volumes of plates.

26 above Giovanni Battista Belzoni of Padua, who was certainly the greatest 19th century explorer of Egypt, made sensational discoveries that included opening the great temple of Abu Simbel, the discovery of the tomb of Sethos I in the Valley of the Kings, and the discovery of the entry to the pyramid of Khafre. (London, National Gallery).

26 center After numerous attempts, Belzoni succeeded in opening a gap between the limestone blocks of the pyramid and penetrating the corridor that led to the sepulchral chamber.

Twenty years later, after playing a major role in epic adventures and great discoveries, including the discovery of the great temple of Abu Simbel and the find of the tomb of Sethos I in the Valley of the Kings, Giovanni Battista Belzoni, the great traveler from Padua in the service of the English consul Henry Salt, discovered the entrance to the pyramid of Khafre, and entered the monument on March 2, 1818. Around the same time, between 1817 and 1819, the Genoese Giovanni Battista Caviglia, a Navy commander also in the service of Henry Salt, performed a lengthy study of the pyramid of Khufu, in which he excavated the so-called Queen's Chamber and explored the first of the five chambers located above the ceiling of the sepulchral hall in order to relieve weight and stress. He also performed excavations of the Sphinx, which partially freed it from the sand.

26 below In a very accurate drawing, the traveler from Padua also showed the first cross-section of the pyramid.

26-27 In his famous work, Narrative of the Operations and Recent Discoveries, Giovanni Battista Belzoni devoted several illustrative plates to the pyramid of Khafre, which prior to its discovery, based on the tradition passed down by Herodotus, had been thought to lack inner chambers. In the drawing Belzoni is shown as he enters the sepulchral chamber of Khafre's pyramid, on March 2, 1818.

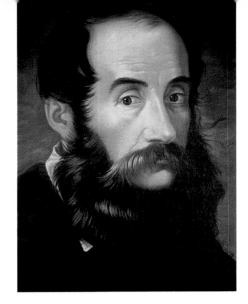

28 above Girolamo Segato, an unlucky but ingenious character who was an artist, scientist and naturalist, traveled to Egypt between 1820 and 1821. Although he is more known for his studies on the petrifaction of anatomical parts, Segato can be credited with entering the pyramid of Djoser at Saqqara, which he explored with the Prussian Baron Von Minutoli.

28 below In 1837 the English explorers Howard Vyse and John Perring discovered the entrances to the three secondary pyramids located next to the pyramid of Menkaure, and then succeeded in penetrating the latter pyramid as well. Inside they found the sarcophagus of the king, which they sent to England. It was lost at sea when the ship that was transporting it sank.

In 1820 Girolamo Segato, from Belluno, discovered the entry to the step pyramid of Djoser at Saqqara, which he mapped and sectioned, making excellent drawings of several details of the underground chambers which comprised the immense funerary apartment.

The English colonel Richard William Howard Vyse also explored and studied the pyramids with great energy and enthusiasm. Between 1835 and 1837 he worked with Caviglia, and then the first time made it possible to make a positive identification of the pharaoh associated with the monument, thus finally confirming the tradition passed down by Herodotus.

Vyse and Perring also explored the satellite pyramids of Khufu and Menkaure, and on July 29, 1837 they made the major discovery of the entrance to the latter pyramid, then unknown. On first penetrating the monument they reached the burial chamber and found there a beautiful

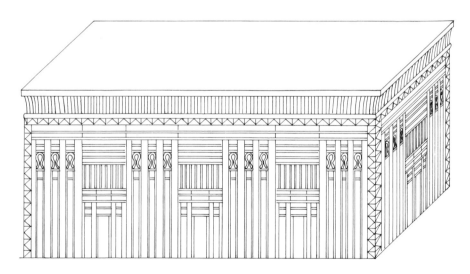

with the engineer John Shea Perring, who did an in-depth exploration of all the pyramids then known. The work of Vyse and Perring made a decisive contribution to the study of the pyramids of Giza: among other things, they are responsible for the discovery of the outside entrance of the lower corridor of the pyramid of Khafre and the exploration of the remaining weight-relief chambers of the pyramid of Khufu. In the last of these chambers they found a royal cartouche which for

basalt sarcophagus with a palace-façade motif, while in an upper chamber they found a wooden anthropoid coffin from a later age, with the royal cartouches. Vyse left for England one month later with the wooden sarcophagus, which was given to the British Museum. The basalt sarcophagus was later lost when the ship which was taking it to England sank in the Mediterranean off the coast of Spain, in an area only recently identified.

28-9 Segato drew the funerary apartments of the pyramid of Djoser, certain areas of which were decorated with blue faience and false door stelae. These first portrayals of the interior were published in the Monumental Atlas of Upper and Lower Egypt, with the contribution of the artist Domenico Valeriani.

29 below Segato also drew the first cross-section of the pyramid of Djoser, although it was somewhat inaccurate due to the complexity of the internal structure of the pyramid. During his exploration Segato also found the remains of a mummified body, which was probably Djoser himself.

30 left The Prussian
Egyptologist Richard
Lepsius worked in
Egypt at the head of
an important
expedition between
1842 and 1845,
smoothly continuing
the work undertaken
by Champollion.
Lepsius wrote a
fundamental work on
the monuments of
Egypt, contained in
twelve volumes that
include 894 large
format plates, with
drawings of not only
many monuments,
but most importantly
of inscriptions and
bas-reliefs, which
were reproduced with
extraordinary
precision.

30 right Lepsius drew
the first true
topographical map of
the necropolises of
Memphis, and
devoted himself to a
study of the internal
structures of the
pyramids, developing
theories on their
construction which
held that these
monuments were
initially built as step
pyramids and were
then enlarged by
superimposing
various layers, so that
their dimensions
would correspond to
the length of the
reign. In Giza, Lepsius
also made the first
survey of the wall
decorations of
numerous private
mastabas in the two
large cemeteries
located to the east
and west of the
pyramid of Khufu.
The pictures show the
extraordinary colors
and delicacy of some
of these wall
paintings, which
Lepsius reproduced
carefully and
accurately.

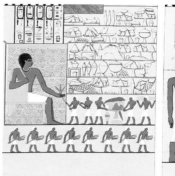

Richard Lepsius, continuing the
work of deciphering begun by Jean
François Champollion, organized an
expedition to Egypt in 1842, sailing
up the Nile to Meroë and spending
three years scientifically exploring all
the principal pharaonic monuments.
The results are collected in a work,
*Denkmaeler aus Aegypten und
Aethiopien*, which is still important
today. Lepsius discussed the pyramids
and in particular drew the first and
most complete map of the necropolis
at el-Lisht, in which he noted the
position of fully 64 pyramids, and
studied those of Abusir, Saqqara and
Meidum, developing the theory that
all pyramids were constructed in
steps, the interstices of which were
filled in later, and that their
dimensions corresponded to the
length of the reign. In addition he
completed excavations in the funerary
temple of the pyramid of Hawara.

In 1858 the founder of the Egyptian
Museum of Cairo and the first
Egyptian Antiquities Service, Auguste
Mariette, devoted himself to the
excavation and study of the
archeological areas of Giza and
Saqqara, the exploration of the
Mastaba el-Fara'un and the large
mastabas of the Old Kingdom, and
the publication of works which are
important to this day. He is also
responsible for the discoveries of the
Serapeum in Saqqara, with the tombs
of the sacred Apis bulls, and for what
he thought was the tomb of Prince
Khaemwaset, the son of Rameses II
(whose tomb has never been found).

31 Auguste Mariette (shown to the right), the founder of the Cairo Museum, continued the work of Lepsius at Giza (he can be credited with the discovery of Khafre's lower temple) and above all at Saqqara, where he excavated and studied numerous mastabas from the Old Kingdom, and was the first to explore the Mastabat el-Fara'un, the tomb of King Shepsekaf, the son of Menkaure and the last pharaoh of the Fourth Dynasty, and the Serapis complex where the sacred Apis bulls were buried. In the northern sector of the necropolis of Saqqara, Mariette discovered and studied the mastaba of Hersire, a high level official of the Third Dynasty, whose splendid wooden door (to the left) is one of the most significant artistic expressions of this period. It is now on display at the Cairo Museum.

32 The Great Gallery of the pyramid of Khufu, here shown in the famous interpretation by the painter Luigi Mayer, was carefully examined by Petrie, who studied the devices used to close off its entrance. Petrie also noted that there was a relationship between the height of the pyramid and the ray of a circumference with a perimeter the length of the base.

33 above left Sir William Matthew Flinders Petrie excavated and studied numerous archeological sites all over Egypt, making a fundamental contribution to the development of Egyptology. Petrie worked on the pyramids of the Memphis necropolises from 1880 to 1882 and made the most precise measurements of these monuments ever completed to that date, using techniques based on the principle of triangulation and quite sophisticated instruments.

33 above right Jacques de Morgan, appointed as director of the Antiquities Service in 1894, made a series of fortunate excavations in the Middle Kingdom pyramids in the Dahshur area, attributed to Sesostris III, Amenemhat II and Amenemhat III. His most important discovery was the tombs of the princesses Khnumit and Iti, which contained sumptuous funeral trappings known as the treasure of Dahshur. They are now on display at the Cairo Museum.

Meidum, Mazghunah and el-Lahun, where he discovered the vestiges of one of the extremely rare urban settlements of ancient Egypt, which he named Kahun. In 1920 he discovered near the pyramid of Sesostris II the tomb of a royal princess whose extraordinary funerary trappings soon became famous as the Treasure of el-Lahun.

In 1894 the Frenchman Jacques de Morgan, appointed director of the Egyptian Antiquities Service, excavated the pyramids of the Middle Kingdom in the area of Dahshur, discovering the so-called Treasure of Dahshur in the unprofaned tombs of the princesses Khnumet and Ita near the pyramid of Amenemhat II, while

*33 center
This general view of the pyramid area of Giza was published by Petrie in 1883 in his book* The Pyramids and Temples of Gizeh.

33 bottom View of the pyramid of Hawara in an engraving by one of its first visitors, the Frenchman Jean Jacques Rifaud, who arrived in Egypt in 1805.

However, the work of the English Egyptologist William Matthew Flinders Petrie, who went to Egypt in 1880 to begin a series of systematic excavations, proved to be the most enormous step forward in scientific knowledge of the Egyptian pyramids. Petrie performed an immense amount of research and published an incredible quantity of scientific reports on his work on almost all Egyptian archeological sites. With respect to the pyramids, he conducted excavations and performed a systematic and complete study of the necropolis of Giza, published in 1883 under the title *The Pyramids and Temples of Gizeh.* He extended his studies to Hawara,

during the same period the French Institute for Oriental Archeology undertook an expedition to el-Lisht, directed by Gustave Jéquier and J. E. Galtier, who identified the tomb of Sesostris I.

Finally, early in the twentieth century the Italian Alessandro Barsanti began research at Saqqara on the pyramid of Unas, which led to the discovery of the funerary temple of this king and three important tombs from the Persian period. Between 1905 and 1912, at Zawiyet el-Aryan, between Saqqara and Giza, he discovered an immense rectangular trench 21 m deep that marked the remains of an enormous pyramid from the Fourth Dynasty.

PYRAMIDS AND MASTABAS

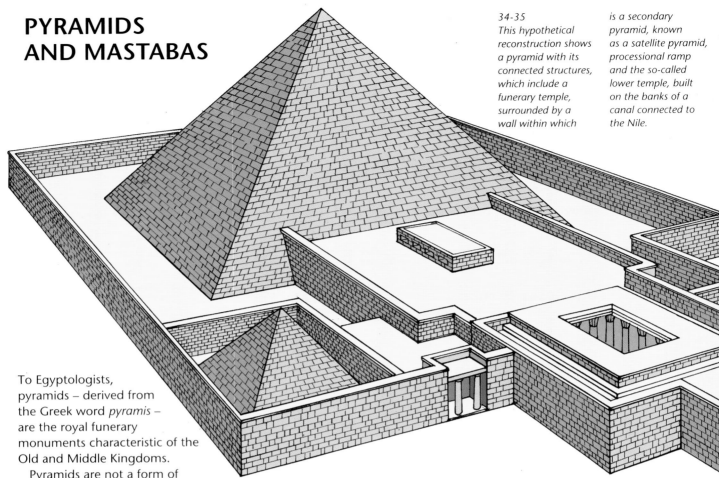

34-35
This hypothetical reconstruction shows a pyramid with its connected structures, which include a funerary temple, surrounded by a wall within which is a secondary pyramid, known as a satellite pyramid, processional ramp and the so-called lower temple, built on the banks of a canal connected to the Nile.

To Egyptologists, pyramids – derived from the Greek word *pyramis* – are the royal funerary monuments characteristic of the Old and Middle Kingdoms.

Pyramids are not a form of architecture exclusive to ancient Egypt, as this form was developed by other cultures as well, including Sumeria, Assyria–Babylonia and numerous Meso-American civilizations. Nevertheless, what characterizes the Egyptian pyramids and differentiates them from those of other cultures is their function as royal tombs.

The pyramids, which the ancient Egyptians called *mer* and indicated by the hieroglyph $\triangle$, can be divided into step and true pyramids, which are an evolution of the former. In both cases, the pyramids are the principal, but not the only, elements of the so-called 'funerary complex' which, in its most developed form in the Fourth Dynasty includes other essential structures with special theological and symbolic meanings: the funerary temple, wall, processional ramp, valley temple and satellite pyramids. Starting in this period the pyramids were also named, using a non-verbal phrase which Egyptologist Gustave Lefèbvre believes described the king himself: for example, the three pyramids of Giza are named 'Khufu belongs to the horizon,' 'Khafre is great' and 'Menkaure is divine'.

The pyramids, an expression in rock of the rays of the sun, were used to

house and protect the royal mummy. They were built on three axes: the vertical axis, which joined heaven and earth and the pharaoh to his divine father Ra, with whom he would be eternally reunited; the north–south, or polar axis, running parallel with the Nile, which runs from south to north from Upper to Lower Egypt, and which relates to the royal function; and the east–west, or celestial axis, parallel to the daily course of the sun, which rises,

sets and is eternally reborn, regenerating itself each day.

In the pyramid, the royal polar axis is expressed by the entrance located on the northern side and by the descending corridor which runs south to the sarcophagus chamber. This direction is sometimes marked on the outside by a so-called satellite pyramid, which in general is situated to the southeast and also served as a cenotaph, a vestige of the Abydos

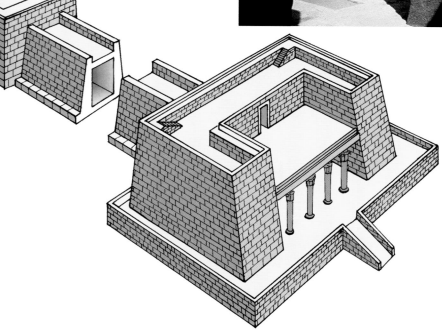

35 above The processional ramp of Khafre's pyramid (in the background), which connects the lower temple to the funerary temple, built on the east side of the pyramid, is still in excellent condition. On the right are the Sphinx and the pyramid of Khufu.

35 below Khafre's lower temple, constructed of large, perfectly square blocks of granite, is the most beautiful example of this type of edifice, used to house the mortal remains of the king before his burial. It has long been debated whether the lower temple was also used for embalming, but more recent studies do not seem to support this theory.

34 below The ruins of Khafre's funeral temple do not adequately express the magnificence of this edifice, which occupied a surface area three times larger than the lower temple and was built within a vast rectangular courtyard with columns, which preceded the actual sanctuary and offerings room. The funerary temples were used for the cult of the deified king, who connected the human and the divine to guarantee continued world order.

origins of the predynastic kings.

The east–west celestial and solar axis relates to the concept of resurrection: indeed, the funerary temple was located on the eastern side of the pyramid, where the living practiced the cult of the dead king who had become divine, thus guaranteeing order on earth, as the union of the earthly world with the celestial realm took place through the royal function. The funerary temple itself was preceded by a courtyard used for offerings, and by a vestibule where important dignitaries probably gathered for the funeral of the king.

The three structural elements of pyramid, funerary temple and satellite pyramids were enclosed within a wall known as the *temenos*, which delimited and separated the sacred area from the rest of the complex.

A processional ramp led from the funerary temple down to the valley temple which expressed the passage of the king from the world of the living to the pyramid tomb in the west, just as the sarcophagus in the burial chamber was placed facing west. The valley temple, located on the edge of a canal connected to the Nile, was used to house the dead pharaoh during embalming and purification rites prior to entombment, before he was transferred to the pyramid.

Its port structures (wharves, piers, etc.) were also used during the construction of the pyramid, providing a place where boats transporting slabs of limestone and blocks of granite could dock.

It is not known exactly where the dead king was embalmed. It is hard to imagine that this lengthy and complex process took place in the valley temple, but current knowledge of the royal funerary ritual in the Old Kingdom is not sufficient to confirm or deny the various hypotheses. In any event, the body of the king was washed and purified in a special structure, called the 'purification tent' or *ibw*, and was then mummified in the 'house of regeneration' or *per nefer*. The actual funeral then followed with the burial of the sovereign.

THE STEP PYRAMID

Step pyramids predate true pyramids and reflect a different religious and theological concept.

The step pyramid was not truly a symbol of the sun, but was rather a gigantic stairway that facilitated the access of the pharaoh's soul to heaven. His mortal body was not placed in a burial chamber within the pyramid, but in a shaft covered by the pyramid itself.

Like true pyramids, step pyramids had connected structures which made

36 above Djoser's step pyramid at Saqqara is the first example of this type of architectural structure known in Egypt. The step pyramid, the result of numerous extensions of what was originally a mastaba, symbolized a gigantic ladder that would facilitate the pharaoh's soul in its celestial ascent.

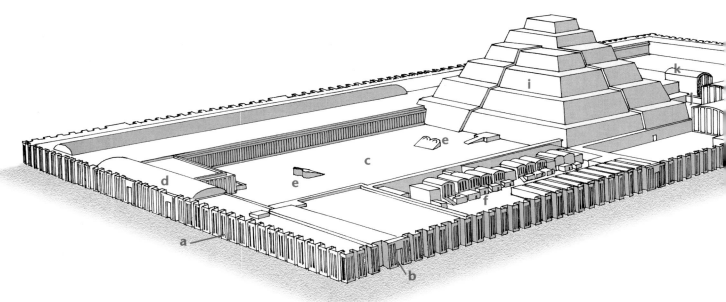

up the 'pyramid complex,' such as the enclosure walls and the funerary temple, but the processional ramp and the valley temple were absent. In addition, the southern portion of the walls – much more massive than those of true pyramids from the Fourth Dynasty – contains a secondary tomb whose function is not certain but which might have been used either to bury the royal viscera or as a cenotaph. In any event, it was connected at the south and the actual polar axis. These secondary tombs eventually evolved into satellite pyramids.

36 center The most typical example of a step pyramid is Djoser's pyramid at Saqqara, where all the connected architectural structures are still visible today, thanks to the restoration work performed under the direction of the French architect Jean-Philippe Lauer. Most of them were used to evoke the Sed

festival (or Heb-sed), which took place during the thirtieth year of the pharaoh's reign and was connected to the concept of regeneration and renewal of royal power. Through these structures, the soul of the king could continue to celebrate the Sed festival and thus permanently renew his power.

a. *Enclosure wall with palace façade*
b. *Entry door*
c. *Large courtyard*
d. *South tomb*
e. *Metae*
f. *South Heb-sed courtyard with relative chapels*

g. *South House*
h. *North House*
i. *Step pyramid*
j. *Serdab courtyard*
k. *Funerary temple (from Stadelman, modified)*

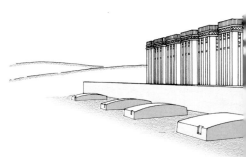

THE MASTABA

37 above The Mastabat El-Fara'un, located in the south section of the necropolis at Saqqara and built for King Shepsekaf, the son of Menkaure, is a splendid example of a mastaba, an Arabic word that means 'bench,' in reference to the outer appearance of this type of tomb, which predates the step pyramid.

The mastaba – from the Arabic *mastabah*, or 'stone bench' – was a much less complex tomb than those described above. It basically consisted of two parts. The deepest portion was a burial shaft flanked by a sometimes large group of chambers that was used to house the funerary trappings and was carefully sealed after the body was placed within it, while the superstructure contained the offerings chapel and storage rooms. In the earliest mastabas the deceased and his funerary trappings were lowered in from above before the roof was constructed; it was not until halfway through the First Dynasty, in the mastaba of Den at Saqqara, that there appeared an access corridor which led to the burial chamber and made it possible to bury the deceased after the tomb was completely finished.

Kings of the early dynastic period were buried in enormous mastabas made of unfired brick. Located in the northern part of Saqqara and in Abydos in Upper Egypt, they were surrounded by a massive wall with an unfired brick façade made to appear like a palace – a precursor of the type used for step pyramids in complexes of the Third Dynasty. These royal mastabas were rectangular, with the longest sides 40–60 m long and the shorter ones about 20 m long, with the brick superstructure also decorated to appear like the façade of a palace. This feature disappeared during the Second Dynasty and was replaced by

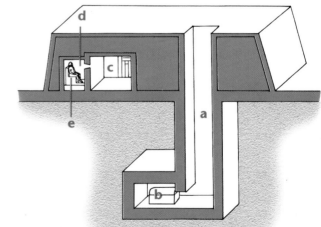

37 center
The mastaba, shown here in an imaginary cross-section, in its simplest form consisted of an underground area comprised of a shaft (a) and the sarcophagus room (b), and a massive quadrangular superstructure which held the offerings chapel (c) and the serdab (d), a closed space which held a statue of the deceased (e), who could magically communicate with the outside world through a small opening.

37 below Hypothetical reconstruction of a royal mastaba from the First Dynasty, based on data obtained from excavations made in the archaic necropolis, located in the northern portion of Saqqara. The mastabas of this period were complex and surrounded by a wall of unfired brick with a palace-façade motif.

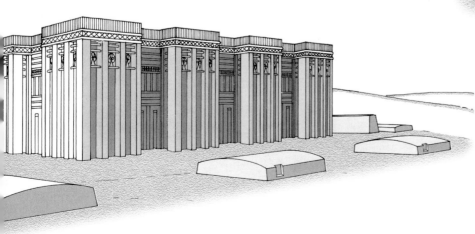

smooth, pale-colored façades, while on the east side niches appeared which seem to be precursors of the funerary temples which developed later on in the Third Dynasty.

Unlike the pyramids, which were reserved for royalty, mastabas were also used for the private burial of important people such as dignitaries, members of the court or relatives of the pharaoh.

THE PRIVATE MASTABAS

Starting with the Fourth Dynasty, in private mastabas the funerary apartment was reduced to a simple sepulchral chamber, while the superstructure, used for offerings to the deceased, became more complex, and was built of blocks of rock. During this period it sometimes included numerous chambers (there are fully 32 in the mastaba of Mereruka in Saqqara) decorated with bas-relief ornamentation covering a surface area of as much as 1,000 sq m.

The subject-matter of the bas-reliefs, which were generally in color, was funerary (the presentation of offerings to the deceased, scenes of funeral banquets with music and dancers, etc.), or agricultural (wine-pressing, work in the fields, the preparation of food and drink, the life of animals), or illustrated the work of craftsmen and artists (the working of gold and metals, carpentry, etc.), hunting in the desert, hunting and fishing in the swamps, or nautical themes. The deceased is generally depicted supervising all these

chamber so that the soul of the deceased could magically leave it to use the offerings made to him.

There is another structure, known as the *serdab*, which was used to connect the world of the living with that of the dead. The *serdab*, an Arabic word which means 'cellar', was a completely sealed room containing a life-size statue of the deceased which could magically communicate with the outside through a small fissure in front of it.

38 left False door stelae, thus called because they were imitations of a door with jambs and lintels, with the name of the deceased generally carved into them, are one of the most common and characteristic decorative elements of Old Kingdom mastabas. Through this device the deceased could magically remain in contact with the world of the living.

38 center There are also numerous private tombs of high level dignitaries or relatives of the royal family in the pyramid area of Giza. It was considered a great privilege to be buried near the tomb of the king, as this made it possible to share his immortal destiny.

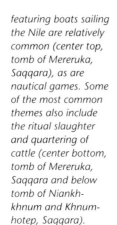

38 right The walls of the chapels of the private mastabas are decorated with bas-reliefs, usually polychrome, which are based on aspects of daily life or the earthly activities of the deceased. Among the most curious subjects are feeding hyenas (above, tomb of Mereruka, Saqqara), while nautical scenes

featuring boats sailing the Nile are relatively common (center top, tomb of Mereruka, Saqqara), as are nautical games. Some of the most common themes also include the ritual slaughter and quartering of cattle (center bottom, tomb of Mereruka, Saqqara and below tomb of Niankh-khnum and Khnum-hotep, Saqqara).

activities, while accompanied by his wife and sometimes his children.

A fundamental element in the internal organization of the mastaba is the false door stela, generally facing west, located in the main offerings room behind the offerings altar. Offerings formulae are carved on the stela, which also bears a depiction of the deceased, again generally accompanied by his wife, along with his name and titles; he is usually seated before a table of offerings. The false door stela may have been located over the underlying funerary

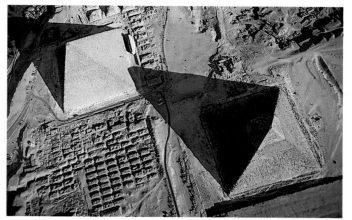

THE PRIVATE NECROPOLISES

Generally the private mastabas of dignitaries, relatives of the king and members of the royal court were built near pyramids, where they formed the large necropolises in which the tombs were carefully located and organized by priests who administered the available spaces, aligning the tombs regularly and separating them with roads which

*39 below
The pyramids of Giza, here shown from the northwest, were built on a limestone desert plateau above the Nile flood plain, so that when the river flooded, the waters of the Nile lapped nearly to their edges but never reached the necropolis. A system of canals connected to the Nile made it possible to use boats*

to reach both the lower temples, where mooring docks were located, and the ports built for the large barges that transported slabs of white Tura limestone, used to cover the pyramids (the quarries where this material was extracted were a only few kilometers away, but on the opposite bank of the Nile).

In this manner the barges could come as close as possible to the ramp systems that connected the ports with the construction sites. To the left in the photograph is the pyramid of Khufu with the western cemetery, in the center the pyramid of Khafre, and to the right the small pyramid of Menkaure.

intersected at right angles, as can be seen in the necropolises located to the east and west of the pyramid of Khufu in Giza.

The chance to build a tomb near the pharaoh's pyramid was considered a great privilege and was a sign of consideration which the king granted as an enormous favor, as it permitted the deceased to benefit from the power of divine resurrection that the dead pharaoh enjoyed for eternity as he shared the celestial throne with his father Ra.

THE CONSTRUCTION OF A PYRAMID

40-41 The phases in the preparation and transport of unfired bricks are depicted In the tomb of the vizier Rekhmire (TT. no. 100) in Thebes. Unfired brick was the most commonly used construction material in Egyptian architecture.

40 above The royal cubit (0.524 m), represented here by a wooden model, was the unit of measurement used in ancient Egypt. The cubit was in its turn divided into palms and fingers. Obviously, all the dimensions of the Egyptian monuments were calculated based on this unit of measurement. (Turin, Egyptian Museum)

The large number of bas-reliefs which illustrate aspects of daily life in the Old Kingdom never depict a pyramid's construction, which was probably considered such a unique event that it could not be reproduced. Thus we have no documents which illustrate the techniques used, and on this subject we can only fashion hypotheses, based on objective data and information collected on site.

The paintings and bas-reliefs in some tombs, especially in the New Kingdom, provide clear information on the techniques used to produce unfired bricks, sculpt large statues, and move enormous blocks using inclined planes, and it is assumed that these techniques were not much different from those used previously during the Old Kingdom.

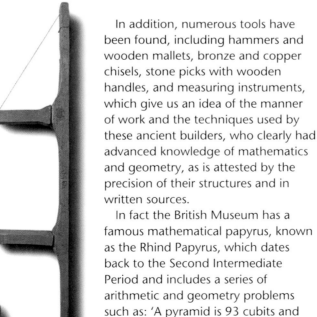

The measurements were based on a unit of size known as the royal cubit, which was 0.524 m in length and was divided into 7 palms (one palm corresponded to about 7.5 cm), which were in their turn divided into 4 fingers, equal to about 1.9 cm each. In order to express the angle of a line, they used the concept of *sekhed*, defined as the horizontal distance of the angle expressed in palms and fingers when the height is equal to a royal cubit.

During construction, architects used simple but effective instruments to verify directions and angles, such as the square, the *bay*, which was a short plumbline, and the *merkhet*, an instrument consisting of a wooden rod with a V-shaped notch that made it possible to sight an object.

The only account of the methods and techniques used to construct the pyramids is that provided by Herodotus (*Histories*, II, 124–35), who makes a number of fanciful and unreliable statements. Nevertheless, he does include some accurate information which should be taken into consideration. According to Herodotus, 100,000 persons worked for twenty years to build the pyramid of Khufu, with ten additional years initially required to prepare the land, the port structures (the wharves, piers, etc.), the ramp and the underground chambers.

It is quite probable that his statements on the number of years necessary to build the pyramid are accurate, but he is totally unreliable regarding the number of persons employed in the operation, which, according to Petrie, was probably closer to 5,000–6,000, while other authors hypothesize even larger numbers – 15,000–16,000 persons according to G. Goyon, or as many as 30,000 according to other writers.

In addition, numerous tools have been found, including hammers and wooden mallets, bronze and copper chisels, stone picks with wooden handles, and measuring instruments, which give us an idea of the manner of work and the techniques used by these ancient builders, who clearly had advanced knowledge of mathematics and geometry, as is attested by the precision of their structures and in written sources.

In fact the British Museum has a famous mathematical papyrus, known as the Rhind Papyrus, which dates back to the Second Intermediate Period and includes a series of arithmetic and geometry problems such as: 'A pyramid is 93 cubits and $1/3$ high. What is the angle if the height of its face is 140 cubits?' A study of this papyrus has, among other things, made it clear that the ancient Egyptians were familiar with and made practical use of Pythagoras' theorem, although they had never theorized or enunciated it.

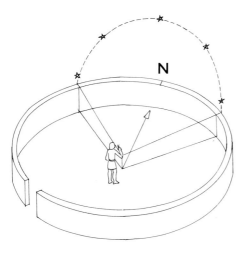

This is not the place to go into detail on the methods and techniques used in building the pyramids, or to examine all the numerous theories put forward on these issues, and we will limit ourselves to describing the principal steps in their construction and mentioning the two leading theories developed to explain it.

After determining the position and preparing a plan which took various essential parameters into consideration (length of the side, anticipated height, and angle of the faces), and using the *merkhet* to determine the position of the pyramid, which took into account factors such as the alignment with other pyramids or places considered sacred, the ground was prepared and leveled, and blocks of local limestone were used as a foundation. At the same time, other teams built a 'pyramid harbor' on a canal especially constructed from the Nile to serve as a means of reaching the necropolises, and prepared wharves and piers to be used to permit the boats loaded with blocks to dock near the building yard.

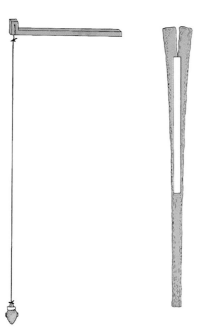

42 left Reconstruction of two instruments, the merkhet *and the* bay *(below), used by architects as early as the Old Kingdom. They were used to determine the exact position of the astronomical North (above), by sighting the position of a determined star at its rise and set, with the aid of an artificial horizon consisting of a vertical limb wall.*

42 below This drawing illustrates the theory of the frontal ramp, which according to Lauer was used to build the pyramids. The ramp became narrower and longer as the structure rose.

42-43 This bas-relief, discovered by Wilkinson, is in the tomb of Djehutihotep, a high ranking official of the Middle Kingdom, who is buried in the necropolis of el-Bersha in Middle Egypt, and shows the transport of a colossal statue by means of a wooden sledge pulled by 172 men. Friction against the runners was reduced by using a mixture of water and lime. Using this system, under ideal conditions the object transported was reduced to one tenth its actual weight.

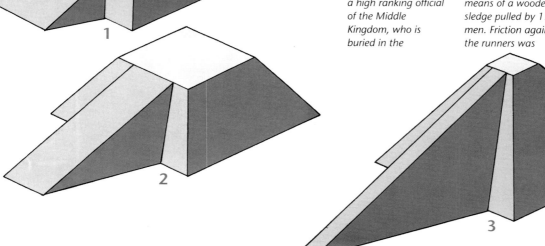

The pyramid building yard was then immediately connected to the port structures by one or more ramps, by means of which sledges loaded with blocks could easily reach the construction. At the same time, teams of quarrymen were already at work in the great limestone quarries of Tura, located on the other side of the Nile in the present-day Maadi and Helwan quarters of Cairo; Tura was famous for the quality of its light limestone, which was used to cover almost all the pyramids.

The exact positions of the sides and angles of the pyramid were then marked accurately on the ground, after determining with great precision the astronomical north, which was identified by observing Ursa Major, or the Big Dipper, which the ancient Egyptians called *meshtyw/meshtin*, 'constellation of the plow' and the constellation *sah*, or Orion. For the pyramid of Khufu, the north was determined with a deviation of only 3'6". At this point the foundation ceremony was celebrated: after driving in the stakes at the corners, the king performed a ritual documented as early as the Second Dynasty and known as *pedj shes*, the 'stretching of the cord'. It consisted of drawing a cord between the stakes at the corners. After purifying the site, the sovereign placed amulets and other ritual objects in a small pit (the foundation deposit), and finally had the first block of stone placed. The real work then began. It was performed by numerous teams, the names of which are found carved on several blocks of the pyramid of Khufu. They prepared the nucleus of the pyramid, placed the corner stones and the covering blocks, and built the funerary apartments and the ramps which would make it possible to transport the limestone blocks to the top of the pyramid.

The innumerable theories offered to explain how these ramps, on which we have no precise information, were built can be divided into two basic groups: theories which hypothesize

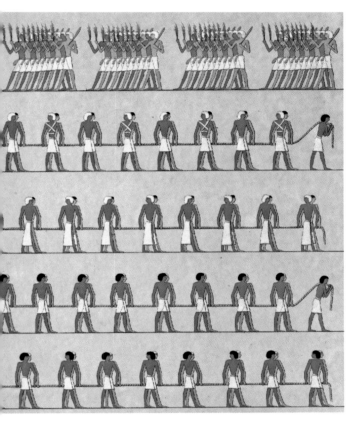

43 below left
Hypothetical reconstruction of the functioning of a floating elevator, one of the machines which may have been used to lift blocks of rock. The debate among researchers who assert that machines or 'machine operators' were used and those who favor the theory of ramps or 'ramp workers,' is still alive today.

43 below right
This object, which dates from the New Kingdom, has been interpreted as a model of a floating elevator. However, no similar models have been found in tombs of the Old Kingdom, and there are many doubts about the actual function of these machines.
(Cairo Museum)

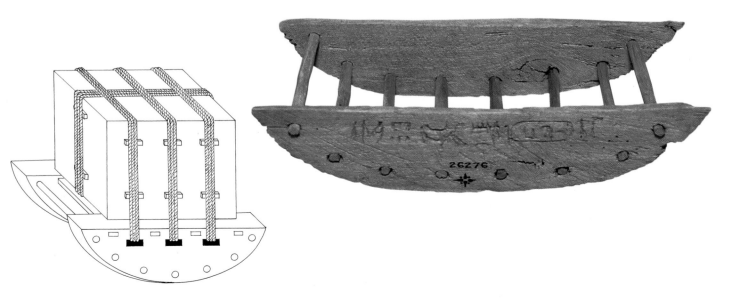

the use of a straight ramp perpendicular to one of the sides of the pyramid, and theories based on the use of a helical encircling ramp. Innumerable variations of both theories have been advanced and supported by valid arguments. Recently a rather plausible new theory has been proposed, according to which numerous small ramps were first employed, followed by a single straight ramp resting on one side of the pyramid. It is not even known what material was used to build the ramps, although for various reasons it

44 above
This bas-relief from the tomb of Rekhmire (Thebes, TT no. 100) illustrates one of the

phases of preparing unfired brick using small wooden molds. This technique is still used in Egypt today.

44 center In addition to the frontal ramp, other types of ramps have been proposed for the construction of the pyramids, such as Hölscher's side ramps (A) or Goyon's encircling ramp (B and C). The encircling ramp has an advantage over the frontal ramp because it is smaller, but at the

same time it poses the problem of having to make sharp curves to the blocks to be lifted. But the true problem posed by the use of ramps is the fact that they were immense structures not much smaller than the pyramids themselves, and would have to be dismantled when the work was completed.

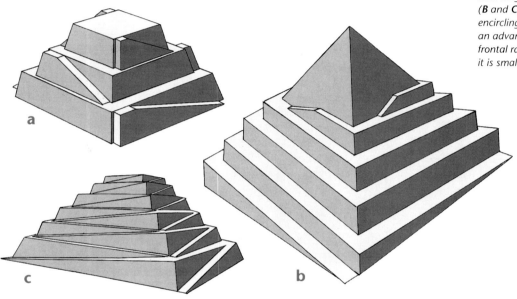

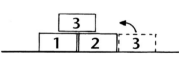

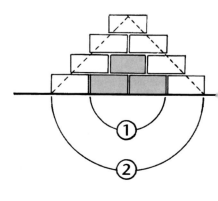

is probable that unfired bricks reinforced with palm trunks were utilized. On the other hand, because these procedures are documented in bas-reliefs on tombs of the period, we know for certain that the great blocks of limestone which made up the structure of the pyramid were hoisted onto the ramps using wooden sledges, whose runners were lubricated to facilitate sliding. It has also been hypothesized that the blocks were lifted using not only levers but also machines, which Herodotus also mentions (*Histories*, II, 125), such as the 'Croon elevator' or the oscillating elevator, a model of

which has been found in tombs of the New Kingdom.

Once the great blocks of limestone were set into place, the final covering of Tura limestone was applied, which is now visible only on the summit of the pyramid of Khafre, and a granite or basalt monolith known as the *pyramidion* was then placed at the top of the pyramid: it has been calculated that the one on the pyramid of Khufu weighed about 7 tonnes.

THE BUILDERS OF THE PYRAMIDS AND THE PYRAMID CITIES

The precision with which the pyramids were built leads one to believe that, in addition to the specialized categories of astronomers, surveyors, architects and master builders, there were also professional workers and simple laborers who, contrary to the statements of Herodotus, were not slaves but peasants. It is probable that this labor was compulsory, but the work was remunerated with food and drink. Living conditions in the building yards were certainly harsh and dangerous, if for no other reason than the enormous masses of rock that were being handled, but workers received food rations three times a day, with a day of rest every ten days.

Little else is known of the social organization of this community of workers, who probably lived in settlements near the building yard known as 'pyramid cities.' However, recent discoveries include a basalt wall from one of these cities, located 2.4 km east of the pyramid of Khufu, and a necropolis located a few hundred meters south of the pyramid containing tombs belonging primarily to the master builders and persons who held important positions in the building yards. Study of the numerous open tombs, now numbering about sixty, in this necropolis will certainly shed new light on this still little-known aspect of the organization of labor during the Old Kingdom.

*45 left
The decorations of the tomb of Rekhmire (New Kingdom, Nineteenth Dynasty) also illustrate the technique utilized to sculpt large statues. This technique must have been similar to that used in the Old Kingdom.*

45 right This copper utensil found at Giza was probably used during the Fourth Dynasty to chisel limestone rock. (London, Petrie Museum)

44 bottom right According to Crozat's theory, the pyramid was constructed through the progressive super-imposition of outer layers onto the original nucleus. This procedure involved a continuous change in the function of the blocks utilized for the construction of the various layers added to the pyramid; they served first as surface blocks and then as support blocks, thus providing an explanation for Herodotus' use of different names for these blocks: bomides and crossai (see Histories, II, 125). The use of levers or machines which, according to Herodotus, were equipped with 'short rods,' and were located on the steps of the continuously growing pyramid, made it possible to lift and position limestone blocks weighing an average of 2.5 tons each in a practical and economical manner, eliminating the need for outside ramps.

THE PYRAMIDS AND NECROPOLISES OF GIZA

PLAN OF THE NECROPOLIS AT GIZA
a. Pyramid of Khufu
b. Secondary pyramids
c. Western cemetery
d. Eastern cemetery
e. Remains of funerary temple of Khufu
f. Pits for Khufu's solar barges
f₁. Pit of Museum for Khufu's solar barge
g. Pyramid of Khafre
h. Chephren's funerary temple
i. Processional ramp
j. Sphinx
k. Lower temple
l. Temple of the Sphinx
m. Funerary monument of Queen Khentkawes
n. Pyramid of Menkaure
o. Funerary temple of Menkaure
p. Remains of processional ramp
q. Remains of lower temple

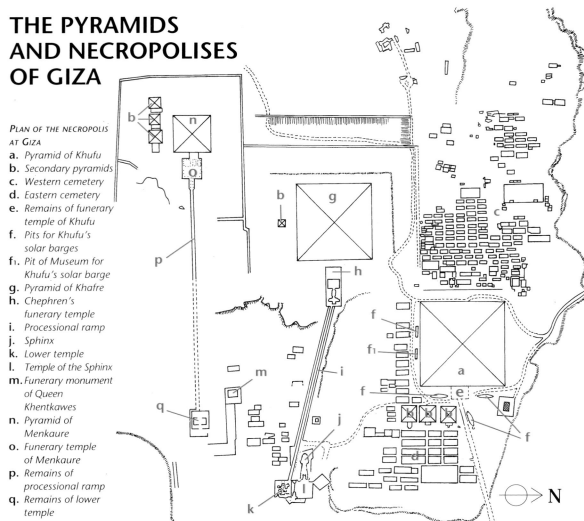

RECONSTRUCTION OF THE GIZA PYRAMID AREA, LATE FOURTH DYNASTY (BY STADELMANN, MODIFIED)
a. Pyramid of Khufu
b. Secondary pyramids
c. Western cemetery
d. Eastern cemetery
e. Funerary temple of Khufu
f. Pits for solar barges
g. Processional ramp
h. Khufu's lower temple
i. Khufu's palace and city of the pyramid
j. Pyramid of Khafre
k. Khafre's funerary temple
l. Sphinx
m. Khafre's lower temple
n. Temple of the Sphinx
o. Funerary monument of Queen Khentkawes
p. Pyramid of Menkaure
q. Menkaure's funerary temple
r. Menkaure's lower temple
s. Port structures
t. Habitation structures
u. Camp of the workers

A few kilometers south of Cairo, several hundred meters from the last houses in the southernmost part of the city, a limestone cliff rises abruptly from the other side of a sandy desert plateau dominated by the imposing and unmistakable form of the last monument on the list compiled by Philo of Byzantium in the second century BC, inspired by the poet Callimachus. Famous as the Seven Wonders of the Ancient World, this list has survived to the present and includes the great pyramid of Khufu (Cheops), the pyramids of Khafre (Chephren) and Menkaure (Mycerinus), and the Great Sphinx.

The ancient Egyptians called this place *imentet*, 'The West' or *kher neter*, 'the necropolis.' Two thousand years later, this site is known as Giza, from a nearby city founded in the seventh century which has now become a populous quarter of Cairo. Even today it is pervaded by an aura of magic and mystery, where suddenly all the noise and clamor of the city fade away into a

A

B

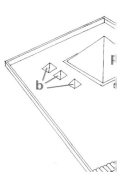

A - The pyramids of Giza seen from the south. In the foreground are the three secondary pyramids and the pyramid of Menkaure.

B - The pyramid of Khufu seen from the southeast, with the solar barge museum, the secondary pyramids and the eastern cemetery. In the foreground are the Sphinx and Khafre's lower temple.

silence interrupted only by the wind whispering through the sand.

Giza was the northernmost necropolis in the Memphis area and became the most important one during the Fourth Dynasty, when the great pyramids were built, but this area contains tombs dating from the first three dynasties as well.

The fame and extraordinary nature of the pyramids of Giza have made this place the symbol of Egypt, and, along with the Valley of the Kings, it is the country's most popular attraction for tourists from all over the world. But while the pyramids and the Sphinx are by far the most well-known monuments at Giza, it should not be forgotten that the area also contains an enormous private necropolis consisting primarily of the tombs of dignitaries of the Fourth Dynasty, with walls decorated with exquisite bas-reliefs.

C - Full relief limestone sculptures that reproduced the features of the deceased, like this one depicting a member of Khafre's family, were found in certain tombs at Giza. It is believed that they may have had a magical function as substitutes for the deceased. (Cairo Museum)

D - Some painted limestone statuettes were found at Giza and appear to be inspired by scenes of daily life. Most of them are from the Fifth Dynasty, like this one that portrays a woman as she prepares the barley paste used to make beer. (Cairo Museum)

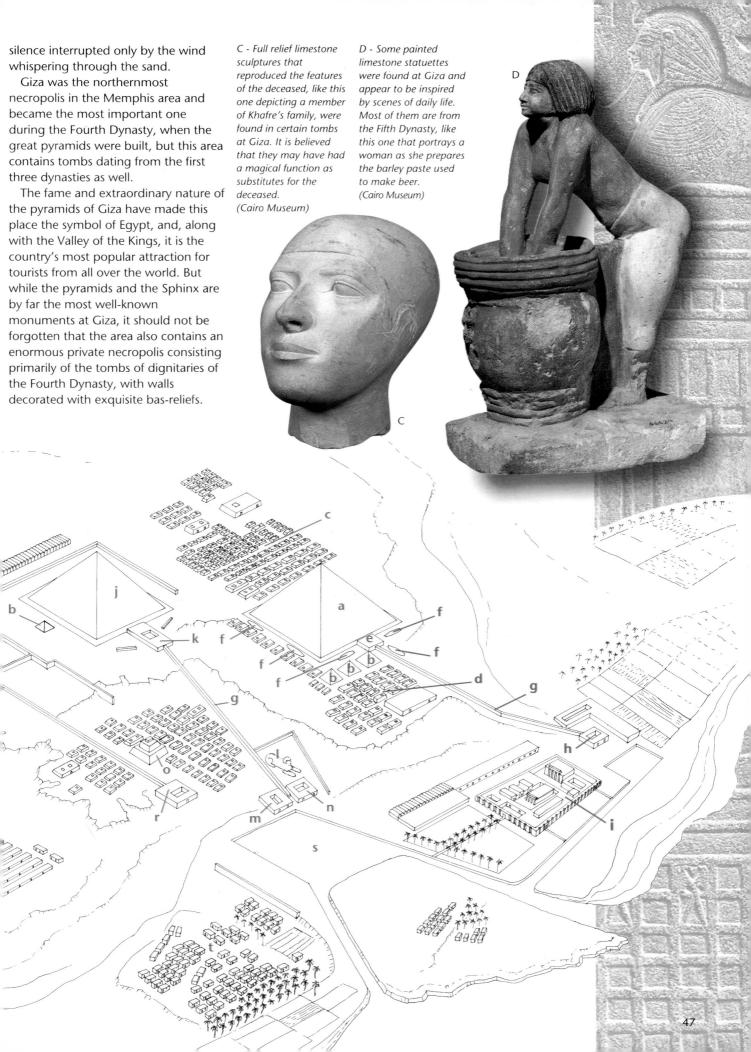

THE PYRAMID OF KHUFU (CHEOPS)

Ancient name: 'Khufu belongs to the horizon'
Original height: 146.6 m
Current height: 138.75 m
Length of side: 230.37 m
Angle: 51°50'40"
Estimated volume: 2,521,000 cu m

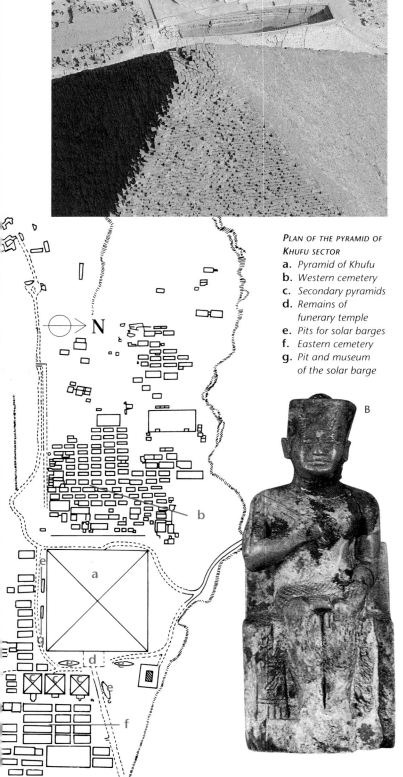

A

Plan of the pyramid of Khufu sector
a. *Pyramid of Khufu*
b. *Western cemetery*
c. *Secondary pyramids*
d. *Remains of funerary temple*
e. *Pits for solar barges*
f. *Eastern cemetery*
g. *Pit and museum of the solar barge*

B

Also known as the Great Pyramid, this was built by King Khufu, the son of Sneferu. Known as Cheops through the writings of Herodotus, he reigned for about 23 years.

Considered a prodigious structure even in ancient times and rightfully included among the Seven Wonders of the Ancient World, 2,300,000 blocks of limestone were used in its construction, originally placed on 210 piers which have an average weight of about 2.5 tonnes each. The average height of each block is about 50 cm, but there are blocks as high as 150 cm, most of which, strangely, are placed on the higher piers.

The northern side contains an enormous gap and the original entrance, which is located at the level of the thirteenth pier, about 15 m high. The entrance leads into a descending corridor 1.20 m high, which after 18 m splits into two parts: the upper portion continues as an ascending corridor, which at this point is blocked by three large granite slabs, and the lower one descends for another 91 m to an underground rock chamber, left unfinished, perhaps due to technical problems related to the

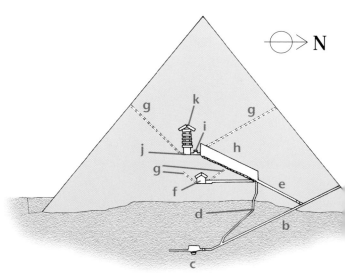

A - Without its pyramidion, the summit of the pyramid of Khufu is a square platform made of blocks on which many travelers have carved their names.

B - This 7.5 cm tall ivory statuette comes from Abydos and is the only surviving likeness of Khufu in existence. (Cairo Museum)

D

C

C - This photograph shows the pyramid of Khufu from the southwest. In the foreground, note the rows of mastabas in the western cemetery, while to the right, on the south side of the pyramid, the solar barge museum can be seen among the structures. Behind the museum are the three secondary pyramids and the eastern cemetery. In the background, at the base of the plateau, are the green lawns of the Golf Club and the houses of the southern districts of Cairo.

D - A small temple dedicated to the goddess Isi can be seen before the southernmost of the three pyramids, which belonged to Queen Henutsen, on the eastern side of the pyramid of Khufu.

E - The original entrance to the pyramid of Khufu is about 15 m high and is surmounted by a double vault. Farther down is the entrance which the Caliph al-Mamum opened in the 9th century, currently used by tourists entering the monument.

E

CROSS-SECTION OF THE PYRAMID OF KHUFU
a. Entrance
b. Descending corridor
c. Underground chamber
d. Service corridor
e. Ascending corridor
f. Queen's chamber
g. Air shafts
h. Great Gallery
i. Antechamber
j. King's chamber
k. Weight relief chambers

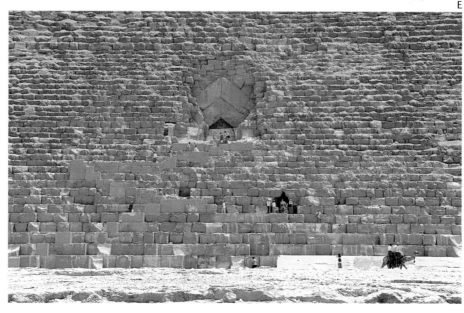

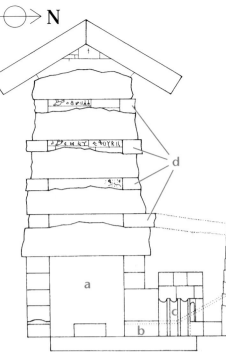

A

50 above left The inscriptions in red ink left by workers are the cartouche of Khufu, the true name of the pharaoh that the Greeks called Cheops. They and the year of his reign appear on the walls of the highest weight relief chamber, explored for the first time by Vyse and Perring in 1837. These are the only known inscriptions in the entire pyramid (from Lepsius).

50 above right The king's chamber (a), preceded by the antechamber (b), in which there were three large slabs of granite (c) blocking the way, is under the so-called weight relief chambers (d), a system of superimposed empty spaces which are believed to have relieved the static weight on the roof of the king's chamber.

B

lack of air, or perhaps for ritual reasons, as it could have represented the domain of Sokar, the god of the underworld.

The present entrance, which follows a tunnel dug by ancient grave robbers, is located approximately 17 m above ground level and reaches the original corridor where it continues as the ascending corridor, beyond the point where it is blocked. This ascending corridor is 38 m long and leads to the Great Gallery. Two openings at the beginning of the Great Gallery lead, respectively, to a second horizontal tunnel, 35 m long, which leads to the so-called Queen's Chamber located on the vertical axis of the pyramid, and

C

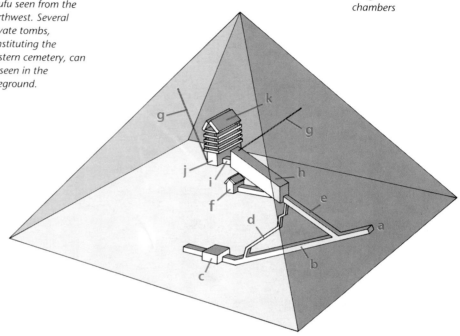

AXONOMETRIC VIEW OF THE
PYRAMID OF KHUFU
a. Entrance
b. Descending corridor
c. Underground chamber
d. Service corridor
e. Ascending corridor
f. Queen's room
g. Air shafts
h. Great Gallery
i. Antechamber
j. King's chamber
k. Weight relief
   chambers

A - Not far from the southeast corner of the pyramid of Khufu is the tomb of Seshemnefer, a high-ranking dignitary who lived around the end of the Fourth Dynasty. The chapel is preceded by a vestibule with two columns.

B - The pyramid of Khufu seen from the northwest. Several private tombs, constituting the western cemetery, can be seen in the foreground.

C - The Great Gallery, 47 m long and 8.48 m high with corbelled walls, was used here for the last time. It is considered a masterpiece of Old Kingdom architecture. The exact significance of this magnificent structure is still not clear.

into a tunnel 60 m long which winds tortuously down to connect with the descending corridor. It has been theorized that this tunnel was designed to permit workers to leave the burial chamber after it was blocked off with the three large granite slabs.

The Great Gallery is one of the architectural masterpieces of ancient Egypt: 47 m long and 8.48 m high, it has corbeled walls, with blocks superimposed with such precision that they extend about 6 cm from each pier.

The tunnel ends in an antechamber originally closed off by three more granite slabs, and leads into the so-called King's Chamber, which is 10.45 m long, 5.20 m wide and 5.80 m high. The sarcophagus is located by its western wall and has no decorations or inscriptions. The ceiling consists of nine slabs of granite, the weight of which has been estimated at 400 tonnes, surmounted by a complex system of five superimposed chambers. They were created in order to relieve the weight and stress caused by the enormous mass of the pyramid resting on the ceiling of the burial chamber. It was in the highest of these chambers that Vyse and Perring found the only ascription of the pyramid: the cartouche of Khufu.

On the northern and southern walls of the King's Chamber, two extremely narrow, straight shafts measuring 20 x

20 cm, inaccurately called 'aeration tunnels,' lead out to the two sides of the pyramid at heights of 71 and 53 m. The significance of these structures has been discussed at great length, and recent research by the German Archeology Institute has demonstrated that they have a purely ritual function: to facilitate the direct ascent to heaven of the soul of the king. Similarly, the three vertically aligned chambers (the underground chamber, the Queen's Chamber and the King's Chamber) do

not appear to be related to changes in design, which have never been proven, but rather serve a ritual purpose.

D

D - All that was found in the granite-walled king's chamber is a monolithic sarcophagus in red granite. The uncovered sarcophagus, located on the west wall, is 2.24 m long and 0.96 m wide. Given its size, it may have been brought in while the room was being constructed.

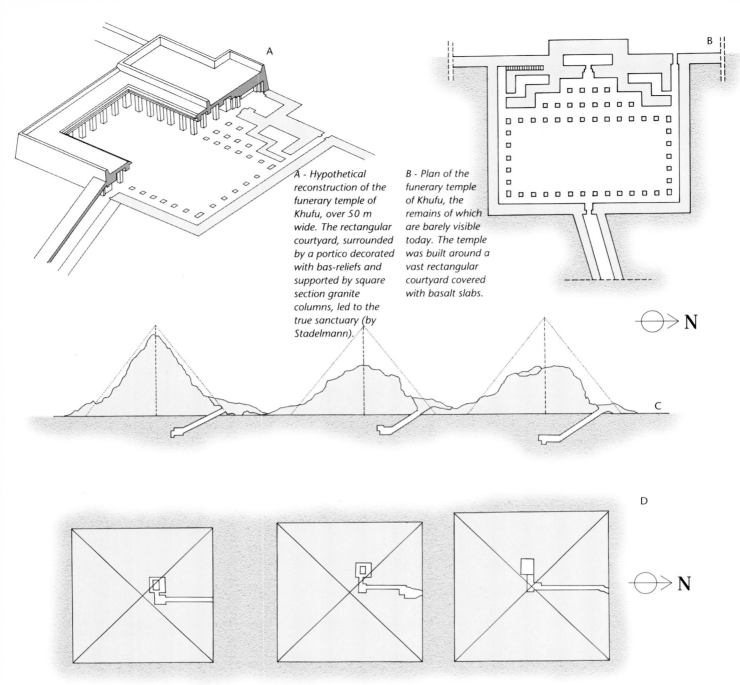

A - Hypothetical reconstruction of the funerary temple of Khufu, over 50 m wide. The rectangular courtyard, surrounded by a portico decorated with bas-reliefs and supported by square section granite columns, led to the true sanctuary (by Stadelmann).

B - Plan of the funerary temple of Khufu, the remains of which are barely visible today. The temple was built around a vast rectangular courtyard covered with basalt slabs.

C and D - Plans and cross-sections of the three secondary pyramids, located on the south side of the pyramid of Khufu. These pyramids, which archeologists identify by the initials G1c, G1b and G1a, are respectively dedicated to the queens Henutsen, Khufu' half-sister, Meritetis, and Hetepheres, the mother of Khufu. A few dozen meters from the pyramid is the queen's shaft tomb.

E - On the south side of Queen Henutsen's pyramid is a temple dedicated to the goddess Isi, the 'Lady of the Pyramids,' built during the Twenty-First Dynasty on what may have been the site of an earlier chapel from the Eighteenth Dynasty, which in its turn occupied the area of Henutsen's funerary chapel. The temple to Isi was expanded during the Saite Twenty-Sixth Dynasty by adding a series of side chapels, when the Giza area became a necropolis, a role it played until the Roman era.

On the eastern side of the pyramid there are two large boat-shaped pits, used for the royal boats, and three secondary pyramids: the one to the south is attributed to Queen Henutsen, daughter of Sneferu and the half-sister of Khufu, the one in the center to Meritetis, and the third one, to the north, to Queen Hetepheres, the mother of the king, whose shaft tomb, discovered in 1925 just a few dozen meters away, by the Harvard University and Boston Museum expedition headed by George A. Reisner, provided the beautiful funerary trappings on display in the Cairo Museum.

Only a few traces of foundations attest to the presence of the funerary temple, which must have had a rectangular plan 52.50 m wide. The processional ramp leading from the temple was 810 m long and abruptly changed direction, running 32° northeast. It led to the valley temple, which probably had already been destroyed in ancient times. The temple foundations and original floor of basalt slabs were found in 1990 during excavations headed by Zahi Hawass, and are located 125 m from the point where the ramp turned to the northeast.

F - In 1925 the American archaeologist Reisner discovered the tomb of Hetepheres, the wife of Sneferu and mother of Khufu, with its splendid burial trappings, now on display at the Cairo Museum. Among the numerous objects is this wooden chair decorated with elegant inlay work.

F

G

H

I

J

G and H - One of the most remarkable objects in the collection was this gilded wooden sedan chair, the preferred means of transport for important dignitaries. A small gilded wooden box with rings inside was also found.

I - Three solid gold objects were also found in Hetepheres' burial trappings, including this small pitcher with elongated spout.

J - This well-preserved bed, complete with head rest (rather than pillows, ancient Egyptians used simple, rigid supports made of wood or other materials) was part of Hetepheres' burial trappings.

THE SOLAR BOAT

A - General view of the solar barge, reassembled and placed in the specially built museum. The gigantic puzzle contained 1224 pieces and took over ten years to reassemble.

B - The museum that holds the solar barge stands on the south side of the pyramid of Khufu, near the pit where the barge was found. A little farther to the right is the still-unopened pit that contains a second barge.

C - Khufu's solar barge is 43.4 m long and 5.6 m wide. No metallic parts were used in its assembly, only ropes and wooden pegs.

D - There are three large, open, boat-shaped pits on the eastern side of the pyramid as well. It is not known for certain if they were used for real boats or if they themselves are simulacra of boats.

A

B

The boat was not only a means of transportation or an instrument used in fishing and hunting, but was also and above all of symbolic importance: it was the means of transportation of the gods.

The god Amen was led on his sacred boat during great religious processions, and the sun-god Ra himself traveled the heavens every day in what was called the 'boat of the millions of years,' to ensure for humanity the balance of the seasons and the ceaseless succession of day and night. The pharaoh, the son of Ra, followed his celestial destiny and thus needed a boat to navigate the heavens.

The large boat-shaped pits found on the eastern side of the pyramid attest to the ancient presence of boats. In May 1954, during cleaning work, the young Egyptian architect and archeologist Kamal el-Mallakh and inspector Zaki Nur found two hermetically sealed, triangular-shaped ditches, closed off by about 40 gigantic blocks of limestone weighing from 17 to 20 tonnes each. The northernmost one was opened: inside was a large wooden boat disassembled into 1,224 pieces. This extraordinary find was carefully and patiently restored under the direction of Ahmed Yussef Mustafa over a

C

D

period of more than ten years, and the boat was finally fully reassembled in 1968. At the conclusion of the long work, this royal boat, whose planking was assembled through an ingenious system of ropes without using nails or metallic parts, appeared with its elegant lines just as it had been designed and built 4,500 years ago: its form, with the sharply upturned prow and stern, seemed modeled after papyrus boats.

The royal boat, which was built of Lebanese cedar, is fully 43.3 m long, with a width of 5.6 m and a draft of only 1.5 m, which made it suitable only for river navigation. The boat had two cabins: a central one about 9 m long, and a small front cabin which

E - The microprobe inserted through a hole drilled into the pit has provided this endoscopic image, confirming the presence of a boat similar to the one excavated in 1954. With the cooperation of the Egyptian Antiquities Organization and the National Geographic Magazine, it was possible to obtain an image of the pit's contents without having to open it.

F   G

F - The solar barge, now on display in the museum built just a few meters away, was found completely disassembled inside this pit, sealed with limestone blocks weighing between 17 and 20 tonnes each.

G - A night time view of the work yard set up in 1987, above the pit where Khufu's intact second solar barge was found buried.

probably was for the captain. Propulsion was by means of ten pairs of oars, and steering through two large oar rudders located in the stern. As there is no trace of a mast, it would have been impossible to use a sail. The assembled boat is located in a special museum just a few meters away from the site of its discovery.

The Egyptian Antiquities Organization decided not to open the second pit, but its interior was photographed in 1987 by a special probe designed with the collaboration of the National Geographic Society. The probe showed that the pit contains a boat similar to the first one.

The significance of the boat of Khufu has been debated at great length. It

has been asked whether the boat ever sailed (there is evidence it was in water), whether it was the boat or one of the boats used by Khufu during his reign, if it was used to transport the body of the dead pharaoh to his final resting-place, or whether it had a purely symbolic or ritual meaning. In the latter case the boat would have been part of the funerary trappings, along with many other much smaller objects which were buried with the king inside the pyramid, so that they could be used during his trip to the underworld. It may have played yet another role and functioned as a solar boat like that of the god Ra. It is difficult if not impossible to determine the truth with certainty, as there is not

enough information to make anything more than suppositions. Nevertheless, the Pyramid Texts leave no doubt: at the end of his earthly life the soul of the pharaoh ascended in the solar boat to rejoin his father Ra and sail eternally across the oceans of time.

THE PYRAMIDS OF GIZA
by Zahi Hawass

A

The Giza pyramids, with their fabric of large local stones and casing of fine white Tura limestone, are some of the finest examples of pyramids in existence. The use of more and more stone by the Fourth Dynasty builders to create larger pyramids and vast funerary complexes outside the pyramid walls gave awe-inspiring results. One can hardly imagine the number of workmen required for such a huge labor project as that of building the pyramids of Giza.

A ventilation system has been created by the German Institute in Cairo in co-operation with the Giza Inspectorate of the Supreme Council of Antiquities, in order to preserve the pyramid of Khufu (called Akhet-Khufu or 'Horizon of Khufu'), which forms the nucleus of the necropolis.

During our work, a robot was sent through the so-called air shaft from the Second Chamber. It went 65 m inside the pyramid before being stopped by what appeared to be a door with two copper handles. We are still uncertain whether this is a door or

a blocking stone, and this needs to be investigated further.

The Discovery of the Causeway and the Valley Temple of Khufu

During the construction of a new sewage system for the village of Nazlet-es-Samman, located at the base of the escarpment, we found the remains of the valley temple, and the continuation of Khufu's causeway, with some of its paving slabs still in situ. The total length of the causeway from the east face of the Great Pyramid to the site of the valley temple is not less than 810 m. The angle of the causeway changed slightly when it reached the escarpment, but, as it approached the lower temple, it turned more abruptly.

At the valley temple site we found a black-green basalt pavement 56 m long and set at about 14 m above sea level, which is about 4.5 m below the present ground level in the area. At the pavement's edge we found part of a mud-brick wall that may possibly be as wide as 8 m. The configuration of the basalt blocks indicates that this

monumental building is what remains of the valley temple.

To the east of the Great Pyramid of Khufu are the subsidiary pyramids of Khufu. The first to the north belongs to Khufu's mother Hetepheres. The second belongs to Queen Meritetis and the third to Henutsen.

The Discovery of the Satellite Pyramid of Khufu

We found the satellite pyramid at the south-east corner of the Great Pyramid unexpectedly, because the site had been excavated fully by Petrie in 1881 and another clearance had been undertaken in 1940.

The satellite pyramid has a T-shaped style similar to that of the subsidiary pyramid of Khafre, located at the south side of the second pyramid at Giza. The superstructure of this pyramid consists of only about three courses of limestone, and is located on one side of the burial chamber of this pyramid. Nothing has been found in the burial chamber except two large stones, a medium sized one, and a small one. There was also a hole cut into the ground. The ceiling of the burial chamber seems to be vaulted, springing from the south and north walls.

There are boat pits located on the south of the subsidiary pyramids G1a and G1b. The boat pit to the south of G1b is also located on the immediate east of G1d, the newly discovered pyramid. It is possible that this boat belonged to the satellite pyramid because the boat pit is located near it. The problem with this is that G1a has a boat pit on the south and this boat pit is located on the south of G1b, with nothing found on the south of G1c (the southern one).

On the east side of Khufu, there is the so-called Trial Passage. This was intended to be the substructure of the satellite pyramid of Khufu, but was abandoned because of the enlarging of the upper temple. The satellite pyramid was then moved and rebuilt in the south-east corner of Khufu's pyramid. The problem here is that the interior of the Trial Passage is exactly like the interior of the Great Pyramid, though shorter, and the substructure of the new satellite pyramid has a T-shape. This may not be significant, however, because Khufu's reign was an experimental period, in which the development of the Old Kingdom architectural components of the pyramid complex was initiated. It seems that the small area then available for the satellite pyramid, and the limited time available in which to build it, made it necessary for it to have a T-shaped style rather than a trial passage. It seems that the new satellite pyramid was constructed hurriedly.

The function of the satellite pyramid is not known, and has been debated at length among scholars. Among the suggestions for its possible function are: that it was a dummy tomb connected with the *Sed* festival; the burial place for placentas or the viscera; a temporary storage place for the body or a tomb for crowns; or that it was a solar symbol.

The southern tomb of the pyramid complex of Djoser is a prototype of the Old Kingdom satellite pyramids. The reliefs on the panels in Djoser's South Tomb represent the king wearing the white crown and running holding the flail. These scenes in the South Tomb can be interpreted as representations of the *Sed* festival.

I therefore propose a new theory on the function of the satellite pyramid: that it was used as a changing room for the ritual of the *Sed* festival.

There is a very interesting sequence in the wall reliefs of the pyramid complexes of the Old Kingdom. The first scene shows the king in his palace with his officials and courtiers, or seated in his chapel. He wears the crown of Upper and Lower Egypt and his robe, and he carries the flail to show his power over the Two Lands. The second scene shows him wearing the skirt and holding the flail while dancing or doing the ritual of the *Sed* festival. The last scene in the sequence of the wall reliefs always occurs in the offering room and shows the king receiving offerings and divinity. He is accepted by all the gods and becomes equal to them because he has accomplished what the gods required him to do on earth and now he is rewarded by becoming a god.

The king's duty is to build a tomb for himself and temples for the worship of the gods, to unify Upper and Lower Egypt, to give offerings to the gods and to smite the enemies of Egypt.

The scenes of the *Sed* festival occur on the walls of the Southern Tomb, which is the prototype of the satellite pyramid. These scenes also occur in the wall reliefs of the pyramid complexes from the Fourth to the Sixth Dynasties of the Old Kingdom. It is therefore feasible that there is a connection

between the *Sed* festival and the satellite pyramid.

The function of the satellite pyramid is that the king used the burial chamber of this pyramid as a changing room. He left his crown and his robe in the burial chamber, and then emerged through the entrance wearing the skirt and holding the flail. He then performed the *Sed* festival outside, announcing to the gods that he had finished all that they had asked him to do. Therefore, the function of the satellite pyramid during the Old Kingdom was as a changing room for the *Sed* festival rituals.

The Discovery of the Pyramidion of Khufu

On the south side of the satellite pyramid was found a large limestone block with three sloping sides. This block was the base of the pyramidion. We knew that there must be a missing part on the north to make it square, but never expected to find the missing part. A year after the discovery of the satellite pyramid itself, however, the pyramidion was found lying on the north side of the pyramid.

A - Recent excavations at the southeast corner of the pyramid of Khufu have revealed the structures of a satellite pyramid with inner chambers arranged in a T-shape, and a descending corridor that ends in a rectangular chamber. The exact function of satellite pyramids is not known, but these structures may have played a role in celebrating the *Sed* festival.

B - A large block of limestone found near the satellite pyramid proved to be the base of the pyramidion that originally stood on top of the pyramid of Khufu. The pyramidion was restored and completed through the addition of other blocks.

57

THE PYRAMID OF KHAFRE (CHEFREN)

Ancient name: 'Khafre is great'
Original height: 143.5 m
Current height: 136.4 m
Length of side: 215.25 m
Angle: 50°10'
Estimated volume: 1,659,200 cu m

B

*PLAN OF THE PYRAMID
OF KHAFRE SECTOR*
a. *Pyramid of Khafre*
b. *Remains of
    satellite pyramid*
c. *Funerary temple*
d. *Ramp*
e. *Sphinx*
f. *Lower temple*
g. *Temple of the
    Sphinx*

The pyramid of Khafre, the fourth king of the Fourth Dynasty, known as Chephren to the Greeks, is also known as the second pyramid and is somewhat smaller than the pyramid of Khufu. Nevertheless, because it was built in a slightly more elevated position and its faces are more inclined, it gives the impression of being the largest of the pyramids of Giza.

First opened in modern times by Giovanni Battista Belzoni in 1818, it had already been profaned in ancient times and in the thirteenth century. It is the only pyramid which still retains a part of its original covering of Tura limestone, which can be seen near its apex.

There are two entrances on the north side. The first, located at a height of 10 m, leads to an upper corridor, which descends at an angle of 25°55' for 32 m and then becomes horizontal until it reaches the burial chamber. The other one is located at ground level and is

A - Khafre, the son of Khufu and Queen Henutsen, is shown here in the famous diorite statue which Mariette found in the lower temple. Khafre succeeded his half-brother Djedefra, whose rule was quite brief. (Cairo Museum)

B - The pyramid of Khafre is almost as large as that of Khufu, but its internal structure is completely different. Giovanni Battista Belzoni discovered the entrance to this pyramid on March 2, 1818.

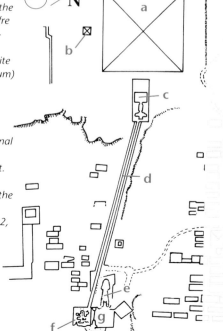

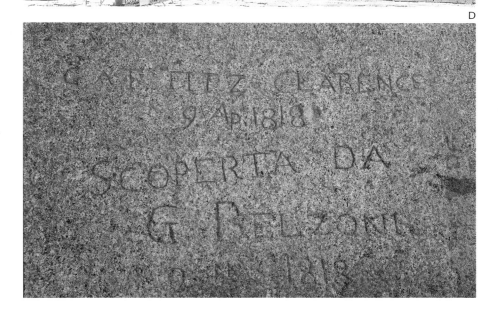

currently used to enter the monument. It leads to a lower corridor, which, after initially descending at an angle of 21°40' and then running horizontally for a brief stretch, rises once again and leads into the horizontal portion of the upper corridor. The burial chamber contains a great granite sarcophagus and its lid with no inscriptions or decorations and the signature of Belzoni dated March 2, 1818, the day of its discovery.

C - There are two entrances on the north face of the pyramid: the present-day entry at ground level, leading to the lower corridor, and the original entrance, leading to the upper corridor. The passageway opened by Belzoni led directly into this corridor.

D - An inscription by the English Colonel Fitzclarence can be seen at the upper entrance, commemorating the opening of the pyramid by Belzoni.

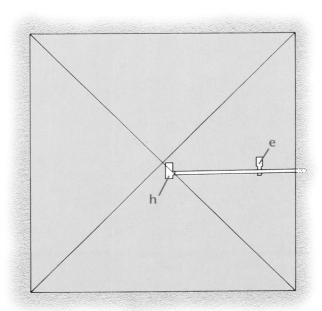

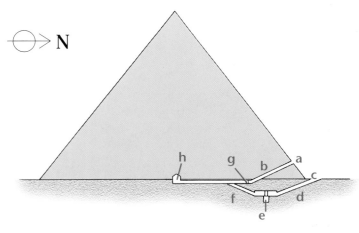

PLAN AND CROSS-SECTION OF THE PYRAMID OF KHAFRE
a. Upper entrance
b. Upper corridor
c. Present-day entrance
d. Lower corridor
e. Underground chamber

(incomplete)
f. Ascending corridor
g. Slabs blocking the way
h. Burial chamber
The great simplicity of the internal structures compared with those in the pyramid of Khufu is quite evident.

Probably the reason for this change is due to problems encountered during construction of the king's chamber and its superstructures, when numerous signs of collapse appeared even before work had been completed.

A - The pyramid of Khafre is the only one on which any portion of the original covering in Tura limestone remains, albeit only on the upper portion. Tura limestone was more valuable than local limestone and was utilized to build the body of the pyramid. It came from quarries located in the Mokattam mountain range on the other side of the Nile.

B - The impressive ruins of the funerary temple, built of enormous blocks of granite, can be seen in front of the eastern side of the pyramid. The temple was gradually dismantled to be reused as construction material.

AXONOMETRIC VIEW OF THE PYRAMID OF KHAFRE

a. Upper entrance
b. Upper corridor
c. Present-day entrance
d. Lower corridor
e. Underground chamber (incomplete)
f. Ascending corridor
g. Slabs blocking the way
h. Burial chamber

It is interesting to note that the blocks covering the burial chamber, unlike those in Khufu's burial chamber, are arranged in 'log cabin' fashion, using a system for lightening static weight that had previously been used in the uppermost weight relief chamber in Khufu's pyramid, and which from this point on would be used in all subsequent pyramids.

C

D

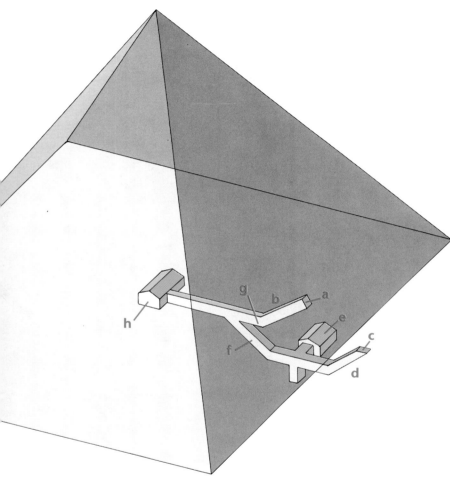

E

C - The words 'Discovered by G. Belzoni - March 2, 1816' appear on the south wall of the burial chamber, to commemorate Belzoni's successful search. In reality, inside the pyramid, which according to Herodotus did not have internal chambers, Belzoni discovered another writing on the west wall of the burial chamber, confirming that the monument had already been profaned in the Islamic era, perhaps around the end of the 12th century.

D - Inside the burial chamber Belzoni found only a large, red granite sarcophagus with a broken cover and no inscriptions, similar to Khufu's sarcophagus. It is 2.02 m long and 1.06 m wide.

E - The final position of the pyramid of Khafre, here seen from the northwest, does not seem to be the one planned in the original design, according to which it should have been located 60 m farther north. This change may explain the presence of two entrances and the asymmetrical position of the rock chamber, which is incomplete. It has also been theorized that the original design provided for a system of three internal chambers, similar to that of the pyramid of Khufu, and that it was later simplified to hasten construction, as Khafre was not a young man when he came to the throne.

61

THE FUNERARY TEMPLE

A - General view, which megalithic architectural style can be seen in the lower temple as well. Unfortunately, only magnificent vestiges of this monument remain, flanked on its two longest sides by four great boat pits (a fifth one can be seen on the north side).

B - Khafre's processional ramp, which is 494 m long and connects the funerary temple to the lower temple, is the most beautiful example of this type of structure. The ramp was originally covered and may have been decorated with bas-reliefs.

On the east side of the pyramid is a colossal funerary temple, which is much larger than that of Khufu (one of its blocks weighs an estimated 400 tonnes). It was excavated in 1910 by Hölscher and von Sieglin. Used for centuries as a quarry for materials, this magnificent temple has sadly been reduced to rubble, and its pylons and granite finishing have disappeared.

The temple was 110 m long and included an entrance with two pylons, a transverse vestibule with fourteen columns, and a rectangular hall

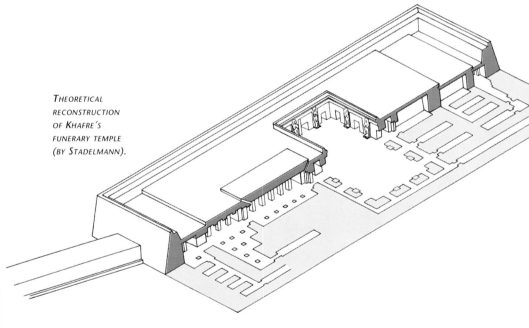

THEORETICAL RECONSTRUCTION OF KHAFRE'S FUNERARY TEMPLE (BY STADELMANN).

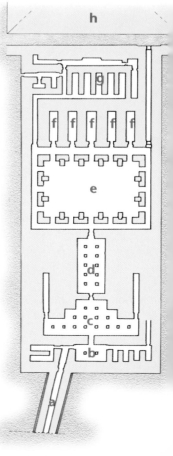

surrounded by columns on the north and south sides, which led into a large courtyard surrounded by a portico with columns where there were large statues of the king. On the western side of the courtyard there were five chapels used in the royal cult. Behind them were located storehouses and a small, intimate sanctuary.

The enormous processional ramp begins at the funerary temple and runs obliquely 494 m south, leading to the valley temple.

PLAN OF KHAFRE'S FUNERARY TEMPLE, ACCORDING TO DATA OBTAINED FROM EXCAVATIONS BY HÖLSCHER AND VON SIEGLIN CARRIED OUT AT THE TURN OF THE CENTURY

a. Processional ramp
b. Vestibule
c. Transverse room
d. Rectangular room
e. Central courtyard

with portico and colonnade
f. Chapels for the statues
g. Storehouses and sanctuary
h. Body of the pyramid

The edifice occupied a surface area of 110 x 45 m and was separated from the pyramid by a court-yard about 10 m wide.

THE VALLEY TEMPLE

C and D - Khafre's lower temple, which at first was erroneously called the 'temple of the Sphinx,' is the only example of this type of structure in existence. Still in excellent condition, its exact function is not yet known.

Discovered by Auguste Mariette in 1852 and erroneously referred to as the temple of the Sphinx, this is the only truly well-preserved valley temple we know of.

Built with large rectangular blocks of Aswan granite, its architectural style is similar to that of the funerary temple: it has a square layout with two front entrances, where there were originally four sphinxes, only fragments of which remain, a transverse vestibule and a large inverted T-shaped hall with sixteen monolithic pillars 4.15 m tall, from the northwest corner of which runs the processional ramp. Along the walls of the main structure of this splendid hall, a true architectural

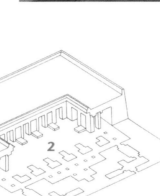

THEORETICAL RECONSTRUCTION OF KHAFRE'S LOWER TEMPLE (1) STANDING BESIDE THE TEMPLE OF THE SPHINX (2) (BY STADELMANN).

PLAN OF THE LOWER TEMPLE (BY RICKE)
a. Processional ramp
b. Corridor
c. Great hall in inverted T shape
d. Vestibule
e. Chapel with three niches
f. Entrances (originally flanked by sphinxes)

masterpiece of the Old Kingdom, there were originally 24 diorite statues depicting Khafre seated. Except for one discovered by Mariette, which can be seen in the Cairo Museum, they have all disappeared (nothing remains but the imprint of the foundation).

Current knowledge is not sufficient to determine the exact role and function of the various parts of this temple, but it does not seem to have been used for embalming the deceased king. In fact, in 1995 traces of the 'purification tent' were found near the temple.

E - A narrow corridor leads from the northwest corner of the temple to the processional ramp.

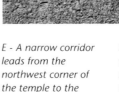

F - The large blocks which form the main structure of the valley temple were positioned with exact precision.

THE SPHINX

A - The Sphinx of Giza is a unique monument in the history of Egyptian art: the head of the king, with his nemes head covering, appears on the 57 m long leonine body. The absence of inscriptions on the monument has led to debates on its age; although many researchers believe it dates back to the reign of Khafre, some believe it may be from the era of Khufu, and certain pseudo-archaeology advocates assert that it is over 10,000 years old.

The word 'sphinx', which may come from the Egyptian expression *shesep ankh* ('living image'), means a sculpture which represents a deity with the body of a lion and a human or animal head.

The Great Sphinx of Giza that rises out of the desert sands, to which the Arabs gave the strange name of *Abu Hôl,* 'the father of terror,' is a unique monument in the history of Egyptian statues, in which sphinxes are typical elements. It fascinated not only voyagers of the eighteenth and nineteenth centuries, but also students of the esoteric sciences and fans of fantasy archeology, who assert that this sculpture is the work of an extremely ancient civilization which disappeared thousands of years before the construction of the pyramids, leaving no other trace.

In reality, although it does exude a certain aura of mystery that easily induces dreams and fantasy, the Sphinx contains no great secrets, nor is it a font of lost knowledge of vanished civilizations. It was sculpted into a rocky spur consisting of three formations of that marly limestone from the Eocene age that makes up the Giza plateau, and had probably already been roughly modeled by the wind before it was sculpted by humans.

About 57 m long and 20 m high, the Sphinx is the image of the king who unites human nature with divine and leonine power. At the same time the Sphinx represented the lord or guardian of the necropolis, and in the New Kingdom was identified with the god Horemakhet, 'Horus on the Horizon,' whom the Greeks transcribed as Hormachis and who, probably beginning in the period of Amenophis II, around 1450 BC, became identified with the god Haurun, a Canaanite desert god of Syrian origins.

During the Eighteenth Dynasty (1550–1397 BC), a thousand years after its construction, the desert sand covered the Sphinx, and a story,

C

D

C and D - Between the front paws of the Sphinx is a large stela which recalls how the pharaoh Thutmosis IV, who lived during the Twenty-Fifth Dynasty, about a thousand years after the era of Khafre, performed the first restoration of the monument, freeing it from the sand that had enveloped it. During the New Kingdom the Sphinx was identified with the god Hormachis, the image of 'Horus on the horizon,' and the Syrian god Haurun.

carved into the great stela located between the front paws of the monument, recounts how the young prince Tuthmosis fell asleep in the shade of its stone body during a hunt. In a dream, the Sphinx, in the form of the god Hormachis, predicted his future ascent to the throne and begged him to free it from the desert sand that was burying it. When Tuthmosis came to the throne years later under the name of Tuthmosis IV, he remembered his youthful dream

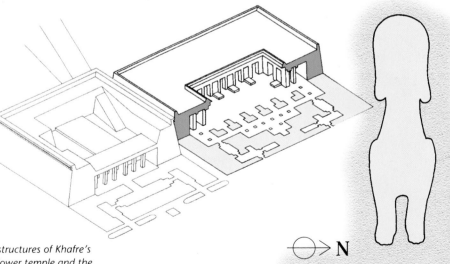

THEORETICAL RECONSTRUCTION OF THE TEMPLE OF THE SPHINX (LEFT) (BY STADELMANN) AND PLAN (RIGHT) Next to the temple (1) is a religious structure from the New Kingdom (2), from the era of Amenophis II (New Kingdom).

B - In front of the Sphinx is a large, roughly four-sided structure which corresponds to the so-called 'temple of the Sphinx,' and which is located within a courtyard surrounded by a colonnade. On its left side are the structures of Khafre's lower temple and the processional ramp that connects it to the funerary temple at the pyramid. To the far right a small religious structure from the New Kingdom can be seen.

A

A - This aerial photo from the west shows the great Sphinx in all its glory, after a series of still incomplete restoration projects that have been under way for over ten years. The leonine body of the sculpture is 47 m long, and its head rises to a height of 20 m. Originally carved from a block of limestone, which may already have been roughly modeled by the wind, the Sphinx was partially covered with blocks of limestone during the Greco-Roman era.

voyage published in 1555, describes it as 'a sculpted monster in the shape of a virgin in front and a lion in back.' Previously, the famous Arab historian al-Makrizi, who lived around the eleventh century, had also expressed interest in the Sphinx, and stated that there was a secret cavity in the monument which hid a cup that had belonged to Solomon, the son of David.

In 1798 scientists of the Napoleonic expedition excavated the monument. They discovered the famous stela of Tuthmosis IV and performed the first scientific investigation of the statue.

The most thorough exploration of the Sphinx, however, was carried out by Giovanni Battista Caviglia, who in 1816 also discovered fragments of the statue, including a portion of the false beard that had decorated its chin, which was then given to the British Museum. Auguste Mariette performed the first systematic excavations, which were continued by his successor Gaston Maspero. Mariette believed that the Sphinx was the most ancient monument of all Egypt, dating to a period before the construction of the great pyramids, and that it contained an underground chamber.

B

and performed the first restoration of the monument.

Despite other excavations during the period of Rameses II, around 1300 BC, the sand once again gained the upper hand and completely buried the colossal structure. This explains why Herodotus never mentions the Sphinx. As the centuries passed, new restoration work, still visible today, was carried out under Marcus Aurelius and Septimus Severus between 160 AD and 211 AD. Then the sands once again prevailed, but the head must still have been visible, arousing the curiosity and wonder of the adventurous travelers of the time, such as the French physician Pierre Belon, who, in his *Relation de*

B - The Sphinx, which name means 'Living idol,' was considered the guardian of the necropolis of Giza.

C - The structures of a small religious building from the New Kingdom, built during the reign of Amenophis II, can be seen to the northeast of the Sphinx.

C

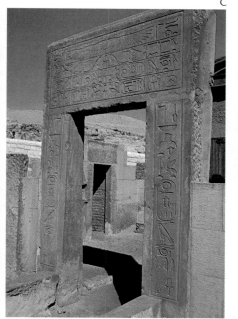

D

E - Excavations carried out by Cavaglia in 1816 led to the discovery of a portion of the ritual beard which originally adorned the chin of the Sphinx. It is now on display at the British Museum.

F - The temple of the Sphinx, seen from the eastern end of Khafre's processional ramp.

In 1925, Emile Baraize consolidated the head with limestone blocks, restored the great 'wings' of the head covering, and discovered the true temple of the Sphinx. Finally, the work undertaken by the University of Cairo in 1935–6, under the direction of Selim Hassan, gave the Sphinx and the structures connected to it their present appearance.

In 1980 the monument had to be restored due to deterioration of the limestone caused by increased humidity, water infiltration and air pollution. The results were disastrous, due to improper use of cement, and the subsequent swelling of the mortar caused numerous blocks of recently applied limestone covering to fall off. It

was then decided to perform another restoration (still under way) without cement-based binders, using much smaller blocks of limestone, to give the Sphinx its original appearance and ensure its survival.

During the course of this last restoration Egyptian archeologists directed by Zahi Hawass actually did find a tunnel at ground level in the northern side of the Sphinx. It led to a cavity, which proved to be empty.

Unfortunately, even the most recent investigations conducted during the restoration work have brought to light no further information which would resolve the problem of dating the Sphinx. While all agree that it does not predate the period of the pyramids, in

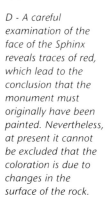

E

the absence of any epigraphic document (no writing of any kind appears on the monument), it can be dated only on stylistic and topographical criteria, and whether it should be attributed to the reign of Khafre, as is commonly accepted by most experts, or of Khufu, is still an open question.

The temple of the Sphinx
A Fourth Dynasty structure known as the temple of the Sphinx was discovered right in front of the Sphinx. It consists of large blocks of limestone and pink Aswan granite, with a double entrance, a courtyard surrounded by large rectangular pillars, and an altar in the center for offerings.

D - A careful examination of the face of the Sphinx reveals traces of red, which lead to the conclusion that the monument must originally have been painted. Nevertheless, at present it cannot be excluded that the coloration is due to changes in the surface of the rock.

F

THE SECRETS OF THE SPHINX
by Zahi Hawass

The Great Sphinx is a national symbol of Egypt, both ancient and modern. But is it more than this. It is an archetype of antiquity whose image has stirred the imagination of poets, scholars, adventurers and tourists for centuries. In recent years, however, the Sphinx has become conspicuous for the rate at which it is deteriorating. Twice in the last decade stones fell from the statue: masonry veneer from the left hind paw in 1981, and a sizable piece of bedrock from the right shoulder in 1988. While experts search for solutions, the surface of the Sphinx is flaking and crumbling.

The Sphinx sits within the Giza necropolis which is dominated by the pyramid of Khufu (Cheops), Khafre (Chephren) and Menkaure (Mycerinus), pharaohs of the Fourth Dynasty (c. 2575–2467 BC). Each pyramid had a long causeway running from a mortuary temple at its eastern side, down to the level of the Nile flood plain, where a valley temple served as an entrance to the pyramid complex.

The Sphinx is intimately connected with the Khafre causeway and valley temple, which suggests that Khafre – perhaps the greatest maker of statues of the pyramid age – had it built as part of his pyramid area. There are emplacements in his pyramid temples for 58 statues, including four colossal sphinxes, each more than 26 feet long and two flanking each door of his valley temple; two colossal statues, possibly of baboons, in tall niches inside the entrances of the valley temple; 23 life-size statues of the pharaoh in the valley temple (fragments of several have been found with his name inscribed on them); at least seven large statues of him in the inner chambers of his mortuary temple; 12 colossal Khafre statues around the courtyard of his mortuary temple; and 10 more huge statues in the Sphinx temple. No other Old Kingdom pyramid temple floor plans indicate so many statues at such a scale. The Sphinx, the largest of all, was carved to a scale of

30:1 for the head and about 2:1 for the lion body.

It is carved directly from the limestone of the Giza plateau, part of the Mokatam formation, which is formed from marine sediment deposited when waters engulfed north-east Africa during the Eocene period. According to geologist Thomas Aigner, formerly of the University of Tubingen and now with Shell International, as the sea retreated northward about 50 million years ago an embankment developed along what is now the north-northwest side of the plateau. Carbonate mud deposited in the lagoon thus formed then petrified, becoming the layers from which the ancient builders quarried their limestone blocks, hauling them up the slope to build the pyramids.

The ancient quarrymen fashioned the Sphinx from the lowest layers, those lying directly on the harder reef. They cut deep into these layers, isolating a huge rectangular block of limestone within a horseshoe-shaped ditch. After sculpting the lion body, they levelled the natural rock floor between the Sphinx and the sides of the ditch. The ditch opened to the east where a broad terrace had already been cut from the hard and brittle reef limestone.

On the south end of this terrace the builders created Khafre's valley temple from huge blocks of limestone, some weighing more than 100 tonnes, that were quarried from the upper layers of rock which correspond to those of the Sphinx head; and possibly higher stone quarried from the Sphinx ditch was taken to the east to build the Sphinx temple. The first known Fourth Dynasty Sphinx shape dates from the reign of Khufu's son and Khafre's predecessor Djedefre. The quartzite head and neck represents the king. The Sphinx represents Khafre as the god Horus giving offerings to his father Khufu, the incarnation of Re who rises and sets on the horizon.

This theory is supported by several

A

B

A and B - The Sphinx, shown in both photos from the southeast, is closely connected to Khafre's processional ramp and the lower temple. Increased air pollution and humidity and the fragility of the Eocene era limestone, part of the so-called Mokattam formation (from the name of the mountain range across from Giza on the opposite side of the Nile), have made it necessary to perform a great deal of restoration work on the monument in order to consolidate the body and paws. Work began in 1980.

facts. First, the Old Kingdom pottery found in the area proves that the Sphinx temple was in use during the Old Kingdom. Second, there are no temples of Re or any other gods dating to the Fourth Dynasty. The Sphinx temple is directed east–west and contains a large open court; thus it is a solar temple.

There is evidence identifying Khufu with Re, thus it is reasonable to suggest that Khufu was worshipped as Re in this temple. This would also account for the lack of priests of the Sphinx and its temple from the Old Kingdom and the great number of mortuary personnel assocated with the cult of Khufu.

Horus is often seen as the son of Re, and there is clearly a close connection between the two gods. The Sphinx obviously represents Horus, as is shown by its later names. Sphinxes in general are closely associated with the sun god Re, as can be seen in representations of sphinxes in the sacred boat of Re from the New Kingdom. The connection between Khafre and Horus can be seen in the diorite statue of the king which shows the hawk behind his head and shoulders, and the generally accepted identification of all Egyptian kings with Horus, as is shown by their titularies.

Since Khafre was the son of Khufu and Horus was the son of Re, it seems reasonable, once we have equated Khufu with Re, to equate Khafre with Horus, and thus to identify Khafre with the Sphinx.

Can the Sphinx be saved?

When Napoleon arrived in Egypt in 1798, the Sphinx was buried up to its neck in sand and its nose had been missing for at least 400 years. In 1816–17 the Genoese merchant Caviglia attempted to clear away the sand that filled the Sphinx ditch. He managed to dig a trench down the chest of the Sphinx and along the length of the forepaws. Auguste Mariette, founder of the Egyptian Antiquities Service, began excavations in 1853. Frustrated by the enormous amount of sand, he abandoned the work to explore the Khafre Valley Temple. Resuming excavations in 1858, Mariette cleared

the sand down to the rock floor of the ditch around the Sphinx and uncovered several sections of the ancient protective walls around the ditch. He also found odd masonry boxes along the body of the monument which might have been the bases for small shrines. Mariette also cleared the Major Fissure where it cuts the Sphinx's back.

C

In 1885, Gaston Maspero, Director of the Antiquities Service, began yet another attempt to clear the Sphinx. Logistical problems forced him to abandon the project after exposing the earlier work of Caviglia and Mariette.

Between 1925 and 1936 French engineer Emile Baraize excavated the Sphinx for the Antiquities Service. As he dug along the Sphinx body, Baraize found many ancient restoration blocks scattered about in the sand. He replaced these and added many of his own small, brick-sized limestone blocks. Baraize added the first buttresses to support the overhanging layers of Member II bedrock on the north side of the Sphinx body.

During World War II, sandbags were stacked against the Sphinx chest and under the chin to support the giant head in the event of aerial bombardment. Restorations in the 1950s and 1970s patched up the masonry veneer around the lower parts of the body.

In 1979 the Sphinx project of the American Research Center in Egypt (ARCE), in collaboration with the

German Archaeological Institute in Cairo, produced the first scale elevations and detailed plans of the Sphinx. The various phases of ancient and modern restoration were color-coded on these drawings. At the time, masonry covered the body for about one-third its height on the north side and for about two-thirds its height on the south side.

It became apparent that the modern and Greco-Roman (Phase III) masonry began to flake and powder more quickly than the Pharaonic masonry (Phase I and Phase II), which developed a light brown patina that has generally protected its surface for thousands of years. The masonry added to the Sphinx as recently as 1926, or even 1973, however, began flaking, probably because of the properties of the stone, the higher salt content of the more recent stone and mortar, and the way the blocks were laid.

In Greco-Roman and modern masonry, joints between small slabs are tight for only a fraction of an inch around their outer faces; the back of each slab is recessed. The narrow space between adjacent slabs is filled with mortar. When the stones deteriorate, the contact between slabs is the first thing to go, leaving the masonry adhering precariously to the backing mortar.

In October 1981 a patch of such deteriorated 1926 and Phase III masonry collapsed from the north hind paw, calling attention to the deteriorating condition of the Sphinx. In 1981–2, a Sphinx Committee of the Egyptian Antiquities Organization (EAO) decided to replace many of the Roman and Baraize restoration stones all around the body. The restoration team used new stones that were larger than those of Phase III, and the older stone material was simply discarded.

Systematic research on the water table, pollution, and on the properties of the stone and mortar

began, but none of the findings and recommendations was applied in the veneer replacement work, which continued until 1987. During this time most of the exposed natural rock on the upper two-thirds of the north side was sealed by stone and mortar buttresses that filled in the weathered recesses and supported the overhanging layers of Member II. The same treatment was given to the rump and the upper one-third of the lion body. A new outer casing was begun over this buttressing, considerably changing the appearance of the Sphinx as it was presented to us by Baraize.

Throughout this work the problems with the rock core body of the Sphinx were never addressed. The buttressing and masonry cladding might stop large pieces from falling, but the effect of the new materials

on the natural rock surface, which had been flaking and crumbling, is unknown. By 1987 the newly applied cladding had already begun to flake because of efflorescing salts in the stone and mortar. Perhaps because of moisture emanating from the core body (particularly along the line of the Major Fissure on the north side), the 1980s restoration slabs began to buckle outward and slip, as though the Sphinx were shedding an unwanted coat. Work on the veneer replacement was suspended in 1987. In February 1988 a large chunk of limestone fell from the south shoulder.

A new Sphinx Committee was appointed in 1989 consisting of scholars from the EAO and Egyptian universities, as well as foreign experts. All agreed that the casing stones and the harmful cement and gypsum mortar of previous restorations should be removed immediately. The idea was to replace the 1982–7 stones, matching the sizes and patterns that existed in 1979, using the plans and elevations of the ARCE Sphinx Project as a guide. Special attention was to be given to maintaining the modeling of the paws and lion body seen in the ancient restorations.

The first part of the project consisted of analyses and restorative work in select areas, including the south forepaw, the south flank, and the tail. The Egyptian National Research Institute of Astronomy and Geophysics studied the water table, which may have dropped as a consequence of the new sewage system installed in nearby Nazlet el-Samman, once one of several villages in the plain below the pyramids, now

A - A worker, employing the same techniques used during pharaonic times, uses a hammer and chisel to finish the new blocks of limestone used in the most recent restoration work.

A

B

C

D

B and D - During the first restoration in 1980, the blocks of limestone used to consolidate the paws of the Sphinx, where water was infiltrating, were set into place using a cement-based glue. Today new blocks have been set into place using more appropriate techniques.

C - A small, dead-end tunnel leading under the monument was found on the northern side of the Sphinx; its walls have no inscriptions.

a virtual suburb of Cairo numbering more than 300,000 people.

Surveys of quarries allowed restorers to select one in Helwan for the new restoration stones, after analysis showed its properties were consistent with those of the well-preserved ancient repair stones. The new team is following the plan of conservation developed in 1989. The 1980s stone veneer is being removed and the mortar packing cleaned out from this and previous modern restorations. Rather than using thin facing slabs that make contact for only a fraction of an inch at the exterior face, the team is laying blocks so that they are in contact for much of their thickness along the bedding plane and vertical joins. They are also employing a system of interlocking adjacent stones that permits ease of replacement if any of the stones begin to deteriorate.

In May 1990 the Getty Conservation Institute installed a solar-powered monitoring station on the back of the Sphinx, designed to measure such potentially destructive environmental factors as wind, particulates, rain, atmospheric humidity, and condensation. Data collected so far indicate a strong, sand-bearing north-west wind as the principal source of wind erosion and that moisture in the atmosphere reacts on a daily basis with salts in the limestone to contribute at least in part to the severe surface flaking of the rock core (Member II).

To address these questions, the Minister of Culture convened the First International Symposium on the Great Sphinx in Cairo in February 1992, attended by geologists, conservationists, art historians, chemists, archaeologists, and Egyptologists.

So far, the Member II deterioration problem has not been resolved. The continuous deterioration of these layers is pronounced on the chest, which has not been covered in modern times by restoration masonry. Some scholars have suggested injecting the chest with a chemical consolidant, while others would like to encase it with limestone to protect it from the wind. The disadvantage of injecting the rock

E

F

core is that there is insufficient data on the long-term effects of various possible consolidants; and the disadvantage of the casing is that it drastically alters the appearance of the Sphinx and we are not sure what will happen to the rock underneath. This is also true for all the filling, buttressing, and casing that has been put up over the rock-core body since 1926 (but mostly from the period 1981 to 1987).

One specialist suggested returning the Sphinx to the state it was in before the 1926 Baraize repairs, and to 'freeze' the statue in that condition.

All agree that coordinated, systematic, apolitical research should be undertaken. For example, different treatments could be tried on temporary limestone walls, or on natural rock exposures in the nearby Giza quarries. These could be monitored over the course of two or three years to determine how the treatment performs. While the Sphinx is deteriorating quickly by the

scale that measures time in hundreds or thousands of years, the deterioration is not so rapid that we do not have time for more and better preliminary studies before we act. Indeed, the lesson of the 1981–7 restoration is that the worst treatments are ill-conceived ones launched in the hope they will quickly remedy, or at least mask, the problem.

E - In 1990 the Getty Conservation Institute installed an electronic device on the Sphinx for purposes of environmental monitoring, in an effort to understand the reason for the problems in conserving the Sphinx. Subsequently, in 1992, an international multidisciplinary symposium was held in Cairo in an attempt to fully address the situation.

F - The Sphinx was restored using the latest technologies, along with more traditional yet effective procedures, especially for moving large blocks without employing potentially damaging mechanical methods.

THE PYRAMID OF MENKAURE (MYCERINUS)

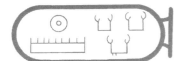

Ancient name: 'Menkaure is divine'
Original height: 65–66 m
Current height: 65.5 m
Length of side: 103.4 m
Angle: 51°20'

A

C

C - Originally the first third of the pyramid was covered by a layer of granite, which can still be seen in the lower piles.

A - There are three secondary pyramids on the south side of the pyramid of Menkaure, the smallest and southernmost pyramid at Giza.

B - During the Mamluk era, a breach was opened into the pyramid at the center of the north face. The entrance to the pyramid was discovered by Vyse and Perring in 1837.

B

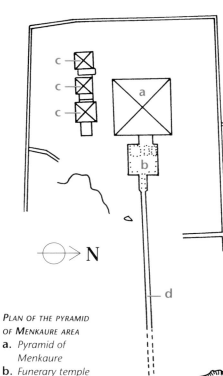

PLAN OF THE PYRAMID OF MENKAURE AREA
a. Pyramid of Menkaure
b. Funerary temple
c. Secondary pyramids
d. Remains of processional ramp
e. Remains of lower temple
f. Tomb of Queen Khentkawes (mother of Userkaf and Sahure)

The pyramid of Menkaure, Khafre's son and successor, known to the Greeks as Mycerinus, is the smallest pyramid at Giza. It was opened by Vyse and Perring in 1837. Unlike earlier pyramids, its faces were covered with blocks of granite on the first third of its height, with limestone slabs only on the upper two-thirds. Some of this granite covering is still visible on the north side of the monument, where the current entrance is located, surmounted by the vast breach resulting from attempts made to penetrate it during the Islamic period.

The pyramid of Menkaure differs from earlier pyramids in the complexity of its funerary apartment, which consists of an antechamber connected to the entry corridor, which is 31.75 m long with an angle of 26°, and an almost horizontal tunnel 12.60 m long, originally blocked at the entrance by three slabs of stone, which opens out on to a large hall. This room was probably the original burial chamber. A wooden sarcophagus and bones from a later period was found in it, with the name of the king painted on it. From here the tunnel descends west to a room which has a number of deep niches used for the funerary

D - The descending corridor, 37.75 m long, leads to an antechamber with walls decorated by bas-reliefs in palace façade motif. From here a horizontal corridor runs toward the primitive burial chamber.

E - A room divided into six small niches is attached to the permanent burial chamber. It was probably used to hold the burial trappings.

F - A general view of the permanent burial chamber, where Vyse and Perring found the sarcophagus of the king. The sarcophagus was lost at sea in 1838 when the ship Beatrice, which was carrying the discovery to England, sank.

D

G - Menkaure, here shown in one of the famous triads found in the lower temple, stands between Hathor and a deity personifying one of the nomes of Egypt. Menkaure was the son of Khafre and was the last king buried in the Giza necropolis.

E

trappings, and then leads to the true burial chamber where Vyse and Perring found the sarcophagus with its palace-façade decoration. The sarcophagus was later lost at sea during transport.

On the southern side of the pyramid there are three satellite pyramids, of which the easternmost one, which is also the largest and best preserved, is attributed to the royal wife of Menkaure, Khamerernebty II. In 1996, during a large-scale study which included cleaning away sand and detritus, a large statue from the Nineteenth Dynasty with no inscriptions was found near the eastern side of this pyramid, depicting Rameses II next to a deity.

F

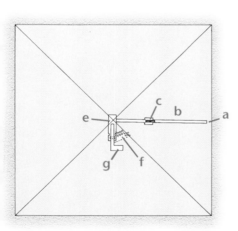

 N

G

PLAN AND CROSS SECTION OF THE PYRAMID OF MENKAURE
a. Entrance
b. Descending corridor
c. Antechamber
d. Primitive descending corridor
e. Primitive burial

chamber
f. Room with niches
g. Permanent burial chamber

The internal structure of the pyramid of Menkaure is quite complex, and shows that a number of changes in design

were made during the course of work, resulting in the expansion of the pyramid northward, as shown by the position of the primitive descending corridor, which was encompassed by the pyramid.

73

THE FUNERARY TEMPLE

A - The funerary temple of Menkaure, the ruins of which are clearly visible, is a complex structure built around a rectangular courtyard from which a double column portico ran, leading into an inner sanctuary. Unfired brick as well as blocks of limestone and granite were used to build the temple, probably in an attempt to hasten its completion. This explains the deterioration of many portions of the temple.

The vestiges of the funerary temple are still visible on the eastern side of the pyramid. It consisted of a complex structure that included a vestibule and a rectangular court that continued west through a portico whose ceiling was supported by a double colonnade. The portico led to the sanctuary, flanked to the north and south by numerous rooms and corridors.

The processional ramp ran from the temple and led to the valley temple, now covered with sand. George A. Reisner led a 1908 expedition to this area conducted by Harvard University and the Boston Museum, and his excavations revealed the four famous triads depicting the king flanked by the goddess Hathor and four other deities which represented the personification of four nomes or provinces. Three of these stelae are in the Cairo Museum, while the fourth is in the Boston Museum.

PLAN OF THE FUNERARY TEMPLE OF MENKAURE
a. Processional ramp
b. Vestibule
c. Rectangular courtyard
d. Portico with double colonnade
e. Sanctuary
f. Annexes structures
g. Pyramid

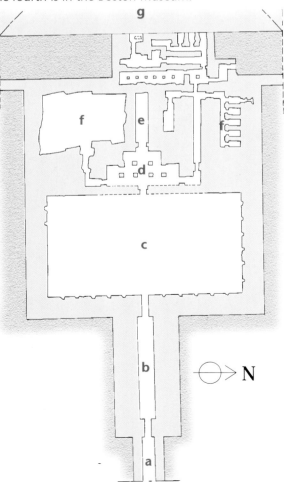

B, C, and D - On the south side of the pyramid of Menkaure are three secondary pyramids. The first, which archeologists identify by the initials GIIIa, is a true pyramid and probably was a satellite pyramid which served a religious function (center photo). The other two, identified as GIIIb and GIIIc, are step pyramids which belonged to the royal wives (lower photo).

THE DISCOVERY OF A PAIR-STATUE OF RAMESES

by Zahi Hawass

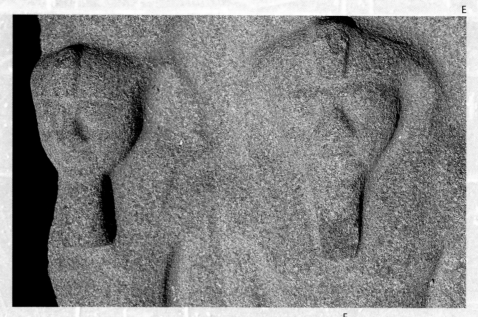

Our excavation around the pyramid of Menkaure began in 1996. The purpose of the excavation was to discover not only the boats of the pyramid, but also the remains of the ramp used to transport the stones for its construction.

We started the excavation to the south side of the third pyramid and to the west side of one of the Queens' pyramids known as GIIIa. The surprise was the discovery of a pair-statue of Rameses II, found under about 3 m of sand. Made from a single block of stone, the joined statues were lying side by side on their backs. They measured about 3 m and 40 cm in height and weighed 3.5 tonnes. The date of the statues is about 1400 years after the pyramid of Menkaure, more than 3000 years ago. The figure on the left depicts Rameses with the false beard of kingship, the royal cobra on his forehead, and the nemes headdress. The figure beside it also represents Rameses, his head now adorned with the sun disk that symbolized the god Ra-Harakhty, 'Horus of the Horizon,' who was identified in the New Kingdom with the Sphinx. Thus the king identified himself both as Horus, the ruler on earth, and as the god, the ruler of the other world.

The cartouches bearing the name of the king had not been inscribed. The statues were left unfinished, perhaps because of a crack across the chests, yet the statues are beautiful. They are the first large New Kingdom statues to be found at Giza. Why are they there? There is an inscription written on the second pyramid, that of Khafre, by a man named 'May,' who was the architect at Memphis for Rameses II. It seems that he ordered his sculptors to carve statues of 'His Majesty Rameses' from the red granite of the third pyramid.

E, F and G - An incomplete statue with no inscriptions depicting Rameses II (lower photo) was found in 1996 in the northeast corner of the easternmost secondary pyramid of Menkaure (GIIIa). The statue, sculpted from a block of granite, was double, and showed Rameses II as the king and as a deity identified with Ra-Harakhty. The sculpture was probably abandoned due to a fracture that split the block of granite in two. It was found next to the pyramid of Menkaure, for which the same material had been used 1400 years earlier to cover the lower piles.

This was not an unprecedented command. During the work on this pair-statue, however, the granite cracked, and the sculptors abandoned the statue – for us to discover. It is for reasons such as these that we say we never know what secrets are hidden in the sands of Egypt.

THE PRIVATE NECROPOLISES OF THE GREAT PYRAMID

To the east and west of the Great Pyramid there are two large private necropolises consisting of hundreds of mastabas arranged in geometrically precise parallel rows. These are tombs of officials and high dignitaries of Khufu who had received the privilege of being buried near the pyramid. A third necropolis, less extensive and important than the first two, is located south of the pyramid. It contains the tomb of Seshemnefer, a dignitary who lived at the end of the Fourth Dynasty.

The tombs of these necropolises were systematically studied for the first time in 1848 by Richard Lepsius, who gave each of them a number. The research was continued by Auguste Mariette, who published an essential work entitled *Les Mastabas de l'Ancien Empire*, and in more recent times, in the 1920s, by the Harvard University

and Boston Museum expedition led by Reisner, who gave the tombs a new and more complete numbering system which is still in use today (the tombs are indicated by a four-digit number preceded by G), and by the Austrian/German expedition led by Hermann Junker, who worked primarily in the western necropolis.

THE EASTERN NECROPOLIS

This necropolis begins to the immediate east of the three secondary pyramids and is formed of seven aligned rows of mastabas arranged into two large groups, with the gigantic mastaba of Prince Ankh-khaf (G 7510) located in the northeast corner. Near the northernmost secondary pyramid, attributed to Queen Hetepheres I, the mother of Khufu, is the burial shaft of this queen, discovered by Reisner in 1925. Its rich funerary trappings, on display in the Cairo Museum, attest to the great level of artistry Egyptian craftsmen had achieved by the middle of the third millennium BC

To the south-east of the pyramid of Hetepheres are the tombs of Qar and Idu, while farther south, near the pyramid of Henutsen, are those of Meresankh III and Khufukhaf.

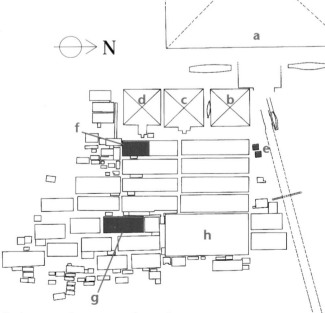

> N

PLAN OF THE EASTERN NECROPOLIS
a. *Pyramid of Khufu*
b. *Pyramid of Hetepheres*
c. *Pyramid of Meritetis*
d. *Pyramid of Henutsen*
e. *Mastabas of Qar and Idu*
f. *Mastaba of Khufukhaf*
g. *Mastaba of Meresankh III*
h. *Mastaba of Prince Ankh-haf (G 7510)*

A - To the east and west of the pyramid of Khufu are two private necropolises known as the eastern cemetery and the western cemetery, consisting of two parallel and aligned rows of mastabas separated by well-defined spaces.

B - Three-dimensional restoration of a portion of the private necropolises of the pyramid of Khufu.

THE MASTABA OF QAR (G 7101)

Principal titles – *Regent of the Pyramid of Pepy I, Overseer of the Pyramid City of Khufu and Menkaure, Supervisor of Priests in the Pyramid of Khafre*
Period – *Sixth Dynasty*

The tomb of this official known as Qar, whose real name was Meryrenefer and who lived during the Sixth Dynasty, probably during the reign of Pepy II, is interesting due to its lovely series of statues depicting the deceased and his family, sculpted in high relief on the southern wall of the first room, in which several elegant bas-reliefs can also be seen decorating the north and west walls.

To the north is a depiction of offerings being presented to the deceased, while on the west wall the scene continues with a depiction of the funeral ritual. Near the southwest corner of the first room is the entry to a second room, where the false door stela can be seen.

D - A pillar supporting a robust architrave, both with hieroglyphic texts, divides the main room of the tomb into two sections. The second section contains a series of statues sculpted in high relief.

E - Qar, a high level official who lived during the Sixth Dynasty, is portrayed here in a polychrome bas-relief on one of the jambs of the door that leads to the second room.

F - The statues, sculpted into the south wall of the first room, portray the deceased, shown to the far right, flanked by a young son and other family members.

C - *The mastabas of Qar and Idu, two high level officials who were probably father and son, are located almost side by side, southeast of the pyramid of Hetepheres.*

G - A statue of the deceased seated can be seen in a niche in the east wall of the first room.

PLAN OF THE MASTABA OF QAR
a. *Entrance*
b. *First room*
c. *Niche with statue with the deceased seated*
d. *Statues of the deceased and his family*
e. *East annex*
f. *Second room*
g. *False door stela*

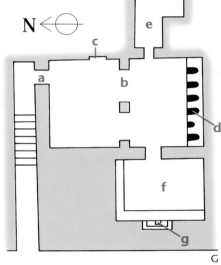

THE MASTABA OF IDU (G 7102)

> **Principal titles** – *The Scribe of the Royal Documents in the presence of the King.*
> **Period** – *Sixth Dynasty*

C

D

The tomb of Idu, who was probably the son or father of Qar, is located a few dozen meters east of the previous tomb and has clear stylistic similarities, although it is much smaller.

The tomb has a single rectangular room with its major axis running north–south. Its west wall is decorated by a series of high-relief statues depicting the deceased, before whom, on the east wall, is the false door stela.

The decorative plan of the tomb emphasizes funerary themes. On the south wall, to the left and right of the door, is a depiction of the deceased's home, the purification tent and the funeral procession, while on the back wall (the northern wall) there are a number of scenes taking place before the deceased, who is seated on a palanquin: they include the preparation of food and drink, music with dancers, and persons bringing offerings.

B

E

A

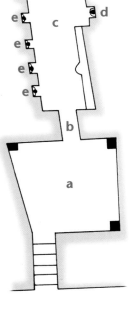

N

PLAN OF THE MASTABA OF IDU
a. *Vestibule*
b. *Entrance*
c. *Offerings chapel*
d. *False door stela*
e. *Statues*

A - A detail of a bas-relief that shows the deceased in front of the offerings table. Idu, whose face is very elegantly sculpted, wears the usual wig and a wide collar.

B - The false door stela is in the center of the east wall of the long rectangular hall, the only room in the tomb. A statue, in an unusual position in the center of the false door stela, shows the deceased seated, his hands on his knees and palms open and upturned to receive offerings.

C - The entry to the mastaba of Idu is a few dozen meters east of that of Qar, who was either Idu's father or son.

D - This bas-relief in the center of the false door stela, above the statue of Idu, shows the deceased and his wife before the offerings table.

E - Six high relief sculptures of the deceased and his family can be seen in a series of niches in the west wall of the tomb. The photo shows the statue of Qar, with a statue of his young son beside him.

THE MASTABA OF QUEEN MERESANKH III (G 7530-40)

Principal titles – Daughter of the King, Royal Wife of Khafre
Period – Fourth Dynasty

F - On both pillars of the first hall, Meresankh III is shown standing, dressed in an elegant white linen tunic.

The mastaba of Meresankh (or Mersyankh) III, is one of the most beautiful tombs in the cemetery due to the quality of its bas-reliefs, whose colors are for the most part well-preserved. This princess, who died at the age of about 50, was the daughter of Kawab and Hetepheres II, both children of Khufu. She later married her half-brother Khafre.

The tomb consists of two rectangular rooms arranged from north to south. In the first the walls are decorated primarily with agricultural, nautical, hunting and commercial fishing scenes. Meresankh and Hetepheres are shown gathering lotus flowers, and catching birds with nets in the swamps. Of particular interest are the scenes on the small portion of the eastern wall to the left of the entry door, divided into five panels showing the production of statues. In this section is a depiction of an artist painting a statue of the queen (beside which Reisner could read a name, probably 'Rehay,' which now is almost completely illegible), and nearby there is a depiction of the sculptor Inkaf, intent on creating a second statue of Meresankh. We do not know if these two individuals were the primary decorators of the tomb, but this is certainly the first known depiction of artists identified by name. On the adjacent south wall there are three niches containing six high-relief statues which depict six men who cannot be precisely identified. On the northern wall there are two square pillars, beyond which there is an extension of the first room. Here, on the rocky wall, an enormous niche has been carved out in which ten large statues depicting various women have been sculpted in high relief, decreasing in size from right to left. As there are no individual

inscriptions it is assumed that these statues depict the deceased, her mother Hetepheres, her daughter Shepseskau and other daughters of Meresankh. The western wall, in the southern portion of which there is also an incomplete false door stela, has two large openings leading to the adjoining offerings room. Here, in addition to the theme of agriculture, which is shown on the small eastern wall, is a scene of the funeral banquet with singers and music (north wall), while on the western wall there are two more niches containing two statues each, probably representing Meresankh and Hetepheres, who flank a second false door stela. This room also contains the shaft that leads to the burial chamber, located about 5 m deep, where in 1927 Reisner found a black granite sarcophagus with the mummy of the queen, which was transferred to the Cairo Museum.

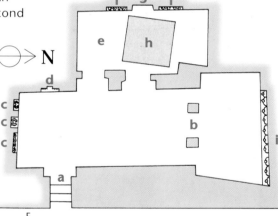

PLAN OF THE MASTABA OF
QUEEN MERESANKH III
a. Entrance
b. Main room
c. Niches with statues
d. False door stela
e. West room
f. Niches with statues
g. Second false door stela
h. Shaft
i. Group of ten statues

G - Two quadrangular pillars set off the northern part of the first large room. In the background, sculpted in high relief, is a row of ten large statues portraying Meresankh III, Hetepheres and other young female members of the family.

H - On the east wall of the first room, to the left of the entry, two artists are shown at work on two statues: their names, Rehay and Inkaf, are indicated beside them.

I - The scenes that show the preparation of food are also in particularly good condition.

THE MASTABA OF KHUFUKHAEF
(G 7130-40)

> **Principal titles** – Chancellor, Son of the King
> **Period** – Fourth Dynasty

The tomb of this prince, the son of Khufu, is located east of the pyramid of his mother, Queen Henutsen, which is in the middle of the group of the three secondary pyramids of Khufu. The bas-reliefs which decorate the walls of this small tomb are quite refined and perfectly preserved, although there is not a trace of color. In the vestibules on the right and left of the door to the offerings chamber, there are two large representations of the deceased with his mother (to the left) and a son (to the right), as he receives the offerings. The theme of offerings continues in the following room, where there is also the false door stela and, in the northern portion, arranged on five panels, procession of people bearing offerings from the possessions of the deceased, who is shown accompanied by his wife. This room leads into the undecorated burial chamber, which is probably from a later period.

A

B

C

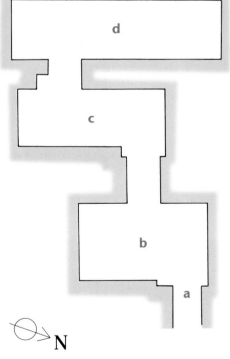

N

PLAN OF THE MASTABA
OF KHUFUKHAF
a. Entrance
b. Vestibule
c. Main room
d. Burial chamber

F

A - Prince Khufukhaf is portrayed seated before the offerings table.

B - The east wall of the main room has three registers depicting persons bringing offerings to the deceased.

C - Khufukhaf, here shown with his mother, receives offerings.

D - On the west wall of the second room a beautiful door, with jambs and lintels decorated with bas-reliefs and texts, leads to the burial chamber.

E - The burial chamber with its undecorated ceiling probably dates from a later period.

F - The deceased receives a lotus flower from a young woman, probably one of his daughters.

THE WESTERN NECROPOLIS

The western necropolis can be divided into three sectors: east, central and west. The tomb of Iasen is located in the first, the second is dominated by the immense mass of mastaba 2000 (corresponding to Lepsius's no. 23), built for a high but unknown dignitary from the period of Khufu or Khafre, and the tomb of Kaemankh, while the tomb of Iymery is in the western section.

G - On the west side of the pyramid of Khufu, here seen from the south, the mastabas that constitute the western necropolis are perfectly aligned in parallel rows.

H - Excavations of the western necropolis are still continuing under the direction of Zahi Hawass, and have led to the discovery of interesting new tombs.

I and K - The paintings in the tomb of Kai are still beautifully colored, as shown in this portrait of the deceased (above) and in the scenes depicting the presentation of offerings on the four registers on the sides of the false door stela (below).

J - This extraordinarily elegant bas-relief represents a dignitary named Kai, whose tomb was recently discovered during excavations in the western cemetery, directed by Zahi Hawass.

PLAN OF THE WESTERN NECROPOLIS
a. Pyramid of Khufu
b. Mastaba no. 2000
c. Tomb of Iasen
d. Tomb of Kaemankh
e. Tomb of Iymery

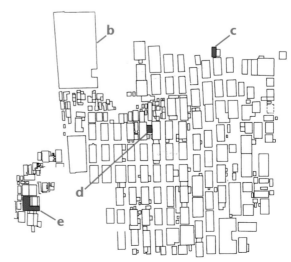

N

A

THE MASTABA OF IASEN
(G 2196)

Principal titles – *Supervisor of Guests of the Great House, Overseer of Priests*
Period – *Fifth–Sixth Dynasties*

This small tomb consists of a narrow corridor that leads to the rectangular-shaped offerings room with its major east–west axis perpendicular to that of the corridor. The bas-reliefs on the east and west walls depict agricultural or fishing scenes, in which the deceased, who is sometimes seated and sometimes standing and accompanied by his wife and child, is shown either supervising or participating. On the west wall there is a large scene of Iasen receiving persons bringing offerings, while music is played for him, food is cooked and cattle are slaughtered. The central portion of the west wall has a niche which holds a large high-relief statue of the deceased.

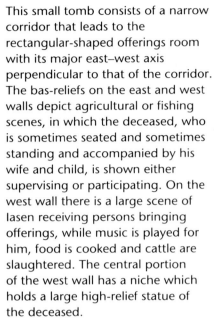

B

A - In the large niche located in the center of the main room there is a high relief statue depicting Iasen, standing, dressed in the classic triangular skirt belted at the waist.

B - Great horned cattle are presented to the deceased.

C - In the corner between the south and west walls are two symmetrical scenes in which the deceased, portrayed in oversize dimensions, is seated at the offerings table to receive offerings.

C

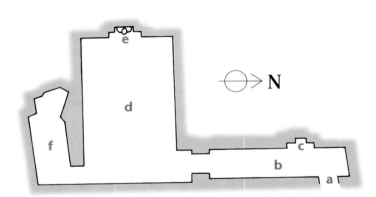

PLAN OF THE MASTABA OF IASEN
a. *Entrance*
b. *Vestibule*
c. *False door stela*
d. *Main room*
e. *Niche with statue of the deceased*
f. *Unfinished room*

D - Iasen, standing, with his wife and young son, who is portrayed smaller in size standing before him, receives offerings which include cattle.

D

THE MASTABA OF KAEMANKH
(G 2196)

Principal titles – *Supervisor of Prophets, Overseer of the Treasury*
Period – *Sixth Dynasty*

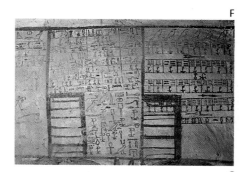

This small tomb to the east of mastaba 2000 and excavated by the Austrian/German expedition of Junker, is notable for its burial chamber, entirely decorated with colorful wall paintings applied directly on walls smoothed with plaster, with no bas-reliefs.

The tomb is L-shaped, and the main structure has a rectangular layout, with the primary axis running north–south.

The walls are decorated with bas-reliefs which depict the deceased as he and his wife attend a concert or various games, and in the side structure as he fishes with a harpoon on a papyrus boat in the swamps. Before this scene is the opening of the shaft that leads to the small burial chamber.

Some of the scenes depicted in the wall paintings are rather unusual and are a precursor to those which would later appear in the Theban tombs of the New Kingdom. On the south wall are representations of the funerary trappings, a man building a bed, various jars and containers, and dance scenes with musicians. On the opposite north wall and on the northern portion of the adjacent west wall are paintings of boats and four storehouses in the form of silos, the contents of which are noted, while most of the west wall contains a beautiful agricultural scene showing cattle, harvesting and gathering.

H - Two registers show a typical agricultural scene with a number of peasants leading large cattle, and a nautical scene with two boats transporting livestock. The artistic style has already begun to foreshadow the style of the New Kingdom.

I - The preparation of the funerary trappings is one of the themes portrayed on the west wall. One of the various objects is a bed, below which is a head support that ancient Egyptians used in place of a pillow.

E - Two men are portrayed as they prepare food and drink. The colors of the paintings in the burial chamber are still in good condition.

F - The small mastaba of Kaemankh is unusual in that its burial chamber is entirely decorated with paintings which are particularly interesting in both style and theme. In the photo a long hieroglyphic text describes the contents of several storehouses.

G - A large sarcophagus, on which the name of the deceased and his titles are written, occupies most of the small burial chamber, which is entered through a shaft.

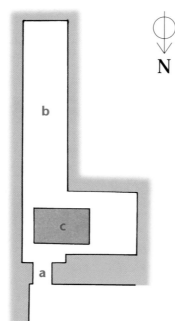

N

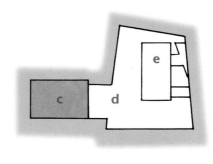

PLAN OF THE MASTABA OF KAEMANKH
a. *Entrance*
b. *Offerings chapel*
c. *Shaft*
d. *Burial chamber*
e. *Sarcophagus*

THE MASTABA OF IYMERY
(G 6020)

A

Principal titles – *Prophet of Khufu,
Overseer of the Great House, Son
of Shepseskafankh*
Period – *Fifth Dynasty*

This tomb, located in the
southwestern corner of the
necropolis, is decorated with colorful,
quite artistic bas-reliefs which deal
with rather interesting subjects.

   The tomb of Iymery was very
popular with nineteenth-century
travelers, who did not hesitate to
leave their signatures on the walls –
especially in the last room.

   The entrance faces east and leads
into a small vestibule decorated with
work scenes (carpentry, goldsmithing
and sculptors at work), and scenes

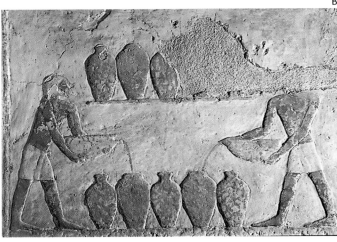
B

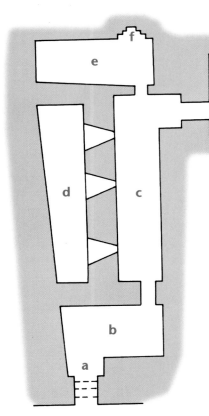

C

*PLAN OF THE MASTABA
OF IYMERY*
a. *Entrance*
b. *Vestibule*
c. *First room*
d. *Serdab*
e. *Second room*
f. *False door stela*

*A and B - This scene,
located on the west
wall of the first room
to the left of the
passageway that
leads to the second
room, is rather rare*

*in the Old Kingdom.
It depicts grape-
pressing (above)
and the preparation
of wine, which is then
poured into jars
(below).*

*C - The mastaba of
Imery is one of the
largest and most
beautifully decorated
tombs in the entire
western necropolis.
It has been popular
with visitors since the
last century, as
attested by numerous
signatures carved into
its walls. The original
colors of the very
elegant bas-reliefs are
still in good condition,
as can be seen in this
scene on two registers,
showing the
preparation of food.*

D - The theme of agricultural work is depicted quite often in tombs: in this scene, four peasants are busy tilling the earth with wooden hoes as they prepare to plant grain.

E - The vestibule contains scenes of offerings made to the deceased: the photograph shows a man leading an oryx to him.

E

F

D

showing offerings made to the deceased, who either is accompanied by his father Shepseskafankh (west wall) or is in his presence (north wall).

The vestibule is followed by a first long room, the south wall of which shows papyrus-gathering, nautical scenes and livestock-raising, offerings being presented to the deceased, the slaughter of sheep, and food and drink preparation. On the opposite north wall there are agricultural, hunting and swamp fishing scenes, with the construction of boats and naval battles taking place in the presence of Iymery.

In the second room of the tomb there are more scenes of offerings in the presence of the deceased, here depicted with his wife and family as they are cheered by music and dancing, while the scribes note how much has been presented to Iymery.

Quite near the tomb of Iymery are the tombs of his son Neferbauptah (G 6010) and that of Ita (G 6030), 'Overseer of Music of the Great House.' Both of these tombs were known to and were visited by nineteenth-century travelers.

G

H

I

F - A common theme in the agricultural scenes of the Old Kingdom is the birth of a calf, here shown with great realism.

G - On the south wall of the second room are two persons bearing offerings, including the thigh of an ox, to the father of the deceased Shepseskafankh.

H - The western portion of the first room depicts musicians (harpists, flautists, etc.) enlivening the funeral banquet.

I - A row of persons bearing offerings, with large baskets full of food and fruit on their heads and birds and flowers in their hands, represents the procession of earthly possessions of the deceased and his family.

THE PYRAMID BUILDERS
by Zahi Hawass

For centuries, scholars and visitors have been drawn to the wonders of the Giza plateau – the pyramids, the Sphinx, and the tombs of officials who served the kings of the Fourth Dynasty. But what of the workers and artisans who for decades struggled to build these great monuments? Where did they live? Where were they buried? When they had finished their colossal assignment, what was the daily life of the people who remained attached to the pyramids and who served in their temples?

Contrary to common belief, the builders of the pyramids were not slaves but skilled artisans and workmen who not only built the pyramid complexes for the kings and nobility, but also prepared and built their own tombs for eternity. The Great Pyramid of Egypt, the last survivor of the seven wonders of the ancient world, at last reveals some of its most closely held secrets – one of which has remained an enigma for centuries.

Who really built the pyramid? First and foremost the pyramid complex is seen as a cult centre for the king, but prior to that it was a labor project. Thousands of workmen needed housing, sustenance, and organization as they went about their daily tasks. The construction process which culminated in the architectural monument we know as the Great Pyramid of Khufu – ruler of the Fourth Dynasty c. 2575 BC – has been under almost continuous investigation since the late nineteenth century, and continues to be so with the on-going excavations directed by the author.

The statistics surrounding the building of the pyramid assuredly alarm the modern mind. The monument measures approximately 230 m in length each side, rises to approximately 137 m at its apex now (it was 146 m), contains 2.6 million cubic metres of stone, the average

weight of which is two and a half tonnes, with the largest blocks weighing fifteen tonnes apiece. Of the many questions which have plagued both scholars and laymen alike, the paramount one is who were the actual laborers on this structure? Traditional thought focused on slave labor as being the only possible solution for the huge workforce required for its construction, a notion that is popularly supported by the biblical references to Moses and apparently endorsed by Cecil B. deMille's compelling images on screen.

The path to more accuracy has been travelled by early scholars, who have put together bits and pieces of information in an attempt to understand the everyday work schedule of the multitudes who

labored under the ancient Egyptian sun. Textual and archaeological evidence during this Old Kingdom dynasty indicates the existence of artisans and workmen who decorated the tombs of the kings, nobles, and associated court officials. We know this from their names – some of the earliest graffiti – which were carved beneath the painted relief scenes of such individuals as the prince Neb-em-akhet, son of Khafre, and scratched in the causeway of King Unas, the last king of the Fifth Dynasty. An artist depicted himself standing between two officials in a tomb from the Sheikh Said tomb complex.

The gangs who built the pyramid were organized in phyles and were divided into four groups, each group having its own name and overseer.

A - About 1 km southeast of the pyramids of Giza, recent excavations have uncovered the structures of a private necropolis which at present contains 30 large tombs and about 600 smaller tombs. This necropolis was used for the burial of the artists, laborers, and master builders who constructed the pyramids, just as the necropolis of Deir el-Medina was used during the New Kingdom for those who built the royal tombs in the Valley of the Kings. The tombs, built primarily of unfired brick, are sometimes similar to, although much smaller than, those of dignitaries of the Fourth Dynasty, and come in a variety of styles. Next to some of the mastabas are vault tombs or tombs with circular structures with cupolas. The necropolis is located on two levels: in the upper cemetery tombs are elaborate and belong to high level personages who held titles such as 'Superintendent of Works' or 'Construction Superintendent.'

Graffiti was left by the workmen inside the second room of the five weight-relieving chambers of the Khufu pyramid and also on the blocks of the Queen's pyramid. The gangs had names, such as 'Followers' or 'Menkaure is drunk.' Recently we also found signs of graffiti inside the boat pit located on the east side of Cheop's pyramid and on the south blocks of the pyramid of Queen Henutsen, wife of the builder of the Great Pyramid.

The Giza necropolis is one of the best and most extensively excavated sites in Egypt. It is here the initial research was begun by the famed Egyptologist Sir Flinders Petrie in 1880–82. Petrie excavated a series of structures located west of the outer enclosure wall of the pyramid of Khafre. He interpreted the groups of rooms discovered as being a city for the workers who labored on the pyramid. The structures consist of long narrow rooms which back on to a square courtyard, the walls of rough limestone blocks being encased in mud plaster. It was estimated that the 111 rooms could house approximately 5500 men. However, settlement debris such as bone, fibre, ash, and charcoal, which gives evidence of human habitation, was missing. This therefore renders Petrie's identification of the site unlikely. In 1988–9 the area was re-excavated, and it was determined that the function of those rooms did not conform to the requirements for a human settlement but, rather, were used as storage for supplies and for cult objects.

G. Reisner in 1955 and more recently, Abdel-Aziz Saleh, investigated the pyramid complex of Menkaure. Reisner found remains of Old Kingdom mudbrick houses in the central open court just east of Menkaure's valley temple. The archaeological evidence indicates that this was the pyramid city of the works associated with that pyramid. Saleh excavated a complex of stone rubble walls located about 73 m south of the causeway of Menkaure, and discovered long narrow foundations in association with an industrial complex of workshops which produced cult artefacts for the king. Fifteen buildings of rubble and mortar with different shapes and number of rooms were found in this area. Ovens for baking or firing ceramics as well as facilities for the preparation of clay were also uncovered.

K. Kromer, an Austrian archaeologist, carried out a series of excavations between 1971 and 1975 in a large mound of settlement debris in the north corner of a bowl-like depression behind a prominent knoll overlooking the main *wadi* (dry creek bed). Finds throughout the excavated strata consisted of pieces of bone, ashes, potsherds, flints, stone bowls, mudbrick debris, and mud seals of Khufu and Khafre. From these remains, Kromer concluded that the mound represented a dump left by the specialized workmen who served under these rulers. This pile of debris had been moved from its original site during the construction process on Menkaure's pyramid. Butzer, in his re-examination of the material, concluded that the mound contained the remains of several settlements for specialized artisans. He proposed to assign the artefacts to five distinct strata and identifies them as typical settlement remains. The most recent excavations have not only proved the existence of a workmen's community but have shed light on their daily life. Excavations have revealed three major areas: the Workmen's Camp; the Institution Area; the Tombs of the Workmen and Overseer. These areas lay south-east of the Great Sphinx and south of the boundary wall along the base of the east–west ridge of the Maadi formation outcrop at Giza.

The modern city of Nazlet-el-Samman (population 200,000) is located under the foot of the Giza pyramids. A recent sewer project has revealed foundations and pottery shards which offer tantalizing evidence that this whole area was heavily inhabited in ancient times. The archaeological site uncovered by Drs Hawass and Lehner is 3 sq km from the south of the recently discovered Valley Temple of Khufu. The archaeological material of the settlement has been consistently recorded, starting at a depth of 3 m below the modern ground level and continuing to a depth of 6 m. All the cores taken within this 3 sq km area east of the Giza pyramids suggest that a continuous spread of the early settlement remains survive throughout. This means that the ancient workmen's communities lay beneath the modern population centres of Nazlet-el-Samman, Nazlet el-Sissi, Nazlet el-Batran, and Kafr el-Gebel.

Further excavations revealed a continuous horizon of mudbrick buildings and associated layers of ash and other rubbish containing large quantities of Old Kingdom pottery. Thousands of fragments of the everyday coarse ware, bread moulds, cooking pots, beer jars, trays for sifting grain and flour, were exposed. Surprisingly, in addition to the expected coarse ware, a large quantity of the fine burnished red ware was uncovered – which lays to rest the belief that this high-quality ceramic was only available to the upper classes. Exceptionally fine South Egyptian food vessels were also excavated, which supports the theory that food was sent to the monuments from other areas. This emphasizes the fact that the united suppport of many communities was needed to back the enormous effort required to build the pyramids.

The diet and lifestyle of the workmen and their families can be established from findings, and reveal a society which was housed, and had access to bread, beer and meat. Evidence for the latter is supplied through the 'butcher's' marks on beef and swine bones. The climate of this period – 4600 years ago – will soon be understood through the analysis of the pollen of the various plants found at the site.

Through the layout of the tombs of the workmen and the overseers it has been determined that there were two communities, segregated by task. The artisans who decorated the tombs and cut the stones lived in one village, and the workmen who moved the stones lived in the other. Estimates of the size of the workforce for the large pyramids of the Fourth Dynasty vary considerably. Herodotus, the fifth century BC Greek historian, stated that 100,000 men were employed in the building of the pyramid of Khufu for three-month periods over twenty years. But this estimate is thought to be overly enthusiastic. A closer approximation would be 30,000 men actually living at the site, with others living in the Memphite region and commuting each day to the work site.

The second area – which is defined as the Institution Area – has revealed two Old Kingdom bakeries. It is possible that this bread factory supplied bread for the whole workforce. Large containers which would hold 14 kilos of dough were found. These baking pots were apparently covered with coals in large vats. A large cache of Old Kingdom bread moulds were discovered, identical to those depicted in the daily life scenes in the tomb of Ti at Saqqara. The grains unearthed in the bakery suggest that the bread was made of barley, making the dark loaves heavy and dense. The vats used for the dough and the bread moulds were stack-heated on open hearths of the bakery rooms. Bread and beer were the common staples of ancient Egypt with protein coming from beef and swine.

Another structure located in this area has been tentatively identified as the storage area for the grain which was used in the barley bread and barley beer. Interestingly, a seal impression was found which showed the incised term 'wcbt.' This means to embalm, or refers to metal-working. More in keeping is the word 'pr-snc,' also found around this stucture. This term could refer to a labor installation or a police district. This same inscription was found in the bakery which was part of a larger complex which included the brewery and grain storage areas. Bakeries and breweries were part of the same production house for the reason that the lightly baked bread dough was used in the mash for the beer, and it is possible that some beer went back into the dough. All of this is evidence for a governmental department or institution responsible for the feeding of the workforce.

Perhaps the most intriguing evidence, however, is that from the cemetery associated with these communities. This is located west of the Institution Area and is now used as a trail for horseback riders. Current excavations have revealed more than 300 tombs, with more to be revealed. Many of these tombs are copies of the grand design used for the pharaoh, nobles, and officials. Some tombs remain in the typical mudbrick 'mastaba' or bench style of the earlier dynasties – but the architecture of some tombs includes vaulted ceilings, miniature replicas of the step pyramid and pyramids with an enclosure wall. Prior to this dynasty all 'mastaba' tomb structures were made with mudbrick. Now tombs are built of limestone, basalt, and granite pieces, the remnant materials from the pyramid construction. There appears to be a kind of hierarchy even in death. The overseer's tomb and the burial shafts for the deceased and his family, painted false doors for the deceased and spouse, and inscriptions which identify the departed as inspector of royal tombs or building director, are situated in front and to the east of the poorer graves which hold the workers who labored under these officials.

The skeletal material of the cemetery is poignant. The workers are buried in the foetal position, and many of the laborers show severe lower back stress. The skull and ribs of one individual show cancer. The tomb of a dwarf pregnant woman was also discovered. Beautifully carved inscriptions which name women as priestesses of Hathor, and votives to the Goddess are found. This may indicate that the Goddesss was the protectress of the workmen. Several fine statues have been found which show the high quality of the grave gifts. Among these is a woman on her kneees grinding grain or pigment with a roller, a smiling artisan, and a fine reserve head. These statues, protected by the sand and arid climate, retain their delicate 4500-year-old colour and minute detail. The associated grave gifts are from the daily life of these people: the beer jars, baking moulds, flower pots, plates and pottery.

The three communities or sites of the workmen were separated from the main building area of the pyramid by a large boundary wall with a bridge in the middle for the workers to pass through each dawn and each sunset. The ancient Egyptians who toiled for the pharaoh on his great pyramid were free men who lived harsh lives by our modern urban standards. It is right and fitting that the focus and emphasis of research now turns from the pharaoh to his subjects who made him immortal.

A - Sometimes the tombs of the laborers' necropolis are decorated with very elegant bas-reliefs, such as this one that decorates the tomb of a superintendent of works, located in the upper cemetery.

90-91 The light of dawn caresses the imposing monuments of Giza: the pyramid of Khafre to the left and the pyramid of Khufu and the Sphinx to the right.

ABU RAWASH

A - The incomplete pyramid of Abu Rawash was built for Djedefre, Khufu's son and immediate successor, whose brief reign lasted eight years. The pyramid, which today is about 9 m high, was supposed to have been about as large as that of Menkaure.

PLAN OF THE PYRAMID OF ABU RAWASH
- **a.** Entrance
- **b.** Descending corridor
- **c.** Burial chamber
- **d.** Satellite pyramid
- **e.** Pit for solar barge
- **f.** Funerary temple
- **g.** Remains of unfired brick wall

About 7.5 km northeast of the pyramids of Giza is the site of Abu Rawash, an important administrative center during the Old Kingdom, with a necropolis, its oldest tombs dating to the predynastic period and the First Dynasty.

Djedefre, who ruled for only eight years and was the son of and successor to Khufu, chose this site for his pyramid. Probably as a result of his short reign, however, his pyramid remained incomplete or in its initial stages. It has been deduced that the length of its side was to have been about 100 m.

Today the structures of the first piers of the pyramid can still be seen, and in particular the enormous trench caused by the gutting of the structure. Thus the ramp of the descending corridor which leads to the burial chamber can be seen out in the open.

On the east side there are a large boat-shaped ditch 35 m long, destined for the royal boat, and the vestiges of the funerary temple in unfired brick. The beautiful heads depicting Djedefre were found here, during excavations by the expedition of the French Institute for Oriental Archeology, led by Émile Gaston Chassinat. The heads are now on display in the Louvre.

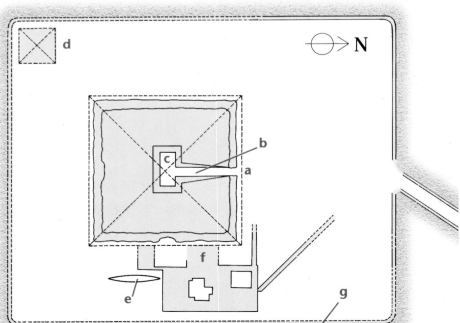

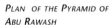

B - On the east side of the pyramid are the structures of a funerary temple in unfired brick, the axis of which does not coincide with that of the pyramid.

C - The internal structure of the temple of Djedefre is quite different from that of the great pyramids of Giza, and consists of an enormous T-shaped pit which includes the descending corridor, 5.70 m wide and 48 m long, and the burial chamber, 24 m long and 11 m wide.

D - Near the southeast corner of the pyramid there is a large boat-shaped pit 35 m long and 9.50 m wide, where fragments of numerous statues portraying Djedefre were found, along with the splendid head which is now on display at the Louvre Museum.

ZAWYET EL-ARYAN

E - The remains of this great incomplete step pyramid are located in the southern portion of the archeological area of Zawyet el-Aryan, located between Giza and Abusir. The monument, discovered by the Italian Egyptologist Alessandro Barsanti in 1900, was later studied by Reisner, who attributed it to Horus Sekhemkhet's successor, King Kaba.

E

The site of Zawiyet el-Aryan, where two incomplete pyramids were discovered, is located about 2 km south of the pyramids of Giza, before the archeological area of Abusir.

The first pyramid, also known as the Layer Pyramid, on the south of the site, is of the step type and even now is about 16 m high. It has been attributed to King Khaba of the Third Dynasty, the successor to Horus Sekhemkhet.

Nothing remains of the second pyramid to the north of the first one, except for a huge trench similar to but even larger than the one at Abu Rawash. Incomplete, this pyramid was studied by Alessandro Barsanti in the early twentieth century. It was about as large as that of Khafre, and has been attributed to a short-lived king of the Fourth Dynasty who probably ruled between the reigns of Djedefre and Khafre and who may have been a son of Djedefre, given the structural similarities between the pyramid of Abu Rawash and that of Zawiyet el-Aryan.

Because it is next to a military zone, the site of Zawiyet el-Aryan is not easily accessible.

F

F - Hypothetical cross-section of the step pyramid of Kaba, the next to last sovereign of the Third Dynasty.

⊕→ N

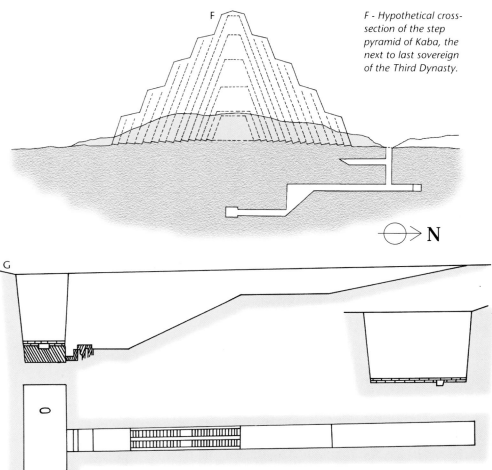

G

G - In 1905, in the northern portion of the Zawyet el-Aryan area, Barsanti discovered an enormous trench quite similar to that at Abu Rawash. It is all that remains of a great pyramid of the Fourth Dynasty that was about as large as Khafre's, and which may have belonged to a son of Djedefre, whose name has now been lost.

THE PYRAMIDS AND TEMPLES OF ABUSIR

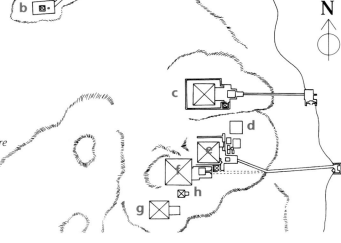

Almost all the pharaohs of the Fifth Dynasty had their pyramids built south of Giza, in the site now called Abusir, halfway between Giza and Saqqara.

Extremely different both architecturally and stylistically from the great pyramids at Giza, the pyramids of the Fifth Dynasty reflect a change in theological concepts, with the increasing predominance of the solar cult of Heliopolis. In terms of names, this change is reflected in the appearance of the suffix -ra in all names of the kings of this dynasty, with the exception of Userkaf and Unas. From the architectural perspective it is marked by the appearance of a new structure: the

PLAN OF THE SITE OF ABUSIR

a. *Solar temple of Niuserre*
b. *Solar temple of Userkaf*
c. *Pyramid of Sahure*
d. *Mastaba of Ptashepses*
e. *Pyramid of Niuserre*
f. *Pyramid of Neferirkare*
g. *Pyramid of Neferefre*
h. *Pyramid of Queen Khentkawes*

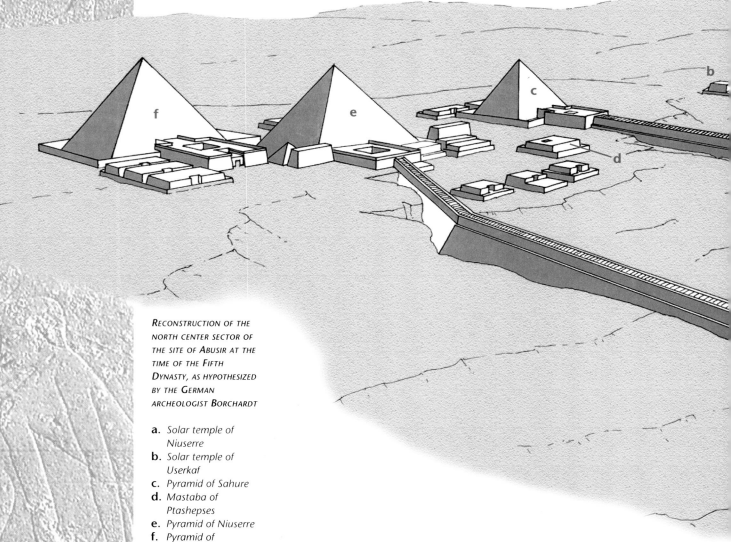

RECONSTRUCTION OF THE NORTH CENTER SECTOR OF THE SITE OF ABUSIR AT THE TIME OF THE FIFTH DYNASTY, AS HYPOTHESIZED BY THE GERMAN ARCHEOLOGIST BORCHARDT

a. *Solar temple of Niuserre*
b. *Solar temple of Userkaf*
c. *Pyramid of Sahure*
d. *Mastaba of Ptashepses*
e. *Pyramid of Niuserre*
f. *Pyramid of Neferirkare*

sun temple, symbolizing the union of the king with the solar deity.

The pyramids of the Fifth Dynasty are also much smaller than those of Giza, and low-quality local materials, cut into small blocks, were used to build them. The precious white Tura limestone was used only for the outer covering, as were expensive materials such as Aswan granite or basalt, which were used sparingly and only for particular structural elements. In general, these architectural decisions reflect the need to keep costs down, with respect both to materials and to labor. On the other hand, the funerary temple seems to have gained in importance and is usually quite large, built of expensive materials and decorated with exquisite bas-reliefs, most of which have unfortunately been lost.

Userkaf, the first king of the Fifth Dynasty, decided to break with the tradition of his immediate predecessors, who built their pyramids on the Giza plateau, and instead chose Saqqara as his burial place (his pyramid is located to the immediate north of the Djoser complex). He built the first sun

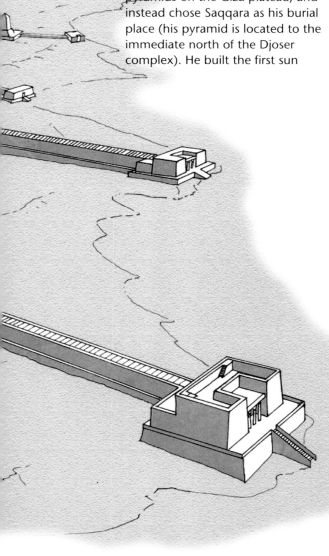

A

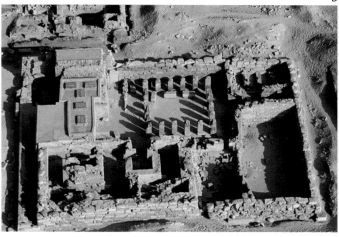
B

C

temple at Abusir, but today only traces of it remain. Written sources state that there were six sun temples, but the locations of four of them are completely unknown.

Sahure, the successor to Userkaf, was the first to build a pyramid at Abusir. It is flanked by those of his successors Neferirkare, Shepseskare, Neferefre and Niuserre, the last king buried at this site, who built a sun temple north of Userkaf's, probably on occasion of the *Heb-sed*, the royal jubilee.

C - The pyramids of Abusir seen from the south: in the foreground are the remains of the pyramid of Neferefre and the great pyramid of Neferirkare.

THE SUN TEMPLE OF USERKAF

Considered the northernmost monument of Abusir, between 1954 and 1957 this temple was studied by an expedition of the Swiss Institute in Cairo, headed by H. Ricke, who uncovered its scanty remains. Research has shown that the temple, in which no bas-reliefs were found, was built in successive periods, and Swiss archeologists have hypothesized that it may be connected to the cult of the goddess Neith, although her name never appears at the site. The Emportrait of Userkaf may, however, be that of Neith!

C - This group of basins is located in the courtyard of the solar temple of Niuserre, probably where sacrificial victims were killed. In the background the truncated pyramid-shaped foundation can be seen, which 19th century travelers called the Righa pyramid. Above it was the great obelisk that symbolized benben, *the rock on which the rays of the sun first shone after the creation of the world.*

D - The basins, probably used to hold water for washing sacrificial victims or for their blood, are carved of blocks of the finest alabaster.

A - This magnificent head of Userkaf, the first king of the Fifth Dynasty, shown wearing the red crown of Lower Egypt, was found in 1957 during excavations of his solar temple in the northern sector of Abusir. Today only traces remain of this solar temple, the first known example of this type of structure. Unlike his immediate successors, Userkaf built his pyramid at Saqqara. (Cairo Museum)

B - In the center of the courtyard of the solar temple of Niuserre, located north of Userkaf's temple at the site known as Abu Ghurab, is a large, extremely beautiful sacrificial altar 6 m in diameter, constructed of five blocks of alabaster. The strange form is due to the fact that the blocks that form the altar surface are sculpted to form four hetep *hieroglyphic symbols.*

THE SUN TEMPLE OF NIUSERRE

This monument, built by Niuserre, the sixth king of the Fifth Dynasty, is about 500 m northwest of the temple of Userkaf, in an area called Abu Ghurab, and is much better preserved. The temple, discovered by John Perring in 1837 and known to travelers of the last century as the pyramid of Righa, was excavated between 1898 and 1902 by a German archeological expedition directed by Ludwig Borchardt, Friedrich W. von Bissing and Heinrich Schäfer. Investigations made it possible to identify the structure and make an accurate graphic restoration.

The sun temple, like the pyramid, was part of a complex that included various structures consisting of three principal elements: the upper temple, the processional ramp running northeast and decorated with bas-reliefs inspired by the theme of the *Heb-sed* festival, and the valley temple. Structural similarities with the pyramids, which have also been confirmed by written sources, have led experts to believe that the sun temple also had a funerary function.

The upper or actual sun temple consisted of a vestibule which led into a courtyard that measured 100 x 75 m. This was surrounded by a stone wall and dominated by a large obelisk constructed of stone blocks on a truncated pyramid-shaped foundation about 15 m high, before which there was a large alabaster sacrificial altar about 6 m in diameter. The obelisk, which was the most important element of the temple, symbolized *benben*, the rock on which the sun's rays first shone when the world was created.

Next to the obelisk on the south side, there was a chapel to which the so-called 'chamber of the seasons' or *Weltkammer* was annexed. Its bas-reliefs, most of which are on display in the Berlin Archeological Museum, celebrate the generating and procreating force of the sun-god over nature, the land, the animals and the three seasons of the Egyptian

B

calendar (*shemu*, or summer, *peret*, or winter, and *akhet*, the inundation), which are represented as human figures followed by representations of the various nomes. (A nome was a sort of province, of which there were 42 during the period of the Old Kingdom.)

Finally, near the enclosure wall at the northeast corner, there were areas which were used for slaughtering sacrificial animals. These were marked by a series of ten large, well-preserved alabaster basins and a row of storehouses. Outside the enclosure wall, along the southern side, a boat-shaped ditch in unfired brick can still be seen; this held the solar boat or was itself a simulacrum of that boat.

C

D

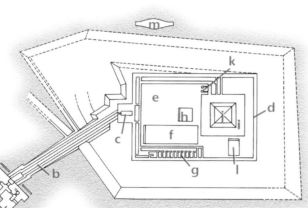

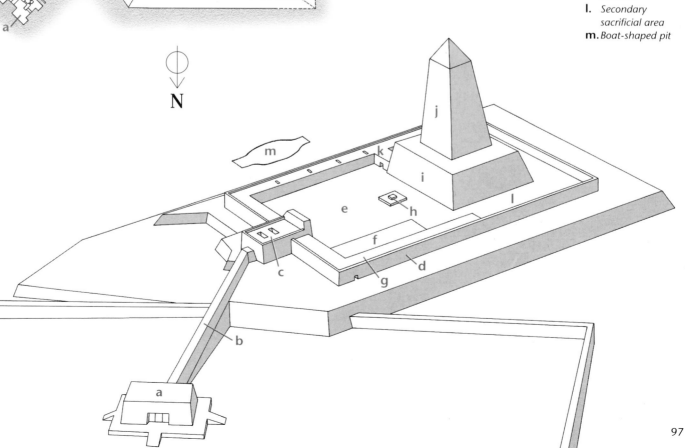

PLAN AND HYPOTHETICAL RECONSTRUCTION OF THE SOLAR TEMPLE OF NIUSERRE, BY BORCHARDT
a. *Lower temple*
b. *Processional ramp*
c. *Upper temple*
d. *Enclosure wall*
e. *Courtyard*
f. *Main sacrificial area*
g. *Storehouses*
h. *Sacrificial altar*
i. *Foundation*
j. *Obelisk*
k. *So-called 'chamber of the seasons'*
l. *Secondary sacrificial area*
m. *Boat-shaped pit*

N

THE PYRAMID OF SAHURE

Ancient name: 'Sahure's *ba* is resplendent, or gleams'
Original height: 48 m
Length of side: 78.5 m
Angle: 50°11'40"

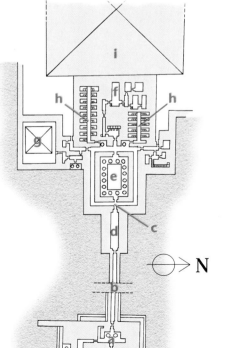

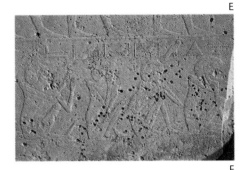

Although the body of the pyramid has deteriorated greatly – at present it is only 36 m high: 12 m less than its original height – its funerary temple and processional ramp are in good condition and the structures of the valley temple are still visible.

The temple, located on the east side, had a complex plan that included a vestibule, a courtyard surrounded by palm-shaped columns (two of which have been restored to their original positions), a double series of storehouses, and a sanctuary, and was decorated with beautiful bas-reliefs which occupied a surface area estimated to be 10,000 sq m.

At present the entire area is being studied and restored by the Egyptian Antiquities Organization under the direction of Zahi Hawass. It will soon be open to the public.

A - Sahure, Userkaf's successor, was the first king to build his pyramid at Abusir: it is a typical example of Fifth Dynasty pyramid structure. The smaller, poorly cut blocks used to build these pyramids and the low resistance of the local limestone utilized explain why the pyramids from this period are in such poor condition.

B - Sahure's funerary temple has a complex plan: built in resistant materials such as granite and basalt, its structures are still in good condition.

C - Two palm-shaped columns are still standing on the east side of the temple courtyard.

D - The cartouche with the name of the king is carved on this enormous granite architrave on the northern side of the courtyard. Like that of his successors, the king's name contains the suffix -ra in honor of the solar deity.

PLAN OF THE COMPLEX OF SAHURE
a. Lower temple
b. Processional ramp
c. Funerary temple
d. Vestibule
e. Central courtyard
f. Sanctuary
g. Satellite pyramid
h. Storehouses
i. Pyramid of Sahure

CROSS-SECTION OF THE PYRAMID OF SAHURE
a. Entrance
b. Corridor
c. Burial chamber

E and F - Two details of the recently discovered bas-reliefs that adorn the funerary temple of Sahure. The first one, which is quite interesting, depicts desert peoples suffering from famine.

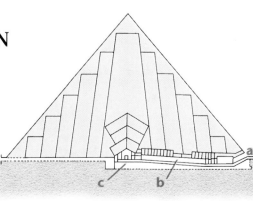

THE PYRAMID OF NIUSERRE

Ancient name: 'Niuserre is the most stable of sites,' or 'The Places of Niuserre are enduring'
Original height: 51.5 m
Length of side: 81 m
Angle: 51°50'35"

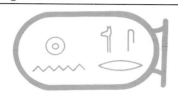

Located directly south of the pyramid of Sahure, the pyramid of Niuserre also has a large funerary temple, with a floor of large basalt slabs. This is distinguished by the fact that it does not follow the median line of the eastern side of the pyramid, but has been shifted south instead. In addition, a good part of the processional ramp and the valley temple, which originally belonged to the nearby temple of Neferirkare, the successor to Sahure, was usurped and reused by Niuserre.

G - The pyramid of Niuserre is midway between that of Sahure, visible in the background, and that of Neferirkare, and has deteriorated more than any other pyramid in the entire complex. Niuserre, who succeeded Neferefre, was the last sovereign buried at Abusir.

H - The funerary temple of Niuserre follows the typical scheme used by Sahure, with the peculiarity that it is not aligned to the east–west axis of the pyramid but is shifted south, and only the sanctuary with the false door stela maintains the traditional alignment. The processional ramp, 365 m long, runs first southeast and then east: the deviation is due to the fact that Niuserre usurped the ramp of his predecessor Neferirkare, whose pyramid is located directly south. The lower temple is now completely covered by sand.

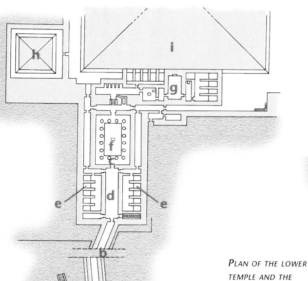

PLAN OF THE LOWER TEMPLE AND THE FUNERARY TEMPLE OF NIUSERRE (BY STADELMANN)
a. Lower temple
b. Processional ramp
c. Funerary temple
d. Vestibule
e. Storehouses
f. Central courtyard
g. Inner sanctuary
h. Satellite pyramid
i. Pyramid of Niuserre

CROSS-SECTION OF THE PYRAMID OF NIUSERRE
a. Entrance
b. Corridor
c. Burial chamber

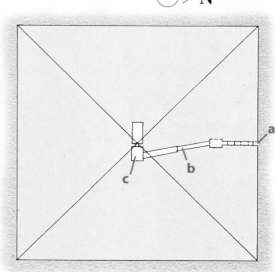

THE PYRAMID OF NEFERIRKARE

Ancient name: 'Neferirkare has become a *ba*'
Original height: 70 m
Length of side: 105 m
Angle: 53°7'48"

The pyramid of Neferirkare, the second pyramid to be built at Abusir, is south of that of Niuserre and is the tallest and most imposing of the pyramids of the Fifth Dynasty. Even now it is about 50 m high.

Both the pyramid and the funerary temple were incomplete upon the death of the pharaoh, and his valley temple and part of the processional ramp were usurped by Niuserre.

During the excavations of this complex, Borchardt discovered a series of extremely important papyruses in the funerary temple; they were part of the temple archives and provided a great quantity of information on the life and economy of the funerary complex and its personnel during the period from the reign of Djedkare Isesi to Pepy II.

A and B - The pyramid of Neferirkare, seen from the south (above) and the east (below), is the tallest and most imposing pyramid in the Abusir complex, and is also the best preserved. It was originally slightly larger than that of Menkaure. Neferirkare, who succeeded Sahure and was also the first king to utilize a double cartouche with his prenomen Kakai written on it, only reigned for about ten years, and both his pyramid and his funerary temple were left incomplete.

C - The funerary temple of Neferirkare, here seen from the summit of the pyramid, was built using for the most part unfired brick to hasten its completion. Blocks of limestone were used only in certain areas, such as the sanctuary and the room with five chapels.

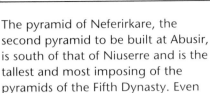

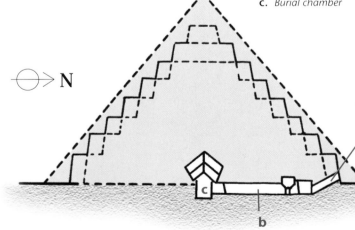

CROSS-SECTION OF THE PYRAMID OF NEFERIRKARE
a. *Entrance*
b. *Corridor*
c. *Burial chamber*

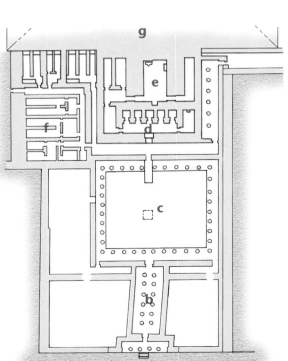

PLAN OF THE FUNERARY TEMPLE
a. *Entrance*
b. *Vestibule*
c. *Central courtyard*
d. *Room with five chapels*
e. *Sanctuary*
f. *Storehouses*
g. *Pyramid of Neferirkare*

THE PYRAMID OF NEFEREFRE (RANEFEREF)

Ancient name: 'Neferefre's *ba* is divine'
Original height: incomplete
Length of side: 65 m
Angle: cannot be determined

E

F

Construction of the pyramid of Neferefre (or, according to a more accurate inscription, Raneferef), the predecessor of Niuserre, located directly south of that of Neferirkare, was interrupted in its initial stages. Excavations performed by the Prague University Egyptology Institute on this area have nevertheless produced extremely interesting results. In particular, even though the pyramid was never completed, it has been

identified as the burial place of Neferefre, and an extremely interesting funerary temple has been discovered on its east side. During this exploration, which also led to the discovery of numerous objects and statues, a papyrus archive similar to those found by Borchardt in the pyramid of Niuserre was discovered.

Finally, a few dozen meters south of the pyramid of Neferirkare and east of that of Neferefre, a complex belonging to Queen Khentkawes, daughter of Menkaure and mother of Sahure and Neferirkare, was found. She also has a tomb in Giza, south of the processional ramp of Khafre, which includes a pyramid and a funerary temple.

D

D - General view of the funerary temple of Neferefre and the Queen Khentkawes complex.

E - Neferefre, here shown in a small painted limestone statue found in 1984–5 during excavations of his

funerary temple, succeeded Shepseskare, whose pyramid has not been found.
(Cairo Museum)

F - The incomplete pyramid of Neferefre rises only a few meters above the surrounding earth.

THE MASTABA OF PTAHSHEPSES

G

H

I

A few dozen meters from the pyramid of Sahure is the large mastaba of Ptahshepses, a high dignitary in the court of Sahure who served as vizier and judge.

The tomb, which is second only to that of Mereruka in Saqqara, was discovered by Jacques de Morgan in 1893 and was studied and restored by the Charles University expedition. It includes an entrance, a portico with two lotus-shaped columns, and a raised room for offerings, with three niches which originally held statues. Farther south is an

enormous square courtyard decorated with pillars, which are sculpted with effigies of Ptahshepses. In the northwest corner of this courtyard a corridor descends to the funerary apartments and the burial chamber, where the sarcophagus is still in its original position.

South of the courtyard are two large boat-shaped pits which held the solar boats or, more probably, served as their simulacra. Such pits are extremely rare in a private tomb, and are otherwise found only in the mastaba of Kagemni in Saqqara.

G - The great mastaba of Ptahshepses, vizier during the reign of Sahure, seen here from the southeast, appears in all its magnificence. It is second only to the mastaba of Mereruka at Saqqara.

H - A great courtyard surrounded by a portico, supported by twenty quadrangular section limestone pillars, is annexed to this monumental tomb.

I - The great granite sarcophagus of the deceased is visible in the funerary apartments.

SAQQARA

A - Userkaf, the founder of the Fifth Dynasty, was the first king to build a true pyramid at Saqqara, northeast of Djoser's step pyramid.

His immediate successors abandoned Saqqara and had themselves buried at Abusir, where Userkaf built a solar temple.

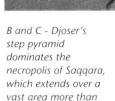

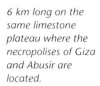

B and C - Djoser's step pyramid dominates the necropolis of Saqqara, which extends over a vast area more than

6 km long on the same limestone plateau where the necropolises of Giza and Abusir are located.

Completely surrounded by the desert sands, the present-day archeological site of Saqqara, located on the western bank of the Nile about 20 km south of Cairo, on the same limestone plateau that extends north to Giza, is the principal necropolis of Memphis, the ancient capital located on the opposite side of the Nile a little farther south. The first pyramid in Saqqara was built during the Third Dynasty, under the reign of Djoser, and thereafter the largest and most beautiful Old Kingdom private tombs in all of Egypt were built here.

Saqqara had had an extremely long history, as it was used as a royal necropolis as early as the First and Second Dynasties. It continued to be a burial place for high officials and dignitaries, as well as for the Apis bulls sacred to Ptah, the principal deity, during the Eighteenth and Nineteenth Dynasties of the New Kingdom. Indeed, during this period, despite the fact that Thebes was the capital of the Egyptian empire, Memphis once again became extremely important as a commercial and industrial center.

The funerary function of the site continued to the Saite and Persian periods around the sixth and seventh centuries BC, a period in which several tombs with extremely deep shafts were dug, such as those situated to the southwest of the pyramid of Unas (the tombs of Psamtik, Djenhebu and Pediese) – and in the Ptolemaic period, then the site was abandoned until the fifth century AD, when it was reoccupied by Coptic Christians who built a large and important monastery here dedicated to St Jeremiah.

Once again forgotten or used as quarries for construction materials during the Middle Ages and thereafter, the monuments of Saqqara which were not lucky enough to be buried in the desert sands were transformed into piles of rubble, but in 1927 Jean-Philippe Lauer began studying them, excavating them and patiently restoring them. Thanks to him and more than 50 years of his work, Saqqara, and the Djoser complex in particular, have stepped out of the mists of time to take on their present-day appearance.

D - The great sycamore statue that shows a priest, Ka-aper, who lived around the beginning of the Fifth Dynasty. Commonly known by the Arabic name of Sheikh el-Balad,

or The Village Mayor, it is one of the masterpieces of Egyptian art. Auguste Mariette made this precious find in 1860, at Saqqara. (Cairo Museum)

E - The famous painted limestone statue portraying Horus Neterikhet, more commonly known as Djoser, as he was later called, was found in 1924 in a special type of closed chapel known as a serdab, annexed to the step pyramid. It is considered the oldest of this type of life-size statue known in Egypt. (Cairo Museum)

E

F

F - This statue, known as The Seated Scribe, dates back to the early Fifth Dynasty, and along with the statue of Djoser and Ka-aper, is one of the most famous statues of the Old Kingdom and one of the great masterpieces on display at the Cairo Museum. This sculpture was also found at Saqqara, during an excavation campaign carried out in 1893.

N

GENERAL PLANT OF THE ARCHAEOLOGICAL AREA OF SAQQARA

1. The central sector, dominated by the pyramid of Djoser and its annexes, and, to the north, the pyramid of Userkaf.

2. The northern sector, which includes the archaic necropolises of the First and Second Dynasties.

3. The sector of the Teti pyramid, which, in addition to the pyramid of this pharaoh, also includes several important tombs, such as the mastaba of Mereruka and that of Kagemni.

4. The western sector, which includes the important mastabas of Ti, Ptahotep and Akhethotep as well as the immense underground structure of the Serapeum.

5. The sector of the pyramid of Unas, with the mastabas of Irukaptah, Niankh-khnum and Knumhotep, Nefer, Idut, Mehu and the remains of the wall and pyramid of Horus Sekhemkhet.

6. The eastern sector, situated at the foot of the limestone plateau at the very edge of the Nile plain, at this point covered with a dense palm grove near the gate that leads to the site. The lower temple buildings of the pyramid of Unas are found here, along with the ruins of the monastery of St Jeremiah and the immense stone tomb of the vizier Bakenrenef, who lived during the time of Psammetichus I. It was excavated between 1974 and 1996 by the University of Pisa expedition, directed by Edda Bresciani.

7. The southern sector (which can be entered only with special permission from the Egyptian Antiquities Organization), which contains the pyramids of Pepy I, Pepy II and the Mastabat Faraun.

a. Serapeum
b. Pyramid of Teti
c. Pyramide of Userkaf
d. Pyramid of Djoser
e. Pyramid of Sekhemkhet
f. Monastery of St Jeremiah
g. Pyramid of Pepy I
h. Pyramid of Djedkare Isesi
i. Pyramid of Merenre
j. Pyramid of Pepy II
k. Mastabat Faraun
l. Pyramids of the 13th Dynasty

103

THE CENTRAL SECTOR

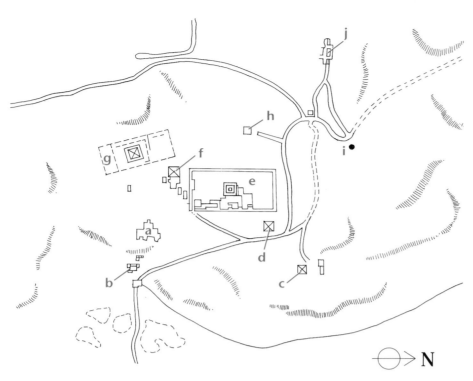

A

A - The Djoser pyramid is about 58 m high and is the result of three successive enlargements of an original mastaba built above a funerary shaft 28 m deep.

B - The step pyramid, here seen from the northwest, dominates the entire archeological site at Saqqara and is part of a large group of structures which constitute one single functional entity known as the Djoser complex, occupying a surface area about 15 hectares in size.

THE DJOSER COMPLEX

The step pyramid, according to tradition, was built for Horus Netcherykhet, better known as Djoser, the first sovereign of the Third Dynasty, by the famous architect Imhotep (who was subsequently deified during the New Kingdom and identified by the Greeks with Asclepius, the god of medicine). It dominates the entire site, which it has come to symbolize.

The pyramid and the related structures which constitute the Djoser complex are surrounded by an imposing wall in light Tura limestone with the characteristic palace-façade motif, interrupted by simulacra of fourteen doors, which probably follow the form of the wall of Memphis, at the time called *Inebhedj*, or 'the White Wall.' The wall surrounds an area of 15 hectares, in the center of which is the pyramid. It is broken by a single entry door with no closing system located on the southeast side, which leads through a narrow passageway into a long corridor originally bordered by a double row of 20 engaged columns about 6.6 m high, tapered at the top. From here one enters a transverse hypostyle room with eight columns connected in pairs by blocks of limestone.

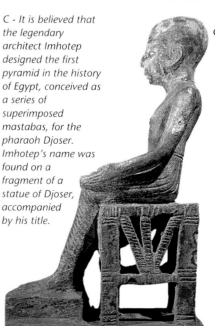

C - It is believed that the legendary architect Imhotep designed the first pyramid in the history of Egypt, conceived as a series of superimposed mastabas, for the pharaoh Djoser. Imhotep's name was found on a fragment of a statue of Djoser, accompanied by his title.

D - The enclosure wall that delimits the Djoser complex, made of blocks of white Tura limestone, has a single small entrance.

D

E

E - The Djoser wall, decorated with molding that uses a geometric motif known as palace façade, is an average of about 10.5 m high.

B

F

G

F and G - The great entry colonnade, consisting of a double row of twenty fascicular columns 6.60 m high, ends in a transverse hypostyle room with four groups of columns, each of which is formed by two joined columns. The present appearance of this structure is the result of the patient work of anastylosis carried out by the famous architect Jean-Philippe Lauer.

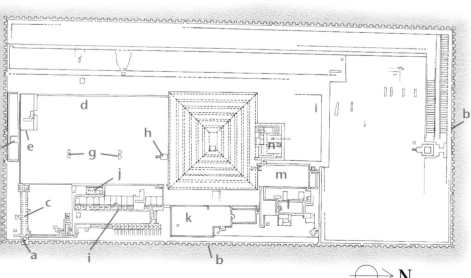

PLAN OF THE DJOSER COMPLEX
a. Entrance
b. Enclosure wall with palace-façade motif
c. Entry colonnade
d. Large courtyard
e. Cobra wall
f. South tomb
g. Metae around which took place the ritual course of the king
h. Entry to Saite gallery
i. Heb-sed courtyard
j. Royal pavilion
k. South house
l. North house
m. Serdab courtyard
n. Funerary temple and entry to pyramid

N

The great courtyard, the cobra wall and the canopic-jar shaft

This hypostyle room leads to the great courtyard, in the northern portion of which is the step pyramid, originally delimited by high walls with a palace-façade motif, portions of which have been recomposed.

On the south side of the wall are the impressive shaft of the so-called South Tomb, 28 m deep, and a rectangular bastion supported by a wall of limestone blocks with a palace-façade motif, decorated on the east side by a magnificent frieze of cobras – the sacred serpents which protected royalty and were the incarnation of the goddess Wadjet of Buto, the protectress of Lower Egypt. The shaft is entered at the bottom through a narrow, deep trench and leads to a true funerary apartment similar to that located under the step pyramid.

This is a second royal tomb, in which were found bas-reliefs depicting Horus Netcherykhet with his name,

and was probably intended to contain the canopic jars holding the viscera of the king. The significance of this structure is not yet fully clear, but, given its position at the extreme southern end of the wall, it is possible that it was intended to evoke the tombs of the first kings of Egypt built in Abydos, in the southern part of the country.

The center of the courtyard is occupied by two crescent-shaped columns constructed of limestone blocks, around which the ritual run of the pharaoh took place during the *Heb-sed* festival, held during the thirtieth year of his rule.

A - In the southwest corner of the great courtyard, standing against the enclosure wall, is a massive four-sided structure whose east side is decorated with a frieze depicting a group of uraeuses, the sacred cobra and protector of sovereignty.

B - Two B-shaped foundations located north and south of the courtyard constitute the metae within which the king had to make his ritual run during the Heb-sed.

C - Next to the cobra wall is a large shaft 28 m deep, at the bottom of which begins a complex system of passageways. This is the so-called south tomb, whose significance has not yet been clearly determined, but which is assumed to have served as either a ritual tomb for the king as the sovereign of Upper Egypt (the southern portion of the country) or as a tomb for the canopic jars containing the king's viscera.

D, E and F - The so-called royal pavilion is on the east side of the great courtyard, and was probably used to hold the royal ka during the Heb-sed ceremony.

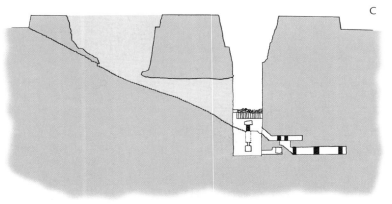

N

The royal pavilion

In the center of the eastern side of the courtyard are three fluted columns which precede the remains of the royal pavilion (or temple T, also called the *Heb-sed* temple), in which the royal *ka* (the 'double,' an aspect of the soul), represented symbolically by a statue, probably was present during the preparatory phases of the *Heb-sed*. Probably all the structures connected to the *Heb-sed* celebrations were exact reproductions of similar structures actually used and of which no trace remains, and were utilized not so much for a royal celebration as for a symbolic ceremony that permitted the *ka* of the deceased king to celebrate the *Heb-sed* eternally, thus being regenerated.

The **Heb-sed** *courtyard*

From the southern portion of the pavilion, whose wall is at this point rounded into a quarter circle, one enters the so-called *Heb-sed* courtyard, which is rectangular in form and parallel to the great courtyard. On the east and west sides of the *Heb-sed* courtyard are the remains of two groups of chapels, some of which have been reconstructed using their original materials. These chapels reflect three different architectural styles.

The three chapels of the first type, located at the north and south ends and in the center of the west side, had a flat roof and façade without columns; the other chapels on the west side, probably ten of them, are of a second type and are decorated by fluted columns, with capitals which are unique in the history of Egyptian architecture: their cubic abacus is flanked by a depiction of two leaves and has a cylindrical hole used to hold a baton that bore divine or royal insignia. Each chapel contains a small sanctuary, which is reached through a narrow, winding, roofless passage with walls on which there are images of doors and wooden latches.

The first two chapels of the second type, starting from the south, have

G - Two of the thirteen original chapels have been reconstructed on the east side of the Heb-sed courtyard. They exhibit a different style from those on the opposite side, as their roofs are arched and have no columns. It is believed that the ritual double coronation of the king as sovereign of Upper and Lower Egypt took place here during the Heb-sed festival.

H - The Heb-sed courtyard is located east of the great courtyard, and its longest sides are delimited by two series of chapels built using three different architectural styles. The vestiges of the chapels are more evident on the western side of the courtyard.

I - These incomplete caryatid statues depicting King Djoser are located on the west side of the Heb-sed courtyard; their original position is unknown.

J - The columns of several chapels on the west side are distinguished by a cubic abacus decorated by two leaves, beneath which is a hole, probably used to hold the insignia.

K - Simulacra of wooden barriers are sculpted in high relief in the little passageways that lead to the chapels with fluted columns on the west side of the Heb-sed courtyard.

another special feature: on the outside wall of each one there is a niche connected by a small stairway, probably used to hold the statue of the king. It is believed that these chapels were connected to one of the most important moments of the *Heb-sed* festival: the double coronation of the king as the sovereign of Upper and Lower Egypt.

Finally, on the east side of the courtyard there are thirteen chapels of a third type, with façades without columns and vaulted roofs. Two of them have been reconstructed.

A

C - Three papyrus-form columns decorate the eastern wall of the courtyard opposite the North House. Papyrus was the symbolic plant of Lower Egypt, the northern part of the country.

D - General view of the North House and the courtyard, whose architectural style is similar to that of the nearby South House. It appears that after his ritual coronation at the end of the Heb-sed, the king received tribute from the populace as the sovereign of Upper and Lower Egypt.

A - The so-called South House, discovered in 1924, has been completely restored, including the blocks found in the opposite courtyard. A khekeru frieze surmounts the door lintel, next to which are two fluted columns.

B - Graffiti in hieratic writing left by unknown tourists who visited the site during the Eighteenth and Nineteenth Dynasties can be seen in the South House. These writings are the first reference to Horus Neterikhet as Djoser. The photo shows graffiti from the era of Rameses II that states that in the 47th year of his reign, Hadnakhte, the Scribe of the Treasury, took a pleasure trip west of Memphis.

The South House and the North House

North of the *Heb-sed* courtyard is the so-called South House, located on the northern side of a courtyard at the Djoser pyramid. It is bounded to the east by a wall which is decorated with a cylindrical column. This column originally had a capital in the form of a lotus, the flower that symbolized Upper Egypt.

This building, whose façade has four fluted columns, contains a cruciform sanctuary with three niches, which are entered through a twisting passage with two sharp right-angle turns. Unknown visitors from the New Kingdom left hieratic inscriptions on their walls in which the name Djoser appears for the first time. During the Old Kingdom, in fact, this king was referred to only as Horus Netcherykhet.

Directly north of the South House is a small courtyard, delimited to the east by a wall decorated with three columns with papyrus-shaped capitals, representing the plant symbolic of Lower Egypt. This courtyard holds a building, similar to the previous one, which is known as the North House.

Probably these two buildings were used during a particular part of the *Heb-sed* festival, in which the king, after his double coronation as the sovereign of Upper and Lower Egypt, received tributes from the North and South of the country.

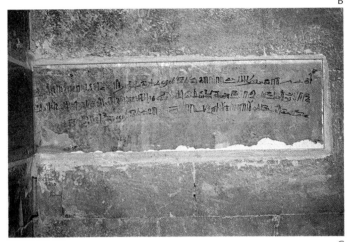

B

C

D

E and F - A peculiar sealed chapel (E) was found in the northeast corner of the step pyramid. Inside was the famous statue of Djoser, now at the Cairo Museum (F).

G - On the north side of the step pyramid are the remains of the funerary temple, used for the cult of the deified king. This is the first example of this type of structure.

The serdab courtyard

To the west of the North House is the so-called *serdab* court, whose name comes from the fact that in 1924–5 a *serdab* was found there, positioned against the northern wall of the pyramid, within which was the famous statue of Djoser now on display in the Cairo Museum.

E

F

G

The funerary temple

On the north face of the pyramid of Djoser are the remains of an imposing funerary temple located west of the *serdab*. Although it is mostly in ruins, it is possible to identify a structure that included a double series of symmetrical architectural elements (courtyard and room for ablutions), probably symbolizing Upper and Lower Egypt.

It is interesting to note that access to the funerary chamber located below the pyramid is through the funerary temple: in pyramids built later, this entry position remained unchanged, but the funerary temple was always built on the east side of the building, and no longer on the north.

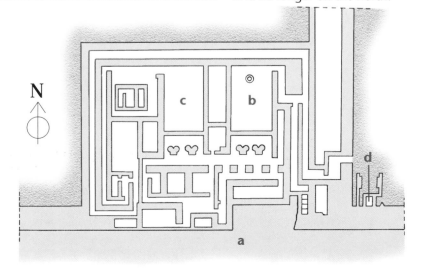

PLANT OF THE FUNERARY TEMPLE OF DJOSER
a. Pyramid
b. East courtyard
c. West courtyard with entrance to the funerary apartments
d. Serdab

N

109

THE STEP PYRAMID

Ancient name: unknown
Original height: 60 m
Length: 173 m east/west; 107 m north/south

A - General view of the Djoser complex, seen from the south. To the southeast of the step pyramid is the royal pavilion and the Heb-sed courtyard. In the foreground is Unas' processional ramp, flanked by a series of large mastabas.

B - By observing the pyramid of Djoser from the southwest corner, one can see the remains of the outermost of the six steps planned for the final phase of the monument (Phase III).

C - The entry to the so-called Saite gallery on the south side of the step pyramid, which leads to the deep funerary shaft that connects to the king's granite burial chamber, above which the first mastaba was built. This tunnel was dug about 2,000 years after the monument was built, in order to explore its interior.

D - This is the original statue of Djoser found within the serdab; it is on display at the Cairo Museum. An exact reproduction of the statue can be seen at the site.

The pyramid of Djoser, which was originally about 60 m high (it is now 58.70 m), has a layout that runs east–west and is based on an initial raised square mastaba about 8 m high, with sides that measured 63 m in length. This mastaba covered a shaft 28 m deep which contained the burial chamber, attached to a system of tunnels used for the funerary trappings (a large quantity of jars and stone recipients was found here) and a system of chambers and passages decorated with blue faience tiles that constituted the funerary apartment, the site of the royal *ka*. On the east side eleven shafts 32 m deep were dug, to each of which a horizontal tunnel was annexed, to be used for the royal harem (the wives and children of the king). These were incorporated into the preexisting structure as it was expanded eastward. It was later decided to make the tomb more imposing by adding a series of steps, giving the monument a stair-like appearance that would symbolically facilitate the ascent of the king's soul to heaven. The mastaba was thus elevated first with four steps (phase II) and then an additional two (phase III), resulting in a total of six steps.

The first known temple for the cult of the dead king was then constructed near the initial entrance on the north side, along with a group of buildings around the pyramid which were connected with the *Heb-sed* jubilee festival (the *Heb-sed* temple and courtyard, North House

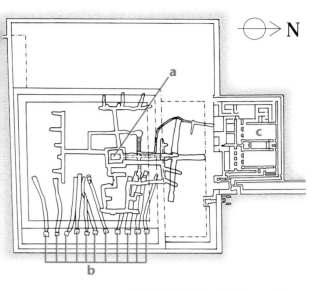

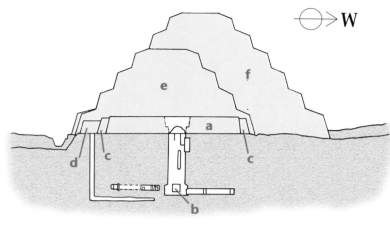

PLAN OF THE COMPLEX
STRUCTURE OF THE STEP
PYRAMID'S FUNERARY
APARTMENTS
a. Burial chamber
b. Funerary shafts
with the connecting
tunnels dug on the
east side, used for
the burial of royal
princes and
princesses
c. Funerary temple

E

F

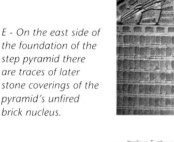

E - On the east side of
the foundation of the
step pyramid there
are traces of later
stone coverings of the
pyramid's unfired
brick nucleus.

CROSS-SECTION OF THE
STEP PYRAMID THAT
SHOWS THE MONUMENT'S
VARIOUS PHASES OF
DEVELOPMENT
a. Original mastaba
b. Funerary shaft
c. First enlargement
of the four sides of
the mastaba

d. Later extension of
the mastaba
eastward (Phase I)
e. First elevation that
resulted in a
pyramid with four
steps (Phase II)
f. Second elevation
and consequent
pyramid with six
steps (Phase III)

H

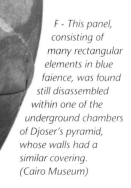

G

F - This panel,
consisting of
many rectangular
elements in blue
faience, was found
still disassembled
within one of the
underground chambers
of Djoser's pyramid,
whose walls had a
similar covering.
(Cairo Museum)

G - This alabaster jar
found beneath the
step pyramid has a
special symbolic and
ritual significance.
Below, the kneeling
man with hands
upraised, the
hieroglyph which
means millions of
years, surmounts
a canopy above

which, carved into
the handle, are the
two thrones of Upper
and Lower Egypt, used
for the king's
coronation during the
Heb-sed, thus
indicating that the
ceremony was
intended to be repeated
for millions of years.
(Cairo Museum)

H - Thousands of jars
in semi-precious
stone, objects
considered quite
valuable during the
Old Kingdom, were
found in the
underground tunnels
of Djoser's pyramid.
(Cairo Museum).

and South House) to permit the royal *ka* to eternally celebrate this fundamental phase of the sovereign's reign, which alone could guarantee his regeneration.

Despite many precautions, the tomb of Djoser was profaned in ancient times, probably as early as the First Intermediate Period.

On the south side of the pyramid there is a fully visible entrance to a tunnel dug in the Saite period (Twenty-Sixth Dynasty), which leads to the great central shaft, making it possible to carry away the over 1,000 cu m of materials which obstructed it – an enormous and extremely risky task. Simple grave-robbers or a first attempt to excavate and study the monument? It is difficult to know for sure, but it is interesting to note that the Saite tombs of Saqqara with their extremely deep shafts certainly draw their inspiration from the monuments of Djoser.

This axonometric cutaway view gives an idea of the complexity and enormity of the underground apartments in Djoser's pyramid, all built around the burial chamber that constitutes the monument's hidden core.

a. *Original descending corridor (phase II)*
b. *Second corridor (phase III)*
c. *Large shaft*
d. *Burial chamber*
e. *Sarcophagus*
f. *The Queen's Chamber*
g. *Chamber decorated with blue faience*

h. *System for sealing off the burial chamber*
i. *The Children's Chamber*
j. *Lepsius' Chamber*
k. *The Star Chamber*
l. *Gallery with stone pottery*
m. *Group of 11 shafts containing the tombs of princes and princesses*
n. *Structures of the original mastaba*
o. *First enlargement of the mastaba*
p. *Second enlargement of the mastaba eastward (phase I)*
q. *First raising of the pyramid (phase II)*
r. *Second raising of the pyramid (phase III)*

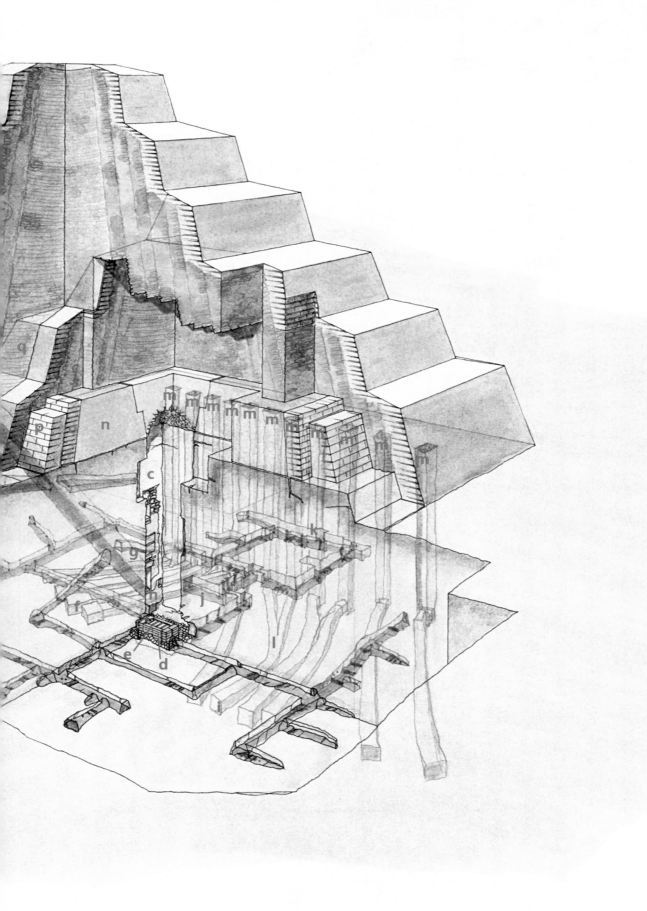

THE PYRAMID OF USERKAF

Ancient name: 'Userkaf is purest
of sites'
Original height: 49 m
Length of side: 73.5 m
Angle: 53°7'48"

C - This colossal red granite head of Userkaf, the founder of the Fifth Dynasty, was found in 1926 by the English archaeologist Cecil M. Firth, inside the funerary temple. The temple was located in an unusual position on the south side of the pyramid. Userkaf, the successor to Shepseskaf, the last king of the Fourth Dynasty, married Khentkawes, the daughter of Menkaure, and ruled for only seven years. (Cairo Museum)

The pyramid of Userkaf, the first pharaoh of the Fifth Dynasty, was identified in 1928 by the English archeologist Cecil M. Firth and is located in the northeast corner of the wall of Djoser. It was built with blocks of rough local limestone covered with Tura limestone. The pyramid was used in ancient times as a quarry for construction materials and has deteriorated greatly, but the remaining structures have made it possible to reconstruct the plan of the entire complex, which has noteworthy architectural details. Only a small sanctuary was found on the east side, while the actual funerary temple was located on the south side, where there was also a satellite pyramid, and where a large shaft tomb was dug during the Saite period. The funerary temple included a courtyard surrounded by granite pillars and paved with basalt slabs. Within the courtyard was a colossal statue of the king, of which only the head remains. It is now on display in the Cairo Museum. South of the temple are the remains of the pyramid of Queen Neferhetepe, containing only a few large limestone blocks which had been the ceiling of the burial chamber.

A - The pyramid of Userkaf, located northeast of the Djoser complex, has been stripped of its original covering of limestone blocks, which were used as construction materials, and now appears quite deteriorated.

B - The funerary temple of Userkaf was originally decorated with elegant bas-reliefs, some of which used naturalistic motifs for the first time in ancient Egypt. This fragment of an originally polychrome bas-relief found in 1928, depicting a group of birds perched on tufts of papyrus in a swamp, is all that remains of the structure's original decorations. (Cairo Museum)

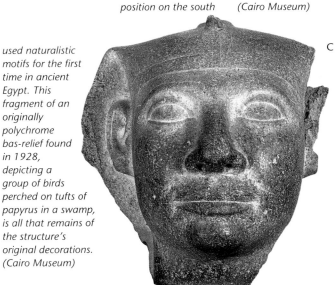

PLAN OF THE USERKAF COMPLEX
a. Pyramid of Userkaf
b. Entrance
c. Funerary chapel
d. Funerary temple
e. Courtyard
f. Vestibule
g. Saite tomb
h. Satellite pyramid
i. Secondary pyramid
j. Ramp

D - Axonometric reconstruction of the funerary apartments of the pyramid of Userkaf (by Stadelmann).

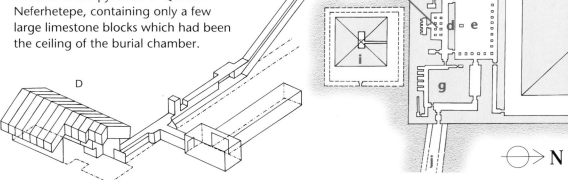

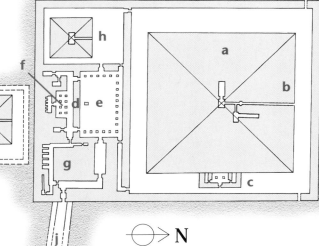

N

THE NORTHERN SECTOR

E - About forty painted limestone disks were found in the mastaba of Hemaka, a high-ranking dignitary during the reign of King Djen, a pharaoh of the First Dynasty. (Cairo Museum)

F - Plan of a large mastaba from the First Dynasty in the archaic necropolis of Saqqara (by Emery).

E

N

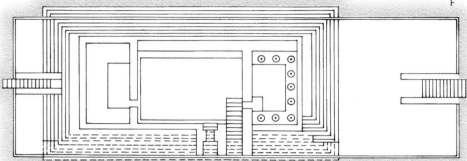

F

THE ARCHAIC NECROPOLIS

In the northernmost portion of the archeological zone of Saqqara is the archaic necropolis with its group of large tombs, discovered and excavated by the English archeologist Walter B. Emery between 1936 and 1956 and identified as royal tombs belonging to the pharaohs of the First Dynasty.

These are large monumental structures in unfired brick, as much as 40 m long, whose walls are decorated with the characteristic palace-façade motif. They contained rich funerary trappings. Nevertheless, because certain tombs of the same sovereigns of the First Dynasty have been found in the royal necropolis of Abydos in Upper Egypt, it has been long debated where the true burial places of these pharaohs were. Are the tombs of Abydos only cenotaphs of the sovereigns, as they also ruled over Upper Egypt, or is the opposite true, and is the real burial ground of the pharaohs of the First Dynasty in Abydos, with the necropolises of Saqqara nothing more than cenotaphs and tombs of high Memphis dignitaries? At present our knowledge is not sufficient to determine where the bodies of these pharaohs were actually buried.

Further north from this archaic necropolis is the huge tomb of Hesire, a high dignitary who lived during the Third Dynasty and bore the title Overseer of Royal Scribes. To the west of this tomb the necropolises of sacred animals were discovered: vast tunnels dating back to the Late Period contain the bodies of over a million ibises and an unknown number of baboons.

G

H

H - The hieroglyphic text of this small ivory tablet, found in a mastaba in the archaic necropolis, mentions King Djet, considered the third monarch of the First Dynasty. (Cairo Museum)

G - The archaic necropolis in northern Saqqara includes large First Dynasty royal mastabas made of brick, their outside walls adorned with palace-façade motif molding, and smaller mastabas from the Second Dynasty. The archaic necropolis was excavated by the great English archaeologist Walter Emery between 1936 and 1956.

THE SECTOR OF THE PYRAMID OF TETI

Located between the archaic necropolis and the Djoser complex, this sector is dominated by the massive pyramid of Teti, around which are several of the largest and most important mastabas of Saqqara, such as the tomb of Mereruka and that of Kagemni.

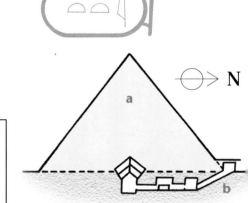

PLAN OF THE PYRAMID OF TETI SECTOR
a. Pyramid of Teti
b. Satellite pyramid
c. Remains of unexplored pyramid attributed to King Merikara (Ninth or Tenth Dynasty)
d. Mastaba of

Mereruka
e. Mastaba of Kagemni
f. Mastaba of Ankhmahor
g. Pyramid of Queen Khuit
h. Pyramid of Queen Iput

A

A - Teti, who succeeded Unas and married Unas' daughter Iput, was the first king of the Sixth Dynasty. His pyramid, here seen from the east side, is located to the northeast of that of Userkaf. The photo shows the remains of the funerary temple and the satellite pyramid.

PLAN AND CROSS-SECTION OF THE FUNERARY APARTMENTS
a. Entrance
b. First descending corridor
c. Second corridor
d. Granite slabs
e. Vestibule
f. Chapel with three niches
g. Burial chamber

THE PYRAMID OF TETI

Ancient name: 'Teti is most durable of sites'
Original height: 52.5 m
Length of side: 78.5 m
Angle: 53°7'48"

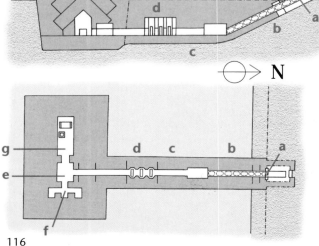

PLAN AND CROSS-SECTION OF THE PYRAMID OF TETI
a. Pyramid of Teti
b. Entrance
c. Remains of small chapel
d. Wall of unfired brick
e. Funerary temple
f. Vestibule
g. Courtyard
h. Storehouses
i. Sanctuary
j. Satellite pyramid
k. Processional ramp

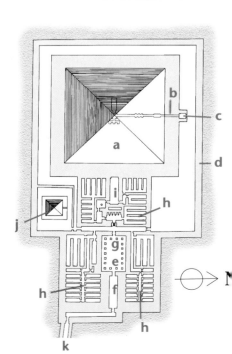

B - On the west wall of the burial chamber is a large bekhen *stone sarcophagus with inscribed texts. Because its dimensions (2.78 x 1.31 m) are greater than that of the entry door, the sarcophagus must have been placed in the chamber while it was still under construction.*

The pyramid of Teti, the first king of the Sixth Dynasty, suffered enormous damage from quarrymen who removed not only the covering and a good part of the blocks of granite in the adjacent funerary temple, but also the limestone slabs within the monument. The position of the pyramid's entrance and annexes is completely conventional. The access passage which opens on the north side and originally included a small chapel, of which a few vestiges remain, leads into a vestibule and then to the burial chamber,

D

B

C

E

C - The texts, elegantly carved in vertical columns on the walls of the funerary apartment, contain formulae and invocations designed to ensure the survival of the king. The decorations in these rooms were never completed, perhaps because of the king's premature death; according to the Greek historian Manetho, he was assassinated by his guards.

in which the sarcophagus, constructed of *bekhen* stone, a graywacke coming from far-off Wadi Hammamat in the Eastern Desert, is still in its original position. The walls of these inner chambers are decorated, as in the pyramid of Unas, with hieroglyphic inscriptions, a good portion of which were smashed by stone quarrymen. Only in recent times have they been restored, thanks to the patient work of the French archeologists of the team directed by Jean Leclant.

On the eastern wall are the remains of a large funerary temple, whose destruction probably began as early as

the Second Intermediate Period. It included a vast courtyard which was originally surrounded by columns, and the remains of an alabaster altar. In the southeast corner a small, relatively well-preserved satellite pyramid can still be seen, while to the northwest of the Teti complex there are the nearly invisible remains of two small pyramids of the queens Iput and Kawit, both wives of Teti.

D - The internal chambers of the pyramid of Teti are decorated with Pyramid Texts, in a custom begun by Teti's predecessor Unas. Unfortunately, the texts in the burial chamber were almost completely destroyed when the monument was used as a stone quarry for construction materials during previous centuries.

E - The enormous limestone slabs arranged in herringbone style, constituting the roof of the vestibule and the burial chamber, were consolidated during lengthy restoration work. The astronomical-style decorations include a myriad of undying stars, likened to the soul of the king.

THE MASTABA OF MERERUKA

Principal titles – *Vizier, Supervisor of the City, Overseer of Prophets in the Pyramid of Teti*
Period – *Sixth Dynasty*

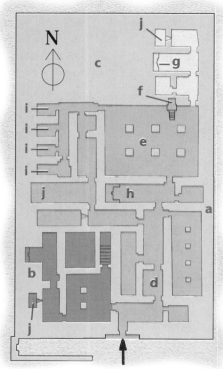

PLAN OF THE MASTABA OF MERERUKA
a. *Mereruka area*
b. *Watethathor area*
c. *Meryteti area*
d. *Room A III*
e. *Main room with six columns (or room A XIII)*
f. *Niche with statue of Mereruka*
g. *Meri Teti's false door stela*
h. *Shaft*
i. *Storehouses*
j. *Serdab*

The mastaba of Mereruka, located to the northwest of the pyramid of Teti and excavated in 1892 by Jacques de Morgan, is the largest known tomb of the Old Kingdom, and occupies a surface area of almost 1,000 sq m. It is a family burial ground divided into fully 32 chambers, 17 of which are reserved to Mereruka (also known as Meri), who held the position of vizier during the reign of Teti. The others are reserved to his wife – the princess Watethathor (known as Seshseshet), the daughter of Teti – and to his son Meryteti. Not all the rooms are decorated, as some served only as storehouses or deposits.

The funerary complex has only one small entrance, which, unusually, is on the south side, and its uprights are decorated by two bas-reliefs depicting the deceased and his wife. The inside layout is such that the entire east part of the tomb (entering from the right) is dedicated to Mereruka and ends in a vast hall supported by six pillars and dominated by a niche containing a life-size statue of the deceased, while a small northern annex is dedicated to his son, and the southwestern portion to his wife.

A - With its 32 chambers, the mastaba of Mereruka, located a few dozen meters northwest of the pyramid of Teti, is the largest of all the private mastabas known. In the tomb were buried Mereruka, his wife Watethathor, Teti's daughter, and their son Meryteti.

B and C - On the jambs of the entry door are two elegant bas-reliefs depicting Mereruka with his titles. Mereruka lived during the reign of Teti, and was his son-in-law and vizier.

D - The life-size statue of the deceased stands in a deep niche before an offerings table on the north wall of the great hall with six columns (room A XIII). Next to the niche are two other representations of the deceased with his wife and mother, shown, as was the custom, smaller in size and standing at his knee. He is watching the scenes shown on the adjoining walls.

E - A small door in the northeast corner of the room with six columns (A XIII) leads to the section of the tomb reserved to Meryteti. The bas-reliefs on the architrave depict young people playing athletic games.

F - The south wall of the room with six columns (room A XIII), west of the entry door, contains a bas-relief showing a group of women crying at the death of Mereruka.

G - This interesting bas-relief is part of a scene dedicated to a rather unusual theme: the forced feeding of hyenas. Two men are preparing to force the animal to swallow pieces of meat. This practice prevented hyenas, which were treated somewhat as pets in ancient Egypt and used as hunting dogs, from eating the wild game.

H, I and J - Metalworking and the creation of jewelry and necklaces were an important part of the decorative scheme of the tomb and are the theme of a large bas-relief located in the small chamber known as room A III. It shows dwarf goldsmiths creating necklaces and jewelry (H and J) and the weighing of precious metals, carefully noted by a scribe (I).

K - Common agricultural tasks are shown on the east side of the room with six columns (room A XIII). The photo shows peasants harvesting grain.

L - In the Meryteti sector (room C III) there is a large false door stela surrounded by a triple jamb. A bas-relief above the lintel shows the deceased before the offerings table.

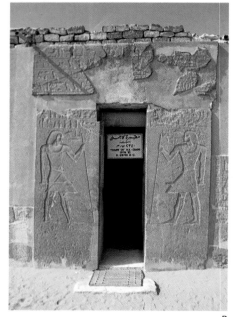

THE MASTABA OF KAGEMNI

Principal titles – *Vizier, Overseer of Prophets of the Pyramid, Supervisor of the City of the Teti Pyramid*
Period – *Sixth Dynasty*

This tomb, discovered by Richard Lepsius in 1843 and excavated by Jacques de Morgan in 1893, by Victor Loret between 1897 and 1899 and by Cecil M. Firth between 1920 and 1926, is located behind the previous one and belonged to Kagemni, known as Memi, who held the position of vizier in the beginning of the reign of Teti and married the princess Nebty-nubkhet, known as Seshseshet.

Although it has only eight decorated rooms, used for the funerary cult, the mastaba is quite large, as it has a series of five storehouses and extends over a surface area of about 1,000 sq m. The mastaba also contained a *serdab*

A - Like Mereruka's mastaba, the jambs of the entry door of Kagemni's mastaba have a double representation of the deceased with his titles.

B - This lovely scene of basket and net fishing in the swamps, using a papyrus boat, is on the north wall of the room with three columns (room III). Lotus plants can be seen in the water.

C - Two people seated in front of one another on a mat hold mallets flared at the end, used to beat the mat and flatten the fibers. The hieroglyphic text explains the scene: 'beating the mat.'

D - This milking scene is quite realistic. The cow's back legs are tied and its tongue is extended in a sign of rebellion.

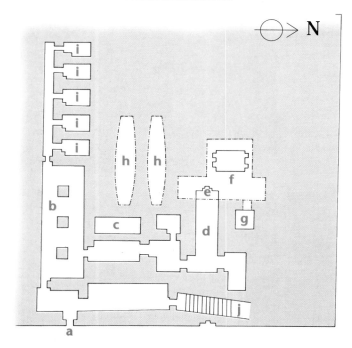

PLAN OF THE MASTABA OF KAGEMNI

A Entrance
B Room with three columns (or room III)
C Serdab
D Offerings room
(room VII)
E False door stela
F Burial chamber
G Shaft
H Boat-shaped pit
I Storehouses
J Stairway

E

F - General view of
room VIII, which
decorative scheme
describes offerings
and the bringers of
offerings. This is the
part of the tomb in
which the original
colors are best
preserved.

G - Kagemni is shown
on the north wall of
room VIII as he greets
a procession of people
bringing offerings,
including jars of
unguents and pieces
of linen, objects
necessary for the
deceased's life in the
Otherworld.

F

*E - The false door
stela surrounded by a
triple jamb has a
narrow opening. On
the upper portion the
deceased is shown
before a table laden
with food: the
formula included in
the text that
comments on the
scene ('thousands of
loaves of bread,
thousands of sweets,
thousands of jars of
beer') magically
ensured the deceased
the food necessary for
his subsistence.*

G

completely walled and isolated from
the rest of the tomb and, something
rather rare in a private burial, two
boat-shaped rooms located on the
roof, which doubtless are an
evocation of the boat-shaped pits of
the pyramid of Unas.

The entrance, located on the east
side, has a decoration similar to that
of the mastaba of Mereruka, with
uprights decorated with bas-reliefs of
the deceased with his titles. The
decorative style is finer than that of
Mereruka, although the colors of the
bas-reliefs are in a much poorer
condition. The themes are typical
of burials of this period: agricultural
scenes, hunting and fishing in
the swamps, and the presentation
of offerings.

*PLAN OF THE MASTABA
ALONG THE NORTHERN SIDE
OF THE PYRAMID OF TETI*
a. *Pyramid of Teti*
b. *Mastaba of
Mereruka*
c. *Mastaba of
Kagemni*
d. *Mastaba of
Ankhmahor*
e. *Pyramid of Khuit*
f. *Pyramid of Iput*

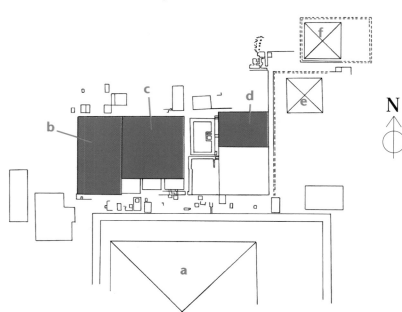

Other mastabas

Other mastabas from the Sixth
Dynasty are located farther east, along
the north side of the Teti wall. They
were excavated by Victor Loret in
1899 and are not yet open to the
public. The most well-known is that of
Ankhmahor, who held the titles of
vizier, 'First after the king' and
Overseer of the Great House. This
tomb is also known as the Tomb of
the Physician, as his bas-reliefs depict
a foot operation and a circumcision in
addition to the usual scenes of daily
life and funerary themes.

THE WESTERN SECTOR

THE MASTABA OF TI

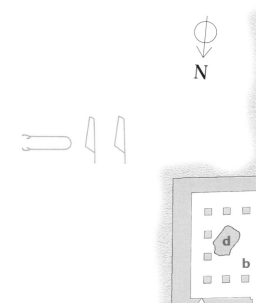

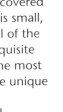

N

A

B

PLAN OF TI'S MASTABA
a. *Entrance*
b. *Courtyard*
c. *Serdab*
d. *Shaft that leads to the burial chamber*
e. *Demedji's false door stela*
f. *Neferhetpes' false door stela*
g. *Corridor*
h. *First room*
i. *Vestibule*
j. *Offerings room*
k. *Ti's false door stela*

Ti was a dignitary who lived during the Fifth Dynasty and held the title of Overseer of the Pyramids of Niuserre and Neferirkare. His tomb, discovered by Auguste Mariette in 1865, is small, yet perhaps the most beautiful of the entire necropolis due to its exquisite decorations. It is also one of the most interesting, due to some of the unique scenes depicted.

The tomb consists of a small entrance that leads into a vast courtyard with a peristyle, the central portion of which is occupied by a shaft that terminates in a descending passage that leads to the burial chamber, which has no decorations or inscriptions. The wall decorations which originally adorned the wall of

C - The most important part of the tomb is the large offerings room, with a ceiling supported by two pillars. There are two false door stelae on the western part of the wall.

D - Ti's false door stela, located on the northern portion of the west wall, is preceded by an alabaster offerings table.

A - A vast courtyard surrounded by a portico supported by twelve square pillars precedes the chapels of Ti's mastaba, one of the most beautiful in the Saqqara necropolis. Near the northeast corner of the courtyard is the first serdab. Ti, a high-ranking dignitary who lived during the Fifth Dynasty, married Neferhetpes, a prophetess of Neit and Hathor, and had a child named Demedji. A large shaft in the courtyard leads to the burial chamber, where the empty sarcophagus of the deceased was found.

B - The first room of the tomb, which probably served as a storehouse for offerings, has a narrow, elongated plan and is completely decorated with painted bas-reliefs on seven registers. The main themes illustrated are the preparation of food and drink, the production of terra-cotta pottery and the presentation of offerings.

C

D

the courtyard with scenes of the family life and activities of the deceased are mostly destroyed and of little interest today. On the north wall of the courtyard is a first *serdab*, while in the southwest corner an extremely narrow passage opens into a corridor which leads to two rooms, both splendidly decorated with colorful bas-reliefs.

The first room, which opens on to the west wall of the corridor, has its main axis perpendicular to the corridor and is decorated with scenes of offerings placed up high on nine

E

panels, along with scenes of the preparation of food and drink. The corridor then leads to the second and larger room, preceded by a small vestibule. This room, whose roof is supported by two columns and which is also known as the Offerings Room, leads to a second *serdab* through a small fissure in its south wall. It contains a replica of the statue of the deceased, the original of which is in the Cairo Museum. Most of the west wall of this room is covered by the famous ship-construction scene, in which we can observe the activity of a shipyard and see a detailed depiction of the construction of wooden boats. The north wall is decorated with a large scene featuring the life-size figure of the deceased as he hunts a hippopotamus in the Delta swamps.

E - The painted limestone statue of Ti, which Mariette found in the serdab*, has now been replaced by a copy, while the original is on exhibit at the Cairo Museum. The dignitary's head is adorned with a rounded wig that falls down on both sides of his head, covering his ears.*

F - The most famous bas-relief in the tomb of Ti, located on the east wall of the offering hall, shows the construction of boats under the deceased's supervision, and is described in full detail. The photograph shows the assembly of the highest part of the broadside, used to support the oars.

F

G

H

I

G - The narrow opening that leads into the serdab *can be seen on the eastern part of the south wall of the offering hall. The* serdab *contained a life-size statue of the deceased, who could thus communicate magically with the world of the living and receive offerings. Two persons can be seen on the sides of the opening; they are the servants of the ka of the deceased, shown as they burn incense. To the right, two craftsmen straighten the poles utilized as tent supports, while to the left are two officials followed by a scribe.*

H - This beautiful bas-relief, which covers a large portion of the northern part of the offerings room, shows Ti on a papyrus boat in the swamps as he participates in a hippopotamus hunt.

I - This scene on the south wall of the offerings room shows carpenters who have chopped down a large tree and are now carving the wood.

THE MASTABA OF PTAHOTEP AND AKHETHOTEP

Principal titles -

Ptahotep – *Vizier and Judge, Supervisor of Prophets of the Pyramids of Menkauhor and Isesi, Supervisor of Priests of the Pyramid of Niuserre.*
Akhethotep – *Vizier and Judge,*

Supervisor of the Pyramid Cities and Supervisor of the Prophets of the Pyramids of Niuserre, Djedkare Isesi and Menkauhor.
Period – *end of the Fifth Dynasty, reigns of Djedkare Isesi and Unas.*

A few hundred meters from the mastaba of Ti is the double mastaba of Ptahotep and Akhethotep. Akhethotep was a dignitary who lived in the Fifth Dynasty. His son Ptahotep, whose sarcophagus, but not his tomb, bears the titles Vizier and Judge, was probably also buried in this sector.

The beauty of the bas-reliefs of Ptahotep's portion of the tomb, which is almost an annex of the main tomb, has given this mastaba its common name of the Tomb of Ptahotep.

The entry corridor with its incomplete decorations leads to a large room with four pillars, on the west wall of which is a door that leads to an inverted T-shaped chapel of Akhethotep. In the southwest corner of the room with four pillars is the passage that leads to the chapel of Ptahotep, which is adorned with marvelous, colorful bas-reliefs. Particularly elegant is the decoration on the west wall, where, framed by

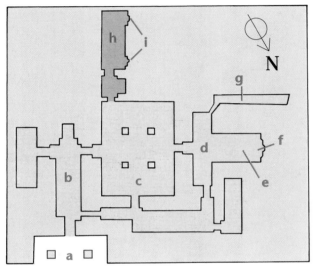

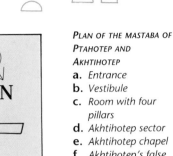

PLAN OF THE MASTABA OF PTAHOTEP AND AKHTIHOTEP
a. Entrance
b. Vestibule
c. Room with four pillars
d. Akhtihotep sector
e. Akhtihotep chapel
f. Akhtihotep's false door
g. Serdab
h. Chapel of Ptahotep
i. Ptahotep's false door

C

D

B

A - The entrance to the mastaba of Ptahotep and Akhtihotep, who lived at the end of the Fifth Dynasty and were probably father and son, is preceded by a portico with two pillars.

B - The false door stela of Akhtihotep is surrounded by a triple jamb, and its upper portion is incomplete. Six small images of the deceased, standing erect, can be seen on the lower portion.

C - There are two false door stelae on the west wall of the chapel of Ptahotep. The opening of the southernmost one is surrounded by a double jamb. Below, there are four representations of the deceased, who is shown standing in the two central jambs, in a sedan chair on the left, and seated in a kiosk on the right.

D - A narrow passageway which begins in the center of the western wall of the room with four pillars leads to the inverted T-shaped chapel of Akhtihotep, at the back of which is the false door stela.

E - In this elegant bas-relief, Ptahotep, seated on a high-backed chair and dressed in the skin of a feline, smells a perfumed unguent in a semiprecious stone container.

F - The first bringer of offerings shown on the central register has a lotus flower in one hand and holds long stalks of papyrus on his left arm.

G - Still in the same portion of wall, this incredibly realistic scene shows a lion sinking its fangs into the muzzle of a terrified cow.

H - The east wall also contains unusual representations of the animal world, including these two porcupines, the first of which has come out of its den to capture a cricket.

I - The deceased is shown at the beginning of the east wall of the chapel, accompanied by his son Akhtihotep, who is presented with cattle driven by herdsmen (upper register), and ducks and cranes (lower register).

E

F

two stelae, is a scene of offerings to the deceased, who is before a table of offerings. Of even greater interest is the decoration on the east side, which depicts two large symmetrical scenes. Each of them shows the deceased seated before nine panels of bas-reliefs, which are not only beautiful, but also depict somewhat unusual subjects, such as nautical and battle scenes and rare animals.

G
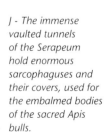

H

I
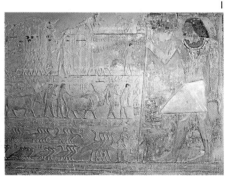

J

J - The immense vaulted tunnels of the Serapeum hold enormous sarcophaguses and their covers, used for the embalmed bodies of the sacred Apis bulls.

The Serapeum
The Serapeum complex is located in this sector, east of the mastabas of Ptahotep and Ti. It was used for the funerary cult of the sacred Apis bulls, as testified by the immense underground tunnels from the Saite period that contain the enormous sarcophagi that originally held the mummies of these animals. This underground complex, discovered as early as 1738 by Pococke, was rediscovered in 1851 by Mariette, who also discovered what he thought was the tomb of prince Khaemwaset, the son of Rameses II.

THE SECTOR OF THE PYRAMID OF UNAS

PLAN OF THE UNAS SECTOR
a. *Pyramid of Unas*
b. *Persian tombs (Psammeticus, Pedenesi and Chennehebu)*
c. *Satellite pyramid*
d. *Tomb of Amen-Tefnackht*
e. *Mastaba of Khenut*
f. *Mastaba of Nebet*
g. *Tomb of Khenu*
h. *Mastaba of Seshsehet Idut*
i. *Mastaba of Mehu*
j. *Outer south wall of the Djoser complex*
k. *Boat-shaped pit*
l. *Tomb of Neferherenptah ('the bird tomb')*

m. *Tomb of Irukaptah ('the butchers' tomb')*
n. *Tomb of Nefer*
o. *Mastaba of Niankh-khnum*
p. *Mastaba of Akhethotep*
q. *Monastery of St Jeremiah*

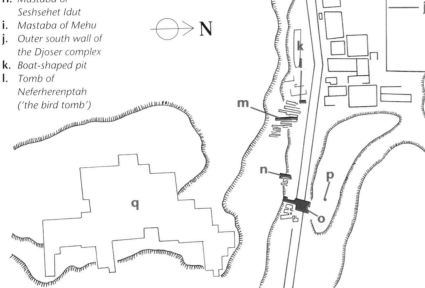

THE PYRAMID OF UNAS

Ancient name: 'Unas is most perfect of sites'
Original height: 43 m
Length of side: 57.5 m
Angle: 56°18'35"

The pyramid of Unas, the last pharaoh of the Fifth Dynasty, is quite dilapidated, and all of its outside covering has vanished except that on the southern face, where a few limestone blocks have been restored to their original positions and where there is a large hieroglyphic inscription which states that Khaemwaset, the high priest of Ptah in Memphis, had restored the pyramid by order of his father Rameses II and had reapplied the name of Unas, which had completely disappeared.

Excavations performed in this area by the Italian Egyptologist Alessandro Barsanti early in the twentieth century, and in 1929 by Cecil M. Firth, made it possible to identify the other structures

A - The pyramid of Unas, here seen from the south, is located a few hundred m southwest of the Djoser complex. Like all pyramids of the Fifth Dynasty, the outer structures of this one are also in poor condition.

PLAN AND CROSS-SECTION OF THE PYRAMID OF UNAS
a. *Pyramid of Unas*
b. *Entrance*
c. *Descending corridor*
d. *Second corridor*
e. *Granite slabs*
f. *Burial chamber*
g. *Antechamber*
h. *Tripartite chapel*
i. *Funerary temple*
j. *Satellite pyramid*
k. *Sanctuary*
l. *Courtyard*
m. *Storehouses*
n. *Vestibule*
o. *Processional ramp*

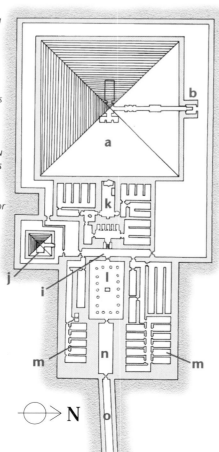

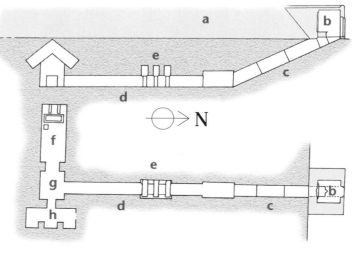

A

D

E

of the complex: the funerary temple, processional ramp and valley temple. Barsanti's excavations also revealed a deep shaft to the southwest of the pyramid, which led to the Persian tombs – the three tombs of Psamtik ('the greatest of physicians'), Pediese ('director of the royal weaving') and Djenhebu ('the head of the king's fleet'), all of whom lived during the reign of Amasis (570–526 BC) and the two following decades. The last's tomb was recently excavated by the University of Pisa archeological expedition to Saqqara, directed by Edda Bresciani.

The funerary temple, located on the east side, is almost completely destroyed, and only traces of the structures remain. Originally this building included a vestibule which connected to a courtyard with peristyle that led to the actual temple.

South of this temple is a rectangular hole that marks the position of the satellite pyramid, while to the north there is a deep shaft dug during the Saite period for the tomb of the general Amen-Tefnakht, containing a sarcophagus with mummy, and farther west a trench with a descending corridor that connects to a system of tunnels running below the temple where Hotepsekhemwy, and perhaps Raneb, the first two pharaohs of the Second Dynasty, were buried.

North of the funerary temple are the large mastabas of Khennut and Nebet, the royal wives of Unas. On the north side is a gigantic block of limestone, weighing about 30 tonnes, that comes from the base of the outer layer, and a descending corridor about 1.4 m high leads to the interior of the pyramid and opens into a vestibule. From here there is a second corridor; the remains of the three large granite slabs which originally blocked the way can be seen about halfway down its length. It leads to a first room, where a small opening located on the east wall leads to a small rectangular chamber in which there are three niches, probably used for the statues of the royal *ka*, while on the opposite wall, to the west, a passageway leads to the burial room, at the end of which is the great diorite sarcophagus of the pharaoh.

Both rooms, which have ceilings made of two large, inclined limestone slabs resting on each other and decorated with

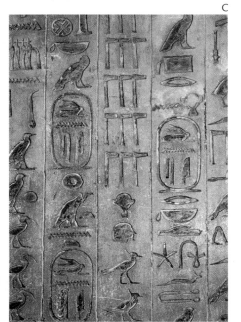

B

C

F

an astronomical motif, are covered in hieroglyphs which were originally colored blue. These are the so-called Pyramid Texts, which include magic formulas that permitted the soul of the deceased king to triumph over hostile powers and overcome the innumerable difficulties encountered in the afterlife before he was reunited with his divine father Ra, to reign eternally at his side. These texts, discovered in perfect condition by Gaston Maspero in 1881, appeared here for the first time and were later adopted by Unas's successors Teti, Pepy I, Merenre and Pepy II. The publication of the texts from these pyramids was edited by Kurt H. Sethe and later expanded by contributions from Gustave Jéquier and R. Faulkner.

THE PROCESSIONAL RAMP
AND THE BOAT PITS

A - The processional ramp of Unas, about 1 km long, first runs east and then changes direction, heading south to the lower temple, the remains of which are located at the entrance of the archaeological area. The ramp was originally covered and adorned with elegant bas-reliefs, of which not the slightest trace remains.

B - Two large boat-shaped pits about 44 m long, made of blocks of limestone, can be seen next to the processional ramp of Unas, 150 m from the remains of the funeral temple. These pits functioned as boat simulacra.

C - One of the most interesting bas-reliefs decorating the processional ramp of Unas is an incredibly realistic scene of the skeletal bodies of a group of starving, malnourished persons (probably Bedouins). A portion of this bas-relief can be seen at the Louvre Museum. (Louvre Museum)

D - The ramp, built using large limestone slabs, is 2.6 m wide and was originally flanked by two walls a little over 3 m high, with the upper portion decorated by beautiful bas-reliefs. It was also covered by limestone slabs, which had an opening in the middle to let in light. This covering was restored for a short distance, as can be seen in the background.

E - The jambs of this large granite door that led to the funerary temple are decorated with the king's cartouches.

F - This bas-relief represents the arrival of boats from Aswan, transporting the large blocks of granite necessary for the construction of the monuments.

A

The processional ramp begins on the eastern edge of the temple and continues for over 1 km, connecting the funerary temple with the valley temple located near the entry to the archeological site. The ramp was originally covered and decorated with beautiful bas-reliefs, including the famous Famine bas-reliefs, now in the Cairo Museum and the Louvre in Paris. Some of the original bas-reliefs have been restored to their original positions, and a small stretch of the ramp has also been covered again to give an idea of its original appearance. Here the bas-reliefs

B

E

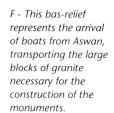

F

C

D

show boat transportation of monoliths in Aswan granite, the manufacture of jars, and the preparation of *electrum*, the famous alloy of gold and silver used in ancient metallurgy. Shortly before the covered portion, the ramp runs past two large boat-shaped pits about 44 m long covered with limestone blocks; these are simulacra of solar boats.

THE HORUS SEKHEMKHET COMPLEX

G

G - The Horus Sekhemkhet complex includes an enclosure wall in limestone slabs decorated with palace facade molding, the remains of an incomplete step pyramid and a southern tomb.

A few hundred meters to the southwest of the pyramid of Unas there is a large complex which includes an enclosure wall similar in appearance to that of Djoser. Construction on it was interrupted when it had reached a height of 3.10 m, and it was incorporated into an embankment at a later stage.

Within the wall there are the remains of an incomplete pyramid used as a quarry. Nothing of it remains but a few piers and the underground structures, including a deep shaft that leads to the burial chamber, in which an alabaster sarcophagus was found, and a funerary apartment containing 136 rooms. This complex, discovered in the early 1950s by the Egyptian archeologist Zakaria Ghoneim, belonged to Horus Sekhemkhet, the successor to Djoser, who reigned for a brief period of about six or seven years. Like the Djoser complex, this also has a south tomb, discovered in 1956 by Jean-Philippe Lauer. Archeological research, however,

has determined that Horus Sekhemkhet was never buried on this site.

Photogrammetric studies made of this area over recent years have shown the existence of another large complex located farther west from that of Sekhemkhet, about which we still know nothing.

H

PLAN OF THE HORUS SEKHEMKHET COMPLEX
a. *Djoser complex*
b. *Royal tomb of the Second Dynasty belonging to Nineter and Hotepsechemwy*
c. *Pyramid of Unas*
d. *Horus Sekhemkhet complex*
e. *Remains of enclosure wall*
f. *Remains of pyramid*
g. *Southern tomb*

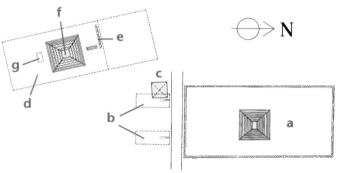

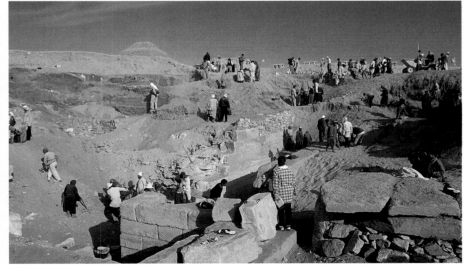

I

H - This small gold box in the form of a shell was found in 1950 in the Horus Sekhemkhet complex, along with other jewelry and necklaces. (Cairo Museum)

I - The excavations of the mastaba of Akhethotep, north of the processional ramp of Unas, are under the direction of the French mission of the Louvre, where the mastaba's chapel was reassembled early in the century.

TOMBS OF UNAS SECTOR

TOMBS NORTH OF THE RAMP

North of the processional ramp, between it and the enclosure wall of the Djoser complex, are the mastabas of queens Khenut and Nebet as well as those of Unas-haichetef, Iynefert (Sixth Dynasty), Unas-ankh (Sixth Dynasty), the vizier Mehu and Princess Idut: the latter is the only tomb of the entire group open to the public.

Closer to the processional ramp is the small tomb of Khenu, while farther south is the mastaba of Akhethotep, a dignitary who lived during the Fifth Dynasty during the period of Niuserre. Its funerary chapel was dismantled in 1903 and reconstructed at the Louvre, where it is today. The mastaba is at present being excavated by a Louvre team directed by Christiane Ziegler.

THE TOMB OF KHENU

A

The upper portion of this small open tomb located next to the north side of the processional ramp of Unas belongs to an official who probably lived in the late Sixth Dynasty and whose titles included Head of the Pyramid of Unas. There are two representations of the deceased on the west wall: the first in a position of adoration with his son Sieunis, and the second as he is seated before a table of offerings with another son, Ihy. Farther in is a beautiful false door stela.

B

C

A - The small tomb of Khenu, a dignitary who lived in the late Sixth Dynasty, is located on the north side of Unas' processional ramp.

B - The deceased and his young son are portrayed on one of the quadrangular pillars in the tomb's vestibule, as he adorns the cartouche of Unas.

C - There is also a well-preserved false door stela in the tomb.

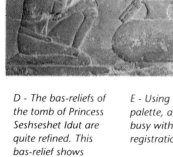

D

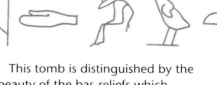

E

THE MASTABA OF SESHSESHET IDUT

This tomb, which was discovered by Cecil M. Firth in 1927, was built for the vizier Ihy, who lived during the reign of Unas in the late Fifth Dynasty. The tomb was later usurped in the early Sixth Dynasty by Princess Seshseshet, known as Idut, who made many changes in the original decorations, which are primarily on the eastern wall of the second room.

This tomb is distinguished by the beauty of the bas-reliefs which adorn five of its ten rooms. In the first two rooms some of the most important scenes deal with nautical, hunting and fishing themes, while the last ones are decorated with more conventional bas-reliefs of funerary offerings and their preparation.

D - The bas-reliefs of the tomb of Princess Seshseshet Idut are quite refined. This bas-relief shows peasants crossing a canal on a papyrus boat, with livestock (not visible in the photograph) and birds.

E - Using the classic palette, a scribe is busy with his work of registration.

PLAN OF THE MASTABA OF SESHSESHET IDUT
a. Entrance
b. First room
c. Second room
d. Offerings room
e. False door stela

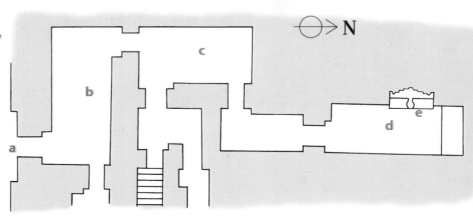

THE MASTABA OF MEHU

Period – early Sixth Dynasty
Principal title – Vizier

The mastaba of the vizier Mehu, who lived during the period of Teti and Pepy I was discovered by the Egyptian archeologist Zaki Saad and excavated by Abdul Salam Hussein in 1940. The tomb, which is aligned in an east–west position and includes four decorated rooms and a courtyard, is located east of and several meters below that of Idut and is decorated with exquisite bas-reliefs which have recently been restored by the Egyptian Antiquities Organization, keeping their original colors almost completely intact.

Beyond the entrance, a passage leads into a small room decorated with scenes of hunting and fishing in the swamps. From here a long, straight corridor, decorated with agricultural, hunting and fishing scenes, runs west and leads to a square offerings room, where there are paintings of offerings and of Mehu as he accepts offerings and watches a dance to the music of four harpists. It then proceeds north to a large chapel, where bas-reliefs project from a beautiful blue-gray background with a splendid false door stela with yellow hieroglyphics that stand out on the dark red background that mimics the appearance of granite. Next, a smaller chapel, dedicated to Merireankh, a dignitary who held the title Supervisor of Prophets for the pyramid of Pepy I, is decorated with paintings of offerings. A large courtyard with two pillars lies north of the straight corridor and is adorned with bas-reliefs depicting Mehu and his son Kahotep.

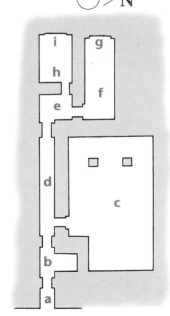

— The splendid false door stela of the mastaba of Mehu is decorated in an unusual style: the limestone used to construct it was painted dark red to imitate granite, while the yellow hieroglyphs stand out clearly on the background.

G - The bas-reliefs of the tomb of Mehu have preserved their beautiful colors. The photo shows individuals bearing offerings of food (a basket of figs) and animals (oryxes and a gazelle) to the deceased, painted on an unusual bluish gray background.

H - Other bearers of offerings present gazelles (partially visible in the photo), a calf and birds.

I - A priest performs a ritual purification with water before the deceased.

PLAN OF THE MASTABA OF MEHU
a. Entrance
b. First room
c. Courtyard
d. Corridor
e. Second room

f. Chapel for Mehu's offerings
g. Mehu's false door stela
h. Chapel of Merireankh
i. Merireankh's false door stela

TOMBS SOUTH OF THE RAMP

There are some impressive tombs south of the processional ramp, almost all of which are rock tombs dug into the limestone rock of the plateau. Built during the Fifth Dynasty and certainly before the reign of Unas, between 2400 and 2310 BC, these were discovered during excavations in this sector performed by Ahmed Moussa between 1964 and 1972. They all have rather similar layouts, generally with a single room with an entrance facing north, and are distinguished by their vivid, well-preserved colors. These are tombs of individuals from various, but never extremely high-ranking, social classes, who lived in the court as officials, craftsmen, royal hairdressers or manicurists. Four of these tombs can be visited upon request.

THE MASTABA OF NEFERHERENPTAH
(the Bird Tomb)

> *Period* – *Fifth Dynasty, around 2315 BC*
> *Principal title* – *Head of the Hairdressers of the Great House*

Several dozen meters west of the preceding tomb, in a slightly more elevated position (access is through a modern stairway located directly below the processional ramp), is the small mastaba of Neferherenptah. Its construction must have been abruptly interrupted by the construction of the processional ramp of Unas, which makes it possible to date this tomb as immediately preceding this king's ascent to the throne, around 2310 BC.

C

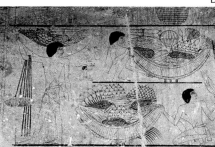

D

E

A

B

PLAN OF THE MASTABA OF NEFERHERENPTAH

a. *Entrance*
b. *Offerings chapel*
c. *Tomb sector decorated with bas-reliefs*
d. *Tomb wall decorated with paintings only*
e. *Incomplete false door*

The unfinished tomb is decorated mostly with simple, finely executed designs which primarily deal with agricultural themes such as milking, preparing meats and beverages, wine-pressing, the gathering of sycamore figs and the cultivation of gardens. On the highest panel there is the large bird-hunting scene that gives this tomb its name.

A, B and C - The small incomplete tomb of Neferherenptah, head of the royal hairdressers during the Fifth Dynasty, is quite different from the other tombs in the Unas sector, as most of its walls have beautiful paintings, first done in red ochre, then corrected and finished in charcoal, on which the sculptors had not yet begun to execute the bas-reliefs. Photographs A and B show paintings of cultivation and gardening, while photograph C shows one of the rare sculpted scenes in the tomb, depicting the milking of a cow.

D - Three peasants gather vegetables and fruit in a garden and place them in large rounded baskets.

E - This splendid representation of a flock of birds gives the tomb its common name of 'the bird tomb.'

F - Kaha, the father of Nefer, leaning on his cane and accompanied by his wife and daughter, watches the presentation of livestock. In the upper register Kaha listens to a report read by an official followed by two scribes, while guards bring two criminals before him.

G - The papyrus collected is used to build a small canoe, used for navigating in the swamps. The lower register shows several peasants caring for livestock.

H - A peasant chops down a tree with an ax.

I - Here is a shepherd trying to drive away the goats who are grazing on the leaves of a tree.

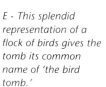

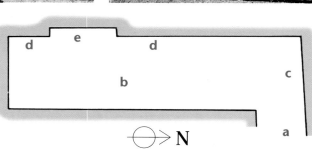

THE TOMB OF NEFER

Period – early Fifth Dynasty, around 2400 BC
Principal titles – Supervisor of Artisans, Head of Choir Singers

This small rock tomb, known as the Tomb of Nefer, has a structure similar to the nearby tomb of Irukaptah. It was a common burial place in which nine people were interred, including Nefer, who lived at the beginning of the Fifth Dynasty and held the title of Head of Choir Singers, his wife Khons, his father Kaha, who also held the title of Head of Choir Singers, and his mother Mertietes, Prophetess of Hathor.

A perfectly preserved mummy was found in one of the nine shafts which contained the bodies of the deceased. Although it was not possible to identify it, it may be the mummy of Nefer himself. The themes of the magnificent, colorful, well-preserved bas-reliefs are classic:

offerings to the deceased and their spouses, agricultural life, grape-harvesting and wine-pressing, hunting and fishing with nets, and the preparation of food and drink, but there are also more unusual scenes showing the construction of a wooden cargo boat and a canoe, a papyrus boat and various types of carpentry.

J - This scene shows the gathering of papyrus, which was collected in large bundles and transported to its place of use.

K - One of the false door stelae is dedicated to Nefer's brother, Werbau and

his wife Khentkawes, who are shown above during the funeral banquet. Werbau is also portrayed on the lintel and on the symbolic opening of the false door, between Khentkawes and his mother Mertietes.

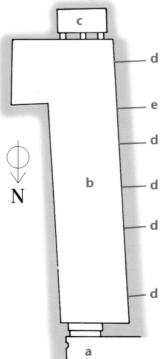

PLAN OF THE TOMB
OF NEFER
a. *Entrance*
b. *Offerings chapel*
c. *Serdab*
d. *False door stela*
e. *False door stela with palace-facade motif*

L - Nefer is shown here aboard a boat with its sail billowing as it heads south. Sails were used when boats traveled against the current up the Nile.

THE TOMB OF IRUKAPTAH
(the Butchers' Tomb)

Period – *Fifth Dynasty*
Principal titles – *Head of the Butchers of the Great House,* Waab *Priest of the King*

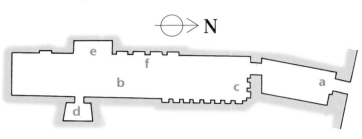

PLAN OF THE TOMB OF IRUKAPTAH

a. *Entrance*
b. *Offerings chapel*
c. *Group of ten polychrome statues*
d. *Niche*
e. *False door stela*
f. *Group of four unpainted statues*

A, D and I - Butchering scenes are quite important in this tomb, whose owner, who lived during the Fifth Dynasty, bore the title of 'Head Butcher of the Great House' (as the royal palace was called). Indeed, this tomb is commonly known as the Butchers' tomb.

B - The east wall has ship scenes on four registers, only the upper two of which are intact and in good condition. These are probably transport ships, with their sails billowing and their closed cabins located aft of the mast, decorated in a checkerboard geometrical motif.

This tomb, dug entirely into the rocky wall, belongs to Irukaptah, a dignitary whose titles included Head of the Butchers of the Great House. It is commonly known as the Butchers' Tomb, due to the butchering scenes that adorn the east wall.

In the eastern part of the tomb, in which at least ten family members of the owner were also buried, ten large, colorful high-relief statues were carved in the rock, using a technique found

elsewhere in only a few tombs of Giza. Above them appears the famous scene of butchering, which takes place in the presence of the deceased.

In the inner part of the tomb there are five shafts, now filled in: the paintings in this section are of naval scenes and hunting in the swamps.

On the opposite west wall there are only four large, unpainted statues and a false door.

E

F

C - The eastern wall of the tomb of Irukaptah is decorated with eight large polychrome statues inlaid in the rock, depicting the family members of the deceased who were buried here. This is the only known tomb in the Saqqara necropolis that uses this type of rock representation, more characteristic of the tombs of Giza.

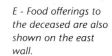

G

C

H

E - Food offerings to the deceased are also shown on the east wall.

F - The deceased, seated before food placed in numerous containers, enjoys the funeral banquet.

G - Detail of one of the statues on the east wall.

H - Here is the preliminary drawing of a statue of a family member, roughly sketched in red ochre. After being finished in black, the sculptors would begin their work, followed by stucco artists and painters.

I

THE MASTABA OF NIANKHKHNUM AND KHNUMHOTEP

Period – mid Fifth Dynasty, around 2340 BC
Principal titles – Prophets of Ra in the Sun Temple of Niuserre, Heads of the Manicurists of the Great House

This great double tomb was built for two dignitaries, Niankhkhnum and Khnumhotep, brothers and probably twins, who both each bore the titles Prophet of Ra in the Sun Temple of Niuserre and Overseer of the Manicurists of the Great House. The tomb, discovered in 1964 under the ramp of Unas, in which a breach was made in order to reach it, is one of the largest and most beautiful in the entire necropolis. It has a complex structure, as it was changed various times and enlarged during its construction.

The oldest part of the tomb, which is the actual chapel, was in fact dug into the rock, while three rooms with a courtyard were added later, built

A - The vestibule contains a beautiful scene of fishing with nets. Among the various fish, depicted quite realistically, the large Tilapia nilotica and Lates niloticus can be identified. Below, to the right, is a fisherman seated in his papyrus boat.

B - Scenes of transporting papyrus on canoes in the swamps.

C - The two owners of the tomb, Knumhotep, accompanied by his son Ptahshepses on the left, and Niankhkhnum with his son Hemra on the right, are shown on the jambs of the door that leads to the second room. Both are also shown in a seated position on the lintel.

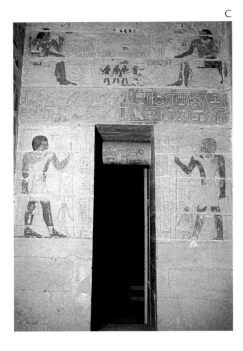

C

A

B

PLAN OF THE MASTABA OF NIANKHKHNUM AND KNUMHOTEP
a. Entrance
b. Vestibule
c. First room
d. Courtyard
e. Second vestibule
f. Chapel
g. Small offerings room
h. False door stela

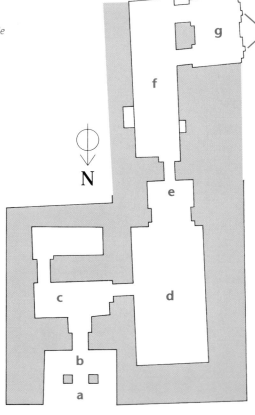

N

D - A priest celebrates
the funerary ritual,
burning incense
before the statues of
the two owners, who
are carried to the
tomb on sledges. The
lower register shows

the ceremony being
performed before a
double statue located
within a shrine.

E - Two men use nets
to hunt birds in the
swamps.

E

F

D

G

with blocks of stone using the
technique employed for the
mastabas.

The tomb includes a vestibule, in
which the two owners and the funeral
procession are depicted. This leads
into two rooms, only the first of
which is decorated with bas-reliefs
that again depict the funeral
procession, followed by scenes of a
market, hunting in the desert, and
Niankhkhnum and Khnumhotep
hunting and fishing in the swamps,
supervising work in the fields and
inspecting the workshops of
craftsmen.

The west wall of this room connects
to the courtyard, on the south
portion of which is the entrance to
the rock portion of the tomb, which
includes the rectangular-shaped
chapel with its longest side running
north–south, to which a small room
for offerings is attached. The east wall
of the chapel is decorated with bas-
reliefs which depict scenes of
agriculture and handicrafts, while the
opposite wall shows hunting and
fishing in the swamps. On the portion

H

I

of the west wall between the two
openings that lead to the offerings
room there is a beautiful depiction of
Niankhkhnum and Khnumhotep
embracing each other affectionately.
In this last part of the tomb there are
two symmetrical scenes, with bearers
of offerings to Niankhkhnum shown
on the south wall and those bringing
offerings to Khnumhotep on the
north wall.

F - The funeral
procession, with
priests and bearers of
offerings, moves by on
the east wall of the
vestibule, before the
two owners of the
tomb (not visible in
the picture). Two
boats are visible on
the lower register.

G - This scene, divided
into two registers,
shows the preparation
and cooking of fish,
with the presentation
of offerings shown
below.

H - A number of
boatmen aboard a
papyrus boat play
water games.

I - The two deceased
brothers, united by
strong ties, embrace
each other
affectionately on the
pillar that sets off the
small offerings room.

THE EASTERN SECTOR

The structures of the valley temple of the pyramid of Unas can be seen at the end of the long processional ramp in this sector, located at the foot of the cliffs of the Saqqara plateau, at the edge of a beautiful palm grove near the entrance to the archeological site. Farther west are the ruins of the monastery of St Jeremiah, founded in the fifth century

and destroyed by the Arabs in the mid tenth century.

Only a few traces of the valley temple remain, including the foundations and two pink granite columns with palm-shaped capitals.

Excavations in the area of the monastery, begun by J. E. Quibell in 1907 and since 1968 conducted by the German Archeological Institute, have revealed the remains of the basilica with a nave and two aisles, dating back to the sixth century, and the hospital and refectory buildings.

THE SOUTHERN SECTOR

Although access is difficult (a special permit from the Egyptian Antiquities Organization is required, along with a guide and an off-road vehicle), this part of the archeological zone of Saqqara is extremely interesting and full of monuments.

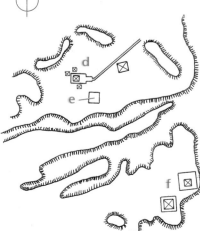

N

A - The archaeological zone at Saqqara is located on a desert limestone plateau that borders the Nile alluvial plain, where there are palm groves and cultivated fields. To the right is the paved road that leads to the site, and to the left the pyramids of Userkaf and Djoser.

B -Numerous trunks of columns and capitals mark the location of what is left of the great monastery of St. Jerome, founded in the 5th century, and dominate the eastern area of Saqqara. The monastery included a basilica with a nave and two aisles, a hospital and a refectory.

C - The first monument that visitors see at the entrance to the archeological area of Saqqara is the remains of Unas' lower temple, marked by two granite columns with palm-shaped capitals. The temple, the excavation of which began in 1937, included a T-shaped wharf.

PLAN OF THE
SOUTHERN SECTOR
a. Pyramid of Pepy I
b. Pyramid of Isesi
c. Pyramid of Merenra
d. Pyramid of Pepy II
e. Mastabat Faraun (Shepseskaf)
f. Pyramids of Mazghuna

THE PYRAMID OF PEPY I

Ancient name: 'Pepy is established
and beautiful'
Original height: 52.5 m
Length of side: 78.5 m
Angle: 53°7'48"

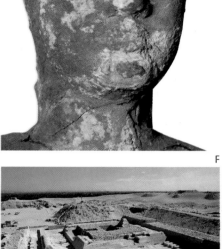

D

Pepy I, the second sovereign of the
Sixth Dynasty, who succeeded his
father Teti, built a beautiful pyramid
in this sector. It was originally about
52 m high and was called *Mennefer*,
'Stable and perfect.' A corruption of
this name gave rise to the word
Memphis, now used to indicate the
capital of the Old Kingdom. In
ancient times it was known as *Ineb-
hedj*, or 'the White Wall.' The name
referred to either a large dam built at
that point of the Nile or to the white
color of its walls, built with blocks of
Tura limestone.

Almost completely destroyed by
continual depredations, this pyramid,
extremely important due to the
written inscriptions on the walls of
the funerary apartments discovered in
1880 and first studied by Gaston
Maspero, has been excavated a
number of times, and excavations
under the direction of Jean-Philippe
Lauer and Jean Leclant, initiated in
1968, are still under way. During the
excavations performed by the French
archeological expedition to Saqqara,
archeologists discovered fully 2,500
blocks of Pyramid Texts from the
inner chambers. These texts, many of
which are unique, were cataloged,
translated and restored to their
original positions.

Excavations have also revealed the
funerary temple on the east side of
the pyramid and the complex
structures on the south side which
included three untitled pyramids,
belonging to royal spouses of Pepy I,
which measured 20.96 m in height
and length of side: no texts were
found in the funerary apartments of
these pyramids.

*D - Pepy I, who
succeeded his father
Teti, was the second
monarch of the Sixth
Dynasty and began*

*the custom of adding
a coronation name to
his birth name: Merira,
or 'beloved of Ra'.
(Cairo Museum)*

E

F

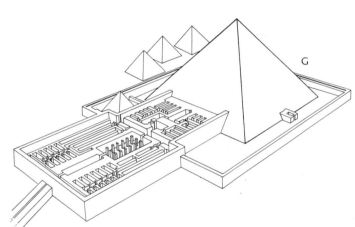

G

*E - The funerary
complex of Pepy I,
which includes the
remains of his
pyramid, was studied
for twenty years
under the direction of
the famous
Egyptologist Jean
Leclant, who
uncovered its
structures and studied
the funerary
apartments inscribed
with the famous
Pyramid Texts.*

H

*F - The pyramid of
Pepy was originally
52.5 m high, and its
sides measured 78.5
m. The structures of
the funerary temple,
on the east side of the
monument, were also
uncovered.*

*G - Reconstruction of
the Pepy I complex
according to data
obtained from
excavations and
research of Audran
Labrousse by the
French Archeological
Mission of Saqqara,
showing the funerary*

*temple on the east
side of the pyramid,
the satellite pyramid
and the three
pyramids of the queens
(by Audran Labrousse).*

*H - Archaeological
excavations have also
made it possible to
use anastylosis to
reassemble the
structures of the
satellite pyramids
located on the
southeast corner of
the pyramid.*

THE PYRAMID OF PEPY II

Ancient name: 'Pepy is most stable in life'
Original height: 52.5 m
Length of side 78.5 m
Angle: 53°7'48"

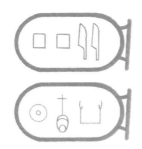

A

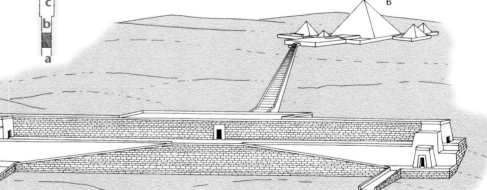

A - The pyramid of Pepy Neferkare, better known as Pepy II, is located directly south of that of Djedkare Isesi, the predecessor of Unas. Despite the length of his reign, which according to Manetho was 95 years, the size of his pyramid is the same as his predecessors Merenre and Pepy I.

PLAN OF THE FUNERARY APARTMENTS OF PEPY II
a. Entrance
b. First corridor
c. Vestibule
d. Granite slabs
e. Second corridor
f. Antechamber
g. Burial chamber
h. Sarcophagus

PLAN OF THE PEPY II COMPLEX
a. Pyramid of Pepy II
b. Pyramid of Queen Ugebten
c. Pyramid of Queen Neit
d. Pyramid of Queen Ipuit
e. Satellite pyramid
f. Enclosure wall
g. Funerary temple
h. Processional ramp
i. Lower temple

B - Reconstruction of the lower temple of Pepy II, characterized by the large terrace with two entry ramps (by Lauer).

The pyramid of Pepy II, the son of Merenre, was built directly north of that of his father, and is one of the best preserved of those in this sector. On the east side of the pyramid of Pepy II, excavated and studied by Gustave Jéquier, are a satellite pyramid and a magnificent funerary temple which connects to its valley temple through the processional ramp. The valley temple is in poor condition. The final part of the descending corridor and the inner chambers are decorated with texts, like the other pyramids of this period.

Around the complex of Pepy II there are also three queens' pyramids: in the southeast corner is the pyramid of Queen Udjebten, while at the northwest corner are those of Queen Ipuit and Queen Neit, the daughter of Pepy I and wife of Merenre. At present the complex of Pepy II is being studied by the Egyptian Antiquities Organization under the direction of Zahi Hawass.

B

THE PYRAMID OF DJEDKARE ISESI

Ancient name: 'Isesi is beauteous'
Original height: 52.5 m
Length of side: 78.5 m
Angle: 53°7'48"

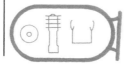

The pyramid of Djedkare Isesi, the predecessor of Unas, is located directly south of the complex of Pepy I, and originally was quite similar in size to that of Pepy I. The layout of the inner chambers of this pyramid, whose external structures even today rise to a height of about 25 m, is similar to that of the pyramid of Unas, but there are no texts on the walls.

THE PYRAMID OF MERENRE

Ancient name: 'Merenre shines with beauty'
Original height: 52.5 m
Length of side: 78.5 m
Angle: 53°7'48"

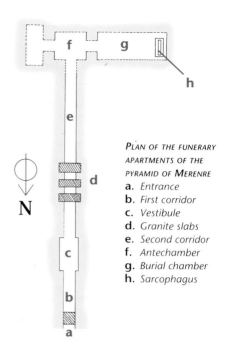

PLAN OF THE FUNERARY APARTMENTS OF THE PYRAMID OF MERENRE
a. *Entrance*
b. *First corridor*
c. *Vestibule*
d. *Granite slabs*
e. *Second corridor*
f. *Antechamber*
g. *Burial chamber*
h. *Sarcophagus*

When Pepy I died after a long reign of about 50 years, he was succeeded by his son Merenre, who built a pyramid not far from that of his father. In 1881 Maspero found the sarcophagus containing the mummy of Merenre in the burial chamber of this pyramid: at present it is the oldest mummy known.

This pyramid, almost completely destroyed, also has inner chambers decorated with Pyramid Texts similar to those found in the pyramid of Pepy I, which are being studied by the French archeological expedition to Saqqara. The combined study of the texts of Merenre, Pepy I and Teti, carried out with the aid of computer technology, has made it possible to create a lexicon and *corpus* including all the Pyramid Texts now known, with a new numeration which takes into consideration their position on the walls.

THE MASTABA EL-FARA'UN

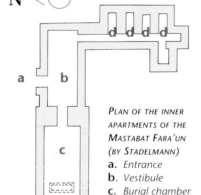

PLAN OF THE INNER APARTMENTS OF THE MASTABAT FARA'UN (BY STADELMANN)
a. *Entrance*
b. *Vestibule*
c. *Burial chamber*
d. *Storehouses*

C

D

The Arabs use the name Mastaba el-Fara'un, 'Pharaoh's bench,' to indicate this gigantic mastaba constructed of enormous blocks of rock originally covered in Tura limestone slabs. It was built for Shepseskaf, son of Menkaure and the last pharaoh of the Fourth Dynasty, who reigned for only four years. The longest side of the monument, which has a rectangular form, measures almost 100 m. The descending corridor, which opens into the north side, leads to a vestibule followed by the burial chamber and a group of storehouses.

C and D - The form of the Mastabat Fara'un, which Mariette opened in 1858, seen from the southwest (above) and the north (below), looks like a sarcophagus. Built of large blocks of limestone covered by slabs of Tura limestone, it was originally 99.50 x 73.30 m in size.

E - Reconstruction of the Mastabat Fara'un, the Arabic name used for the tomb of Shepseskaf, son of Menkaure and the last monarch of the Fourth Dynasty, according to Jequier and Lauer.

E

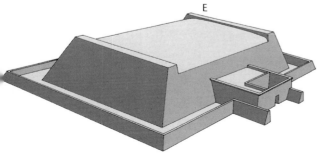

THE PYRAMIDS OF DAHSHUR

A

B

The archeological site of Dahshur, first opened to the public in October 1996, is about 10 km south of Saqqara along a paved road, although in reality the northernmost monuments of the Dahshur area are no more than 2 km south of Saqqara as the crow flies.

Dahshur contains three pyramids from the Middle Kingdom (Twelfth Dynasty) built by Amenemhat II, Sesostris III and Amenemhat III. The pyramids are situated in the eastern portion of the area, in a line running from north to south. Nevertheless, the truly interesting aspect of the site is the two extraordinary pyramids built by Sneferu, the founder of the Fourth Dynasty: the Red Pyramid and the enigmatic Bent Pyramid, which may be considered the first true pyramid built in Egypt. At first it seems difficult to explain the fact that the same sovereign had two pyramids built in the same place, and it has been hotly debated which of the two was built first. Current knowledge leads us to believe that the Bent Pyramid is the older.

Today research and excavations in the Dahshur area being carried out by the German Archeological Institute of Cairo, the expedition of the Metropolitan Museum of New York and the University of Waseda, Japan.

A - The Bent Pyramid (Sneferu's south pyramid) is the most characteristic monument of the Dahshur archaeological site, located about 10 km south of Saqqara and opened to the public in 1996.

B - The Red Pyramid (so-called due to the color of its limestone blocks), or Sneferu's north pyramid, can be considered the first true pyramid built in Egypt, and it is second only to the pyramid of Khufu.

GENERAL PLAN OF
THE DAHSHUR SITE
A *Pyramid of Sesotris III*
B *Red Pyramid (Sneferu's north pyramid)*
C *Pyramid of Amenemhat II*
D *Pyramid of Amenemhat III*
E *Bent Pyramid (Sneferu's south pyramid)*
F *Lower temple of the Bent Pyramid*
G *Fourth Dynasty necropolis*

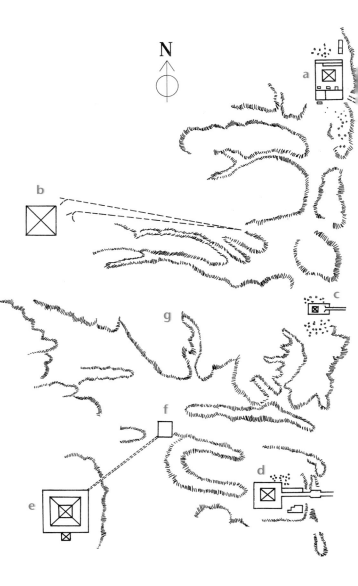

THE PYRAMIDS OF THE FOURTH DYNASTY

THE RED PYRAMID OR NORTH PYRAMID OF SNEFERU

Ancient name: 'Sneferu is shining'
Original height: 104 m
Length of side: 220 m
Angle: 43°22'

C - Sneferu's north pyramid was originally also covered with slabs of Tura limestone. Recent research has led to the conclusion that this is the true burial place of Sneferu, the father of Khufu.

CROSS-SECTION OF THE PYRAMID AND AXONOMETRIC VIEW OF THE INNER CHAMBERS
a. Descending corridor
b. First chamber
c. Second chamber
d. Third chamber (or burial chamber)

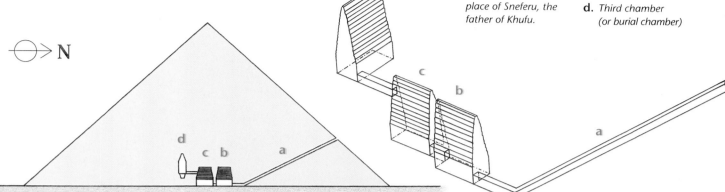

← N

The North Pyramid of Sneferu, commonly known as the Red Pyramid due to the color of the limestone used for its construction, has sides with an angle of 43°22', which corresponds exactly to that of the summit of the Bent Pyramid. This seems to indicate that the architects wanted to take into consideration previous experience, using a plan which was less grandiose but certainly considered safer. In any case, with its side 220 m in length, the Red Pyramid, which was originally covered with slabs of white Tura limestone, to which it owes its name of 'shining pyramid,' is second in size only to the pyramid of Khufu. The entrance to the long corridor that leads to the inner chambers is located on the north side at a height of 28 m from the ground. After continuing for 60 m the corridor opens into an extraordinarily beautiful room with a projecting vaulted ceiling over 12 m high, constructed of eleven beds of limestone blocks, each of which projects a few centimeters out from the one below. From here the corridor leads to a second room, whose center corresponds to the center of the pyramid. It also has a projecting vaulted ceiling. From the second room the corridor ascends for a few meters to reach a third room, with its main axis perpendicular to the preceding rooms. The ceiling of this room,

C

D

E

again vaulted and projecting, is 16 m high. About 400 m east of the pyramid is a vast necropolis from the Fourth Dynasty which has been excavated and studied by the German Archeological Institute under the direction of Rainer Stadelmann.

D - Recent investigations conducted at Dahshur by the German Archaeological Institute of Cairo have revealed the pyramidion that once surmounted the pyramid and which, after restoration, was placed on the eastern side near the remains of the funerary temple.

E - Inside the pyramid are numerous graffiti left by 19th century visitors, including Bernardino Drovetti from the Piedmont region, who was the French consul in Egypt during the early decades of the 19th century.

F - A narrow quadrangular passageway separates the first and second chambers of the Red Pyramid.

G - The roof of the second chamber, with a geometric center that coincides with the base of the Red Pyramid, has a splendid projecting vault over 10 m high.

F

G

THE BENT PYRAMID OR SOUTH PYRAMID OF SNEFERU

Ancient name: 'Sneferu is shining in the south'
Original height: 105 m – planned height 128.5 m
Length of side: 188.60 m
Angle: 54°27'44"–43°22'

A

A - The Bent Pyramid (Sneferu's south pyramid) is located about 2 km from the Red Pyramid (Sneferu's north pyramid). The shift in the inclination of its sides, which gives it its strange form, occurred during the final phase of construction, probably due to the structure's static needs, thus reducing its height by about 23 m. The satellite pyramid can be seen to the right, on the south side.

B - Reconstruction of the sanctuary located on the eastern face of the Bent Pyramid (according to Ricke).

C - A small sanctuary for the royal cult is on the east side of the pyramid. It is similar to that of the pyramid of Meidum, and consists of a table for offerings flanked by two large stelae.

This oddly shaped pyramid, which appears to be older than the North Pyramid, was the first pyramid designed not as a step structure but as a true pyramid. The project was grandiose, and if it had been completed according to plans, the pyramid would have been the largest in Egypt. But during its construction, when it was almost two-thirds of its planned height, the architects suddenly decided to reduce the inclination of the angles by over 10°, from 54°27'44" to 43°22', with a consequent reduction of 23.5 m from its projected height. Nevertheless, it is still the fourth largest pyramid in Egypt, after that of Khufu, the nearby Red Pyramid and the pyramid of Khafre.

The German Egyptologist Ludwig Borchardt hypothesized that the change was caused by the need to complete the pyramid more rapidly due to the unexpected death of the king, but it is much more likely that the architects had noted signs of collapse in the vaults of the inner chambers and thus decided to lighten the static weight by changing the angle of the faces, a solution which gave the pyramid a curious bent form. It also has the peculiarity of possessing two entrances: one on the north side and the other on the west. It may be assumed that this is also related to the signs of structural collapse, and that one of the two descending corridors was blocked because it was considered unsafe.

Access to the funerary apartments was through the entrance located at a height of 11.50 m on the north wall. From here a descending corridor leads to a first room with a vaulted projecting ceiling 17 m high. One must ascend a few meters from the first room to reach two more rooms with vaulted projecting ceilings, located on different levels.

The pyramid had a satellite pyramid on the south side, while on the east side was a small funerary temple built of unfired

B

C

144

PLAN OF THE BENT PYRAMID
a. North entrance
b. West entrance
c. Burial chamber
d. Satellite pyramid
e. Sanctuary for the royal cult (funerary temple)
f. Processional ramp

D - About 700 m east of the Bent Pyramid are the remains of Sneferu's lower temple with its rectangular plan, built of blocks of Tura limestone. It is interesting to note that due to its elevated position far from the Nile flood plain, this temple must have served a different function from that normally attributed to this type of structure, and probably had something to do with the royal cult.

E - The satellite pyramid, originally 26 m high but now reduced to no more than 20, had a small sanctuary on its eastern face. It is believed that this structure had the same function as the 'south tomb' of the Djoser complex.

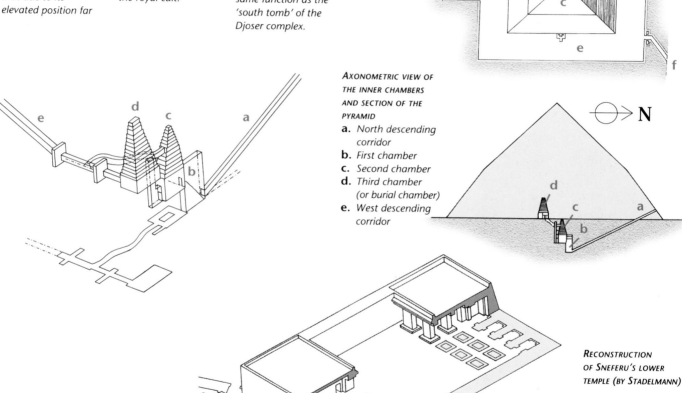

AXONOMETRIC VIEW OF THE INNER CHAMBERS AND SECTION OF THE PYRAMID
a. North descending corridor
b. First chamber
c. Second chamber
d. Third chamber (or burial chamber)
e. West descending corridor

RECONSTRUCTION OF SNEFERU'S LOWER TEMPLE (BY STADELMANN)

brick with two large stelae that framed a table for offerings.

The processional ramp, about 700 m long, began at the northeast corner and ran northeast to the imposing rectangular-shaped valley temple, which measured 47 x 26 m and was built of Tura limestone, surrounded by a wall of unfired brick. The building, which was excavated in the early 1950s by the Egyptian archeologist Ahmed Fakry, included a vestibule in which there were two large rectangular stelae incised with the royal names, and a central court that ended in six chapels.

PLAN OF SNEFERU'S LOWER TEMPLE (BY RICKE)
a. Processional ramp
b. Vestibule
c. Central courtyard
d. Chapels

THE PYRAMIDS OF THE MIDDLE KINGDOM

THE PYRAMID OF SESOSTRIS III

Ancient name: unknown
Original height: 78.5 m
Length of side: 105 m
Angle: 56°18'35"

This is the northernmost pyramid of Dahshur. It was built in unfired brick for Sesostris III, the fifth king of the Twelfth Dynasty. Like all pyramids of the Middle Kingdom, with the exception of that of Amenemhat II, it was originally covered with slabs of Tura limestone which have now almost completely disappeared, and it is now so deteriorated that it looks like a vast pile of rubble about 30 m high. Its nucleus was also severed by a large trench dug by the first explorers, Richard William H. Vyse and John Shea Perring, in 1839, so that they could penetrate the monument.

The entrance to the funerary apartments is no longer on the north side but on the west, where there is a shaft that leads to the funerary chamber, in which a great granite

A - Sesostris III, the son of and successor to Sesostris II, whose pyramid is at el-Lahun in Faiyum, had his pyramid built at Dahshur in the northernmost area of the site. Today this monument, which with its sides 105 m in length was the largest pyramid of the Twelfth Dynasty, is nothing more than a heap of rubble. During the excavation campaign of 1984, de Morgan found the intact tombs of the Princesses Mereret and Sithathor on the northern side of the pyramid.

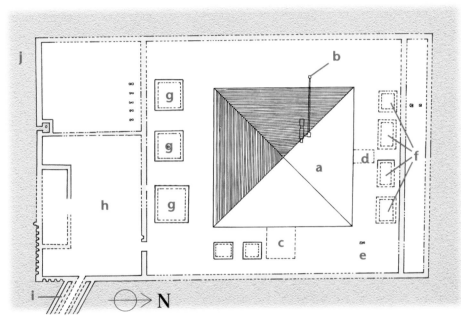

PLAN OF THE SESOSTRIS III COMPLEX
a. Pyramid of Sesostris III
b. Entrance
c. Remains of the east chapel
d. Remains of the north chapel
e. Shaft
f. Mastabas of the princesses
g. Southern mastabas
h. Courtyard
i. Ramp
j. Boat crypt

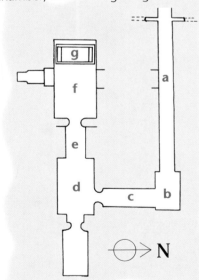

PLAN OF THE INNER CHAMBER OF THE PYRAMID OF SESOSTRIS III
a. Corridor
b. First room
c. Second room
d. Vestibule
e. Antechamber
f. Burial chamber
g. Sarcophagus

B - This gold and amethyst belt and this ankle bracelet were part of the burial trappings of Mereret, daughter of Sesostris III and sister of the future Amenemhat III. The amethyst pearls, arranged in a double row, are interrupted by gold clasps with double feline heads. (Cairo Museum)

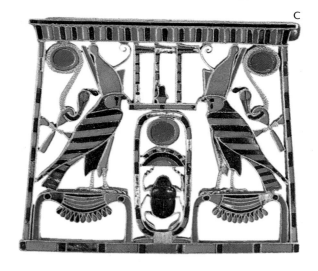

C

D and E - These two magnificent chapel-shaped gold pectorals with amethysts, turquoise, lapis lazuli, carnelian and vitreous pastes, were part of the burial trappings of Mereret. On the first (above), the goddess Nekhbet, with her wings spread, surmounts the cartouche of Sesostris III, beside whom two griffins, representing the power of the king, subject his enemies. In the second one, Nekhbet surmounts the cartouches of Amenemhat III, beside whom the king, this time in human form, is shown destroying his enemies.
(Cairo Museum)

C - This pectoral belongs to the Princess Sathathor, daughter of Sesostris II and sister (perhaps also wife) of Sesostris III. In the center of the chapel-shaped jewel is the cartouche of Sesostris II, beside whom are two hawks with the double crown that symbolized both the god Horus and the king. A similar pectoral is on display at the Metropolitan Museum of New York.
(Cairo Museum)

sarcophagus was found. A second shaft located to the northeast was discovered by Jacques de Morgan in 1894 and is connected to a complex of four tombs of queens and princesses, of which those of Sithathor and Mereret have revealed splendid funerary trappings, now on display in the Cairo Museum. On the south wall of the pyramid de Morgan also discovered three mastabas, two of which he succeeded in entering, and an underground area to the southwest of the pyramid, which contained six wooden boats.

In 1990 the expedition of the New York Metropolitan Museum of Art, under the direction of Dieter Arbold,

D

E

undertook a series of systematic excavations of this area which in 1994 led to the discovery of the entrance to one of the three mastabas discovered by de Morgan on the south side, belonging to Queen Khnemet-nefer-heget, known as Weret, mother of Sesostris III. It contained a rich cache of jewels, some of the most interesting pieces of which include two bracelets with *djed* pillars (which imitated bundles of stalks tied together) and two amethyst scarabs carved with the name of Amenemhat II. The following year the same expedition discovered two new mastabas located north of the pyramid, belonging to the vizier Nebit and his wife Sitwerut.

THE PYRAMID OF AMENEMHAT II, OR THE WHITE PYRAMID

Ancient name: 'Amenemhat is powerful'
Original height: cannot be determined
Length of side: about 50 m
Angle: cannot be determined

A Two gold crowns decorated with semiprecious stones and vitreous pastes adorned the mummy found in the tomb of the Princess Khnumit, discovered by de Morgan in 1894 on the western side of the complex of Amenemhat II. (Cairo Museum)

B This wide collar of gold, lapis lazuli, semiprecious stones and vitreous pastes, with its ends decorated with two hawk heads, may be the most beautiful object found in Khnumit's tomb. (Cairo Museum)

Located about 1.5 km south of the preceding pyramid, the pyramid of Amenemhat II, the son of Sesostris I and third sovereign of the Twelfth Dynasty, was built of limestone, giving it the name of the White Pyramid. Today little more than scattered remains are visible. To the west of the pyramid, excavations by Jacques de Morgan performed in 1894–5 revealed the tombs of Queen Keminub and the chancellor Amenhotep, along with those of the princesses Itaweret, Sithathormerit, Ita and Khnumet. The latter two tombs were still intact and contained sumptuous funerary trappings, now on display in the Cairo Museum.

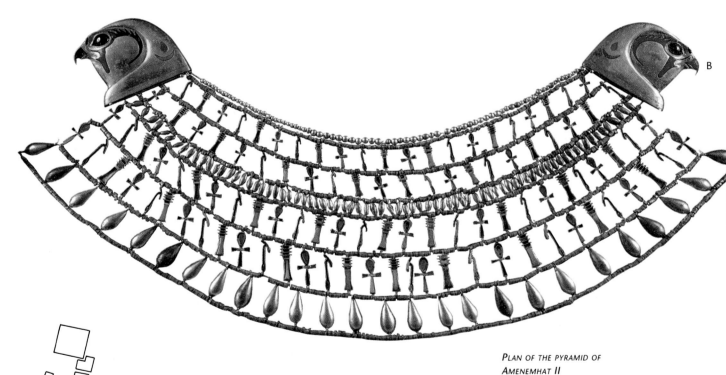

A

B

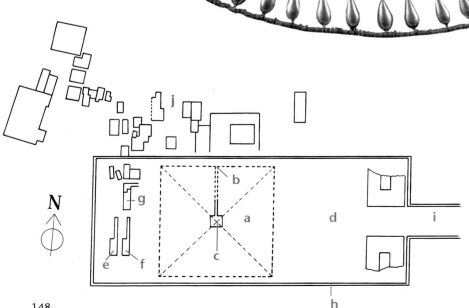

PLAN OF THE PYRAMID OF AMENEMHAT II

a. Pyramid of Amenemhat II
b. Entrance
c. Burial chamber
d. Remains of funerary temple
e. Tomb of Itaweret Sathathor
f. Tomb of Keminub and Amenhotep
g. Tomb of Khnumet and Ita
h. Enclosure wall
i. Ramp
l. Mastabas from the Third Dynasty

N

THE PYRAMID OF AMENEMHAT III, OR THE BLACK PYRAMID

Ancient name: unknown
Original height: 81.5 m
Length of side: 105 m
Angle: 57°15'50"

The pyramid of Amenemhat III, the son of Sesostris III, is commonly known as the Black Pyramid, due to the fact that it was built of dark materials such as unfired brick and basalt, and its black, irregular mass, which rises up about 30 m, stands out uniquely against the horizon.

The pyramid, excavated in 1894–5 by Jacques de Morgan, who also found the basalt pyramidion, now on display in the Cairo Museum, had a complex funerary apartment which

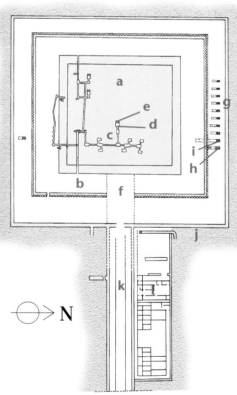

contained a large sarcophagus in pink granite, and its entrance is at the southeast corner outside the wall of the pyramid.

Twelve funerary shafts were also found on the north side, to be used by members of the royal family. King Hor-Auibra of the Thirteenth Dynasty, famous for the marvelous wooden statue depicting his *ka*, now in the Cairo Museum, was buried in one of these shafts.

The pyramid was never used as a royal sepulcher, because Amenemhat III had a second pyramid built at Hawara in Faiyum, where he was buried.

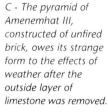

PLAN OF THE PYRAMID OF AMENEMHAT III
a. *Pyramid of Amenemhat III*
b. *Entrance*
c. *Funerary apartment*
d. *Burial chamber of Amenemhat III*
e. *Sarcophagus*
f. *Remains of funerary temple*
g. *Burial shafts of the king and princes*
h. *Burial shaft of King Hor-Auibra*
i. *Tomb of Princess Nubhotep*
j. *Enclosure wall*
k. *Processinal ramp*
l. *Remains of residential building for temple personnel*

C - The pyramid of Amenemhat III, constructed of unfired brick, owes its strange form to the effects of weather after the outside layer of limestone was removed.

D - Like Sneferu, Amenemhat III, shown here, built two pyramids for himself: the first is in Dahshur and the second at Hawara at Faiyum, where he was buried.

E - This wooden statue that represents the ka of Hor-Awibra, the third monarch of the Thirteenth Dynasty, was found in one of the twelve burial shafts discovered by de Morgan in 1894–5 on the north side of the pyramid of Amenemhat II. (Cairo Museum)

THE PYRAMIDS OF MAZGHUNAH

About 4 km south of Dahshur are the remains of two more small Middle Kingdom pyramids in unfired brick. They are known as the pyramids of Mazghunah, after a nearby village.

They may belong to the last two sovereigns of the Twelfth Dynasty, Amenemhat IV and Queen Sobekneferu.

THE PYRAMIDS OF EL-LISHT

Today Lisht is a little village between Saqqara and Meidum, almost parallel to the northernmost part of Faiyum, about 60 km south of Cairo. At the end of the First Intermediate Period, during which Memphis was forced to give up its role as capital to Thebes, the first pharaoh of the Twelfth Dynasty, Amenemhat I, came to the throne and the capital was again moved to the north, the new city being called *Itjtawy*, 'Seizer of the Two Lands.' Located between Memphis and Faiyum, its necropolis was in today's el-Lisht site, just as Saqqara was for Memphis seven centuries earlier. Taking advantage of the proximity of the ancient capital, less than 30 km away, Amenemhat did not hesitate to reuse its

B - The first two kings of the Twelfth Dynasty, Amenemhat I and Sesostris I, founded a new city called It-tawi, located between Memphis and Faiyum. They built their pyramids nearby, at the site known as el-Lisht. In the photo, the pyramid of Amenemhat appears among the palms.

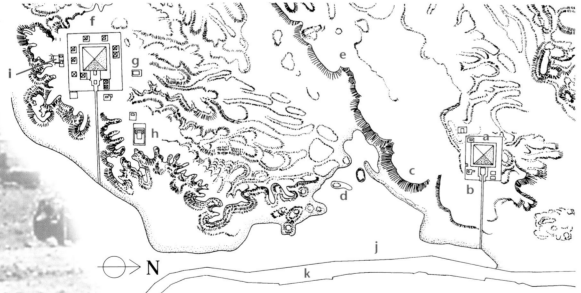

materials in building the new capital, which lasted for almost three centuries, until the Second Intermediate Period.

The necropolis of el-Lisht was explored between 1894 and 1895 by an expedition of the French Institute for Oriental Archeology. Excavations and studies still continue through the work of the American expedition of the Metropolitan Museum of New York.

Excavations have revealed the remains of two pyramids and annexes north and south of the archeological zone. They

date to the reigns of Amenemhat I and Sesostris I respectively. A significant number of private mastabas of high dignitaries and officials of the Middle Kingdom have also been found. When they moved the capital from Thebes to the Memphis region, the first two sovereigns of the Twelfth Dynasty evidently took their inspiration from the traditions of the Old Kingdom, especially with respect to funerary aspects, and they restored the custom of the pyramid as royal tomb.

PLAN OF THE EL-LISHT SITE
a. Pyramid of Amenemhat I
b. Muslim cemetery
c. Tombs from the Old Kingdom
d. Greco-Roman tombs
e. House of the Archeological Mission
f. Pyramid of Sesostris I
g. Northern mastaba
h. Mastaba of Senusret-ankh
i. Southern tombs
j. Village of el-Lisht
k. Canal

THE PYRAMID OF AMENEMHAT I
(North Lisht)

Ancient name: 'Amenemhat is raised to perfection'
Original height: 55 m
Length of side: 78.5 m
Angle: 54°27'44"

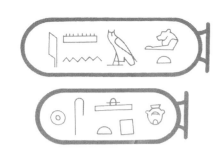

C

The pyramid of Amenemhat I was built on a small embankment, with the annexes, funerary temple and processional ramp located on different levels.

The pyramid was built not only of unfired brick, but also of materials from earlier structures. The funerary temple, located on the east side, was built on a second terrace lower than that of the pyramid, while to the west, outside the wall that surrounds the complex, there was a group of tombs for members of the royal family.

D

E

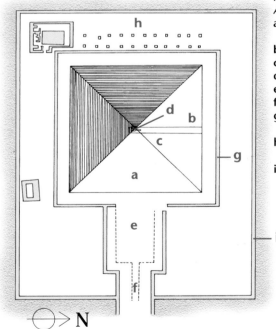

The entrance to the funerary apartment of the pyramid, which has never been thoroughly studied, was located on the north side, where a granite-covered corridor began which led to the burial chamber. As with the pyramid of Teti at Saqqara, the corridor was preceded by a small chapel.

C and D - The pyramid of Amenemhat I is located in the southern part of the el-Lisht archaeological area. Today it is little more than 20 m high. The funerary temple, located on the eastern side, is almost completely destroyed.

E - This head of a woman was found in the area of the pyramid of Amenemhat I, during excavations conducted by the Metropolitan Museum of New York

in 1908. It probably portrays either a princess or a court lady and is sculpted with great skill, using two different kinds of wood.
(Cairo Museum)

THE PYRAMID OF SESOSTRIS I
(South Lisht)

Ancient name: 'Sesostris is most
favored of sites'
Original height: 61 m
Length of side: 105 m
Angle: 49°23'55"

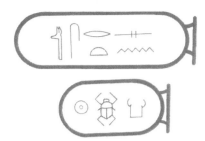

A - This wooden statuette found in a private tomb of el-Lisht, located near the pyramid, represents Sesostris I wearing the white crown of Upper Egypt. (Cairo Museum)

A

PLAN OF THE PYRAMID OF SESOSTRIS I
a. *Pyramid of Sesostris I*
b. *Entrance*
c. *Burial chamber*
d. *Funerary temple*
e. *Satellite pyramid*
f. *Inner enclosure wall*
g. *Courtyard*
h. *Processional ramp*
I. *Secondary pyramids used for female members of the royal family*
j. *Outer enclosure wall*
k. *Pyramid of Queen Nefru, wife of Sesostris*

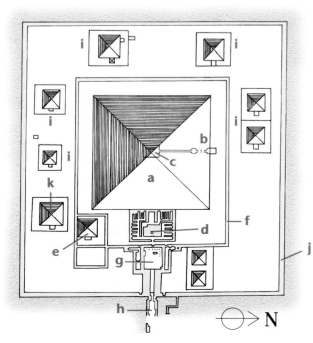

B and D - The pyramid of Sesostris I, or the south pyramid of el-Lisht, has an architectural innovation that would be used in later pyramids as well. Its structure is divided into a series of walls built with large blocks of stone and arranged in a radiating fashion, with the interstices filled with rocks and sand.

The pyramid of Sesostris I, also known as the South Lisht Pyramid, is located 1.6 km south of the previous one, and is more interesting and better preserved.

The monument, discovered in 1882 by Gaston Maspero, was excavated by J. E. Galtier and Gustave Jéquier in 1894 and then by the expedition of the New York Metropolitan Museum between 1908 and 1934. It was built using a technique which would later be used for the pyramid of el-Lahun at Faiyum: first walls were raised using great blocks of limestone radiating from a central nucleus, then the spaces were filled with unfired bricks, and the structure was then covered with slabs of Tura limestone.

The pyramid was surrounded by a double enclosure wall which delimited a rectangular area within which were found ten more secondary pyramids belonging to dignitaries and members of the royal family.

On the east side of the pyramid, where there was also a satellite pyramid, the excavations carried out by Galtier and Jéquier revealed the remains of a funerary temple, of a similar structure to that of the temples built during the Sixth Dynasty, and the remains of a courtyard with a portico supported by 24 columns. Ten beautiful life-size limestone statues were found buried here, depicting the king in a seated position. They are now on display in the Cairo Museum.

The processional ramp ran from the east side of the wall. It is still visible today, bordered by walls decorated with bas-reliefs in a style similar to that of the ramp of Unas at Saqqara. It ran down toward the valley temple, which has not yet been found.

Several mastabas were found near the pyramid, among the most important of which is that of Senusretankh, 'High Priest of Ptah,' located about 200 m east of the outside walls, with a funerary chamber decorated with Pyramid Texts.

C - The funerary temple of Sesostris I is in much better condition than that of Amenemhat I, and uses the plan of the funerary temples of the Sixth Dynasty, on which it is undoubtedly based.

E - During excavations conducted in 1894 by the French Institute of Oriental Archaeology in the area of the funerary temple of Sesostris I, ten large life-size statues of the king were found, now on display at the Cairo Museum.

153

MEIDUM

The archeological site of Meidum is about 50 km south of Dahshur, just a few kilometers from the Faiyum region. Here, in a completely isolated position at the edge of the desert and the cultivated zone, is a strange truncated-cone pyramid within which is a great private necropolis.

THE PYRAMID OF MEIDUM

Ancient name: 'The stable pyramid'
Original height: 93.5 m
Length of side: 147 m
Angle: 51°50'35"

It is traditionally believed that Huni, the last king of the Third Dynasty and successor to Djoser after the brief reigns of Horus Sekhemkhet and Khaba, built a step pyramid at Meidum similar to that of Djoser at Saqqara. It was later covered in a manner which made it look like a true pyramid, but the Arabs continued to call it *el-haram el-kaddab*, or 'the false pyramid.'

In fact the name of Huni never appears in the monument, but some graffiti from the New Kingdom in the small funerary temple refers to his son Sneferu, the founder of the Fourth Dynasty and owner of two pyramids at Dahshur. This written evidence clearly indicates that the Egyptians of the New Kingdom considered Sneferu to be the builder of the pyramid, which his father Huni may simply have begun. In any event, it seems that Sneferu alone was responsible for filling in the steps and transforming the outside appearance of the pyramid. In fact, the various techniques used in constructing the central nucleus and filling in the steps,

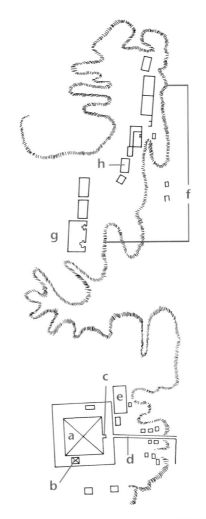

GENERAL PLAN OF THE MEIDUM SITE
A Pyramid of Huni
B Remains of the satellite pyramid
C Offering chapels
D Processional ramp
E Mastaba no.17
F Fourth Dynasty necropolis
G Mastaba of Nefer-Maat
H Mastaba of Rahotep

N

A

B

A - A massive and mysterious pyramid with a strange quadrangular tower form stands at Meidum, about 20 km south of Lisht, in the desert sands at the edge of the Nile alluvial plain, furrowed by a system of irrigation canals. This structure is generally believed to be the remains of the step pyramid of Huni, the last king of the Third Dynasty, later transformed into a true pyramid by Sneferu, the first king of the Fourth Dynasty.

B - The Meidum pyramid, which 19th century travelers knew by the Arabic name of el-haram el-kaddad, or 'the false pyramid,' is considered the transition point between step pyramids and true pyramids. The great novelty is in the position of the burial chamber, which for the first time is incorporated into the body of the pyramid and not in a shaft dug into the rock and surmounted by the pyramid.

C and D - According to one theory, the outer covering of the pyramid slid away due to lack of cohesion with the underlying layers, thus causing the partial collapse that left the central core uncovered. Actually, there is no proof for this theory, and more recent research leads to the conclusion that the pyramid was simply never completed. On the eastern side there is an offerings chapel, followed by a long processional ramp (right).

C

D

along with the graffiti found by the English Egyptologist William M. Flinders Petrie on several blocks dating from the seventeenth year of the reign of Sneferu, would indicate a certain distance in time between the two stages of the work.

Although Mariette was the first to penetrate the pyramid, in 1881, the first systematic excavations in the Meidum area were performed by Petrie between 1888 and 1891. He found several structures, such as the processional ramp and the funerary temple, which later characterized the pyramids of the Fourth Dynasty.

The processional ramp, on an east–west axis, descends toward the cultivated plain, where it disappears, and the valley temple has never been found. On the eastern side of the pyramid there is a chapel for offerings – an early form of the funerary temple, with a much simpler structure that includes two rooms leading to a tiny courtyard with two large stelae that flank a central altar.

On the north side of the pyramid, at a height of 18.5 m, is the entry to the 1.55 m high descending corridor, which leads to the burial chamber with its projecting vault similar to those of the pyramids at Dahshur, and in which no trace of a sarcophagus has been found. Meidum is the first place where the burial chamber is inserted into the body of the pyramid itself, and not in a shaft covered by a superstructure, as in the mastabas. In addition, on the south side, in the space between the pyramid and the enclosure wall, a new structure appears: the satellite pyramid.

Investigations have shown that the pyramid of Meidum was built in three successive phases: the initial pyramid, which had a series of seven super-imposed levels (phase I), was enlarged by raising the steps, of which there were probably eight, and adding a

AXONOMETRIC VIEW OF THE MEIDUM PYRAMID
a. *Entrance*
b. *Descending corridor*
c. *Burial chamber*
d. *Level of detritus*
e. *Phase I*
f. *Phase II*
g. *Phase III*

N

CROSS-SECTION OF THE MEIDUM PYRAMID, BASED ON THE STUDY BY POTRIO AND BORCHARDT
a. *Entrance*
b. *Descending corridor*
c. *Burial chamber*
d. *Level of detritus*
e. *Central core of the seven-step pyramid (phase I)*
f. *Enlargement of the pyramid and raising of the steps (phase II)*
g. *Outside covering (phase III)*

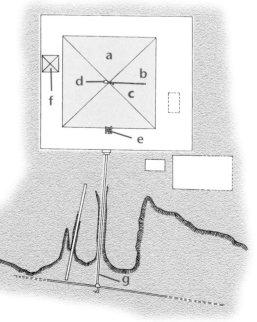

PLAN OF THE MEIDUM COMPLEX
a. *Pyramid*
b. *Entrance*
c. *Descending corridor*
d. *Burial chamber*
e. *Offerings chapel*
f. *Remains of satellite pyramid*
g. *Processional ramp*

new covering layer (phase II). Then during the final phase, probably during the reign of Sneferu, the space between one step and the other was filled in, and a final covering made of smooth limestone slabs that gave the impression of a true pyramid was set into place. The construction of the offerings chapel on the east side of the pyramid seems to date from this last phase.

The transition between the two architectural forms probably reflects a development in theological concepts of the period. While the step pyramid symbolically represented the stairway the soul of the king could use to ascend to heaven, now this celestial ascension could take place along the steep sides of the true pyramid, a purer form that materialized the protecting rays of the sun-god Ra, with whom the soul of the pharaoh would be reunited.

There is a theory that the change Sneferu ordered was not successful, as the outside covering of the pyramid slid off around the lower levels, thus giving the pyramid its present-day curious truncated-cone form. It has been hypothesized that this occurred during the construction of the Bent Pyramid at Dahshur, but this is unlikely. In fact, the presence of a vast necropolis in this area from the Fourth Dynasty, and the graffiti added by visitors from the New Kingdom, lead one to believe that the supposed slippage occurred at a later date.
It has recently been hypothesized that

A

A - The 5.60 m high burial chamber has a projecting vault, constructed using a new technique that would be perfected in Sneferu's pyramids at Dahshur. Mariette was the first to penetrate the Meidum pyramid in 1881.

B - The small offerings chapel discovered by Petrie in 1891, on the eastern side, can be considered a forerunner of the funerary temple.

C

B

D

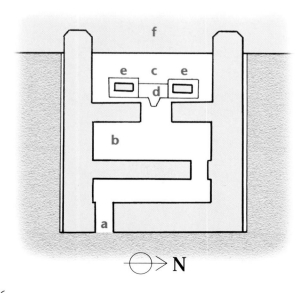

C - The imposing form of anonymous mastaba no. 17, in unfired brick, can be seen a few dozen meters northeast of the pyramid. The mastaba was explored by Petrie in 1917.

D - The chapel consists of a central altar flanked by two large monolithic stelae, preceded by two small rooms.

PLAN OF THE
CHAPEL OF OFFERINGS
a. *Entrance*
b. *Vestibule*
c. *Courtyard*
d. *Offerings altar*
e. *Monolithic stelae*
f. *Pyramid*

the outside layer of filling material never did slip and that the pyramid of Meidum was simply never completed. According to this theory, the accumulation of detritus that still surrounds it today is merely due to the dismantling of the construction ramps.

E

F

Quite near the east side of the pyramid, at the northeast corner, there is an enormous anonymous mastaba of unfired brick which was explored in 1910 by William Flinders Petrie, who labeled it as no. 17. A sarcophagus with a mummy was found inside, but no inscriptions. About 600 m north of the pyramid is a large necropolis for princes and dignitaries of the Fourth Dynasty, from the time of the reign of Sneferu. Several sumptuously decorated tombs were found within it.

In the chapel of mastaba 116 of Prince Neferma'at, probably the son of Sneferu, and his wife Itet, excavated by Auguste Mariette in 1871, a famous painting of geese was found. Known as the Geese of Meidum, it is one of the masterpieces of art of the Old Kingdom, and is now on display in the Cairo Museum. In 1892, in the same tomb, Petrie found two color bas-reliefs

F - One of the most important private mastabas in the necropolis north of the Meidum pyramid belongs to Prince Nefer-Maat, probably the son of Sneferu and his wife Itet.

G

E and G - Two important discoveries were made in the mastaba of Nefer-Maat: in 1871 Mariette discovered the famous painting of a group of geese (E) and in 1892 Petrie found two more paintings (G) of animals and hunting scenes, which used a new technique employing encrustations of vitreous pastes; this technique was subsequently abandoned. (Cairo Museum)

H

depicting small animals and hunting scenes. They used a completely new technique that involved the application of colored vitreous pastes into figures cut into the limestone walls, a technique later abandoned due to its fragility. The mastaba of Prince Rahotep, also probably a son of Sneferu, and his wife Nofret, contains two splendid, colorful limestone statues depicting the deceased, now on display at the Cairo Museum.

H and I - The mastaba of Prince Rahotep is decorated with palace façade molding. This is where Mariette found the two famous painted limestone statues of Rahotep and his wife Nofret, now on display at the Cairo Museum (right).

I

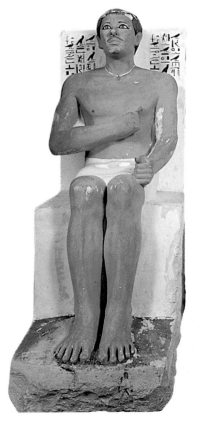

THE PYRAMIDS OF THE FAIYUM

A

B

C

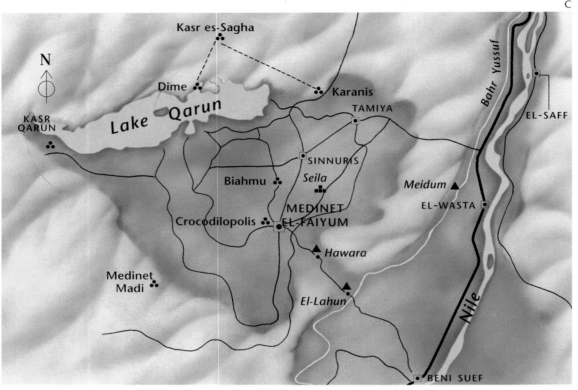

C - Faiyum, a vast verdant region located directly south of Lake Qarun, was extremely important during the Middle Kingdom, when the capital was transferred to el-Lisht. The monarchs of the Middle Kingdom tried to regulate the water system of the area, which received water from the Nile through a great canal called Bhar Yussef, by building major hydraulic works.

A and B - Amenemhat III built a large temple at Faiyum, at Medinet Madi, dedicated to the two principal deities of the region, the crocodile god Sobek and the cobra goddess Renenutet. The temple was further enlarged during the Ptolemaic period, when an important city called Narmuthis rose on this site, and various structures were added, including a dromos surrounded by lion-headed sphinxes.

The Faiyum, often inappropriately called an oasis, is a green, fertile region consisting of a vast, vaguely circular depression connected to the Nile through the *Bahr Yussef*, the 'Canal of Joseph,' with its northwest portion occupied by Lake Qarun (Lake Moeris to ancient authors).

The Coptic name for this area, *Peiom*, gave rise to the name Faiyum. The ancient Egyptians called this region *She-resi*, 'the southern lake' or *Merwer*, 'the great lake.' At the time it was a vast swamp full of animals and luxuriant vegetation.

The Faiyum became quite important during the Middle Kingdom, when the capital was transferred near to el-Lisht, and was selected as a burial ground by two important sovereigns of the Twelfth Dynasty, Sesostris II and Amenemhat III, under whose reign the first dam systems were

D

constructed to regulate the flow of waters of the Nile in the region and improve the crop irrigation system.

Although the pyramids of el-Lahun and Hawara are by far the most important pyramids of Faiyum, they are by no means the only ones. West of Meidum, at the site of Seila, there is also a small step pyramid which is not well-known and has never been studied in depth. It may have been built in the Third Dynasty.

D - The remains of two large foundations which originally supported two colossi of Amenemhat III, located at Biahmu, north of the city of Medinet el-Faiyum next to a large dam, testify to Middle Kingdom efforts to control the waters of el-Faiyum.

THE PYRAMID OF EL-LAHUN

Ancient name: 'Sesostris is shining'
Original height: 48 m
Length of side: 106 m
Angle: 42°35'

Sesostris II, the successor of Amenemhat II and fourth pharaoh of the Twelfth Dynasty, wanted to build his pyramid at el-Lahun near the point at which Bahr Yussef enters Faiyum, a few kilometers from the site of Kom Medinet Ghurab, a settlement which gained some importance during the Eighteenth and Nineteenth Dynasties. The name of the site seems to derive from the Egyptian *ro-hent*, 'entry of the canal,' which in Coptic became *lehoné*.

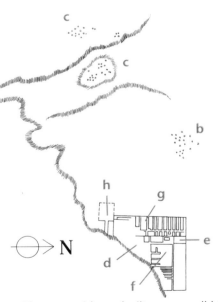

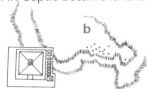

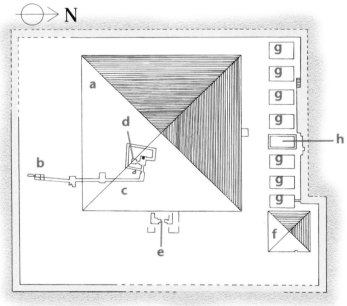

E - The pyramid of el-Lahun was built using the new technique of limestone walls arranged in a radiating fashion, with interstices filled in with unfired brick. This technique was used for the first time in the pyramids of Sesostris I at el-Lisht.

F - The entrance to the funerary apartments was on the south side and had been shifted, probably in order to make it more difficult for any potential grave robbers to find.

The pyramid was built on a small hill 12 m high, using a special technique which involved the preparation of large blocks of limestone placed in a radiating fashion, the spaces between them being filled with unfired brick and then covered with limestone slabs. Access to the funerary apartments was through the eastern portion of the south side, through two shafts. A sarcophagus of pink granite was found in the funerary chamber, which is constructed entirely of granite.

Shaft tombs were also dug on the south side, including the tomb of the princess Sithathoriunet, the daughter of Sesostris II, in which Petrie, who explored the site, found sumptuous funerary trappings known as the Treasure of el-Lahun. On the north side of the pyramid, placed in a parallel position, are a series of small mastabas, and farther east the remains of the queen's pyramid.

Plan of the site of el-Lahun
a. Pyramid of Sesostris II
b. Necropolis
c. Underground tombs
d. Remains of the city of Hetep-Senusret (Kahun)
e. Acropolis
f. Eastern district
g. Western district
h. Remains of lower temple

Plan of the pyramid of Sesostris II
a. Pyramid of Sesostris II
b. Entrance
c. Corridor
d. Burial chamber
e. Remains of an offerings chapel
f. Secondary pyramid
g. Mastabas
h. Tomb of Sithathoriunet

A - A row of
mastabas can be
seen on the northern
side of the pyramid.
They were used for
members of the royal
family. A secondary
pyramid, used for the
queen, is located at
the northeast corner.

C - General view of
the Kahun settlement,
with the acropolis in
the background. The
city was essentially
home to priests and
administrative
personnel employed in
the service of the
pyramid.

B - The masonry
structures of the
acropolis are much
better preserved than
those of the lower
districts. In this part
of the city, where the
royal residence may
have been, the
houses are large, with
central courtyards
and numerous rooms.

D - Petrie found this
gold uraeus, the
sacred cobra, with its
lapis lazuli head and
encrustations of
amazonite and
carnelian, in the
funerary apartments
of the pyramid. The
jewel probably
adorned the king's
crown or wig.
(Cairo Museum)

The valley temple was discovered
east of the pyramid about 1 km away,
not far from the remains of a city which
Petrie named *Kahun*. This is an
extremely important site, as it is one of
only three ancient cities currently
known in all of Egypt. Excavations of
this city, which in ancient times was
known as *Hetep-Senusret*, or 'Sesostris is
satisfied,' were recently recommenced
by a Canadian archeological expedition
under N. B. Miller of the Royal Ontario
Museum, which discovered a working-
class area with small and medium-sized
houses, a residential area with larger
houses and courtyards, and an upper
part of the city forming a sort of
acropolis. This city, in which a myriad
of papyruses written in hieratic script
was found, was undoubtedly
connected to the pyramid, and it may
be considered the only extant example
of a so-called 'pyramid city.'

F - In 1914 Petrie
discovered shaft tombs
on the south side,
including the tombs of
Sithathoriunet, one of
the daughters of Sesostris
II, whose burial trappings
included many pieces of
jewelry, such as this gold
crown decorated with
an uraeus, two plumes
and three double bands:
a series of rosettes is on
the band around the
head.
(Cairo Museum)

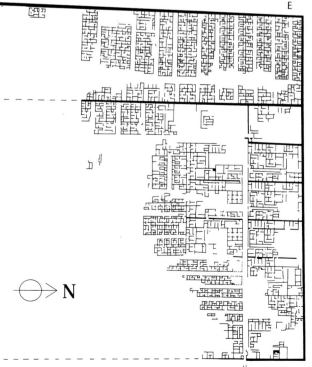

E - Plan of Kahun,
one of the extremely
rare examples of
ancient Egypt cities.
Excavations have
shown the acropolis,
a residential district
and working class
districts.
(by Petrie)

N

THE PYRAMID OF HAWARA

Ancient name: uncertain
Original height: 58 m
Length of side: 100 m
Angle: 48°45'

The site of Hawara is about 8 km southeast of Medinet el-Faiyum, the present-day capital of the Faiyum region. Here, Amenemhat III, after abandoning the plan of being buried in his pyramid at Dahshur, built a second pyramid in unfired brick, originally covered with limestone slabs. Almost 60 m high, it may be considered the last large pyramid built in Egypt.

In the funerary apartments, which are no longer accessible, due to water seepage from a nearby canal, Petrie, who explored the site in 1888–9, found the quartzite royal sarcophagus and a similar but smaller one which has not been positively identified.

On the south side of the pyramid was a vast funerary temple, now reduced to a jumbled mass of muddy heaps from which occasionally

H - Axonometric view of the funerary apartments of the pyramid of Hawara, based on findings by Flinders Petrie.

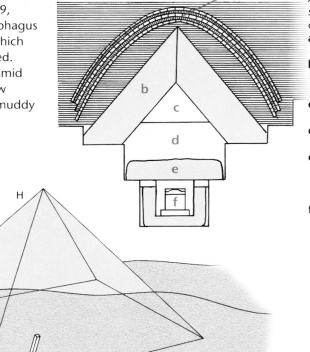

ARCHITECTURAL STRUCTURE OF THE BURIAL CHAMBER
a. *Vault of unfired brick 90 cm thick*
b. *Herringbone-style vault in limestone slabs*
c. *Upper weight relief chamber*
d. *Lower weight relief chamber*
e. *Roof of the burial chamber, formed of three large quartzite slabs*
f. *Sarcophagus*

G - The pyramid of Hawara was the second pyramid built by Amenemhat III, and it is second only to the pyramid of Dahshur in size. It was the last of the great pyramids built in Egypt. The funerary apartments, now inaccessible due to flooding from a nearby canal, were excavated by Petrie in 1888-9, who found the sarcophagus of the king there.

PLAN OF THE HAWARA COMPLEX (BY STADELMANN)
a. *Pyramid*
b. *Entrance*
c. *Corridor*
d. *Burial chamber*
e. *North chape*
f. *Remains of*

funerary temple, known as the Labyrinth
The funerary temple located on the south side of the pyramid of Hawara covered a surface area of 60,000 sq m, and according to

Herodotus had three thousand rooms. The Greeks called this temple the Labyrinth, a word which is a corruption of the coronation name of Amenemhat III, Nimaatra.

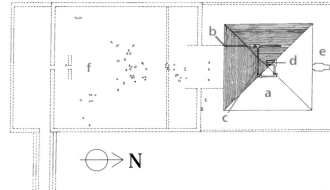

A

B

A and C - The pyramid of Amenemhat III at Hawara, about 10 km northwest of that of Sesostris II at el-Lahun, is located farther within Faiyum, a region in which the monarch wanted to increase his influence. Amenemhat, who reigned for over 40 years, was famous not only for his hydraulic works, but also for his architecture, due to the size and complexity of the funerary temple annexed to his pyramid; Greek historians called it the Labyrinth.

emerge the poorly preserved remains of ancient structures. This temple, mentioned by Herodotus (*Histories* II, 148), Strabo (*Geographica*, XVII, 1, 37) and Pliny (*Nat. Hist.*, XXXXVI, 19), covered a surface area of 60,000 sq m and had an unusual structure consisting of a series of independent rooms placed in three or four rows, connected by a complex system of corridors. Herodotus also states that it contained 3,000 rooms on two levels. The Greeks gave this building the name of 'labyrinth,' according to a theory a corrupt form of Nimaatra (the coronation name of Amenemhat III), which then became Lamares or Labares. North of the pyramid there is a vast necropolis in which, in 1888, Petrie found the celebrated Portraits of Faiyum. These were paintings from the Roman period which use the encaustic technique. They were fitted to the mummy-case at death, reproducing the appearance of the deceased.

The unprofaned tomb of the princess Neferuptah, a daughter of Amenemhat III, was found in 1965, about 2 km south of the pyramid. Funerary trappings, which were found at the same time, are now on display in the Cairo Museum.

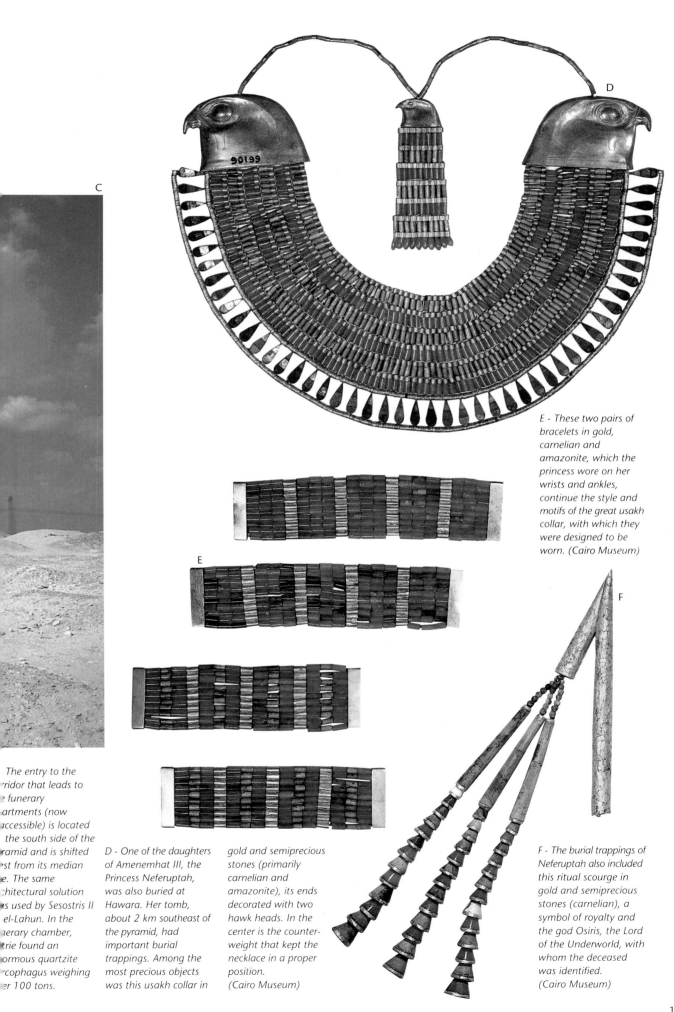

C

D

E

F

E - These two pairs of
bracelets in gold,
carnelian and
amazonite, which the
princess wore on her
wrists and ankles,
continue the style and
motifs of the great usakh
collar, with which they
were designed to be
worn. (Cairo Museum)

The entry to the
rridor that leads to
e funerary
artments (now
accessible) is located
the south side of the
ramid and is shifted
st from its median
e. The same
chitectural solution
s used by Sesostris II
el-Lahun. In the
erary chamber,
trie found an
ormous quartzite
rcophagus weighing
er 100 tons.

D - One of the daughters
of Amenemhat III, the
Princess Neferuptah,
was also buried at
Hawara. Her tomb,
about 2 km southeast of
the pyramid, had
important burial
trappings. Among the
most precious objects
was this usakh collar in

gold and semiprecious
stones (primarily
carnelian and
amazonite), its ends
decorated with two
hawk heads. In the
center is the counter-
weight that kept the
necklace in a proper
position.
(Cairo Museum)

F - The burial trappings of
Neferuptah also included
this ritual scourge in
gold and semiprecious
stones (carnelian), a
symbol of royalty and
the god Osiris, the Lord
of the Underworld, with
whom the deceased
was identified.
(Cairo Museum)

GLOSSARY

ANUBIS
Jackal-headed deity who presided over the embalming process and accompanied the dead to the underworld.

ATUM
A deity representing the sun as Atum-Ra (the demiurge of the cosmogony of Heliopolis); he represented the setting sun in particular.

CANOPIC JARS
Four jars used to hold the lungs, stomach, intestines and liver removed from the body of the deceased during the mummification process.

CARTOUCHE
Beginning in the Fourth Dynasty, the name of the pharaoh was written within this depiction of a loop of cord with a knot at the base. The cartouche, which evokes cyclic rhythms and the universal power of the sun god Ra and thus of the king, who was considered his son on earth, was used for the two most important of the pharaoh's five names, his family name and the name he assumed at his coronation.

CENOTAPH
A symbolic burial place or site of a funerary cult used in lieu of the actual tomb.

HATHOR
Cow-headed (or simply cow-eared) goddess who was the protector of women, music and the dead.

HEB-SED (see Jubilee)

HEDJET
White crown symbolic of dominion over Upper Egypt.

HELIOPOLIS
A city in Lower Egypt, whose ancient name was On (or 'column'); it was the center of the sun cult.

HEKA (scepter)
Symbol of royalty associated with the god Osiris.

HORUS
Extremely ancient sun deity depicted in the form of a hawk (later anthropomorphized), who was identified with the kings of the Early Dynastic period. Horus was in fact considered the protector of royal power.

KA
One of the human souls, representing the life force. Also known as the 'double,' it was created along with the human being but was immortal and ensured the strength necessary for life in the underworld.

KHEPER (or Khepri)
Deity representing the rising sun, depicted as a scarab beetle.

MASTABA
Name used to indicate the non-rock tombs of the Predynastic Period and the Old Kingdom. The word mastaba is of Arabic origin and means 'bench,' and alludes to the outside superstructure of this type of tomb.

MUMMY
Dehydrated body of the deceased, wrapped in narrow strips of cloth. The word comes from the Persian *mumiyah*, which means bitumen, although this substance was used in the mummification process only during Roman times.

NAOS
A stone or wooden tabernacle where the statue of the god was kept within the sanctuary.

NECROPOLIS
Greek word utilized to indicate a burial ground.

NEKHBET
Vulture goddess worshipped at El-Kab and protector of Upper Egypt.

NEKHEKH
Scourge, symbol of authority, associated with the god Osiris.

NOME
Greek word used to indicate the various administrative provinces of ancient Egypt, which were originally called sepat. This system of administrative division of the country probably dates back to the Early Dynastic period, and reached its apex during the Ptolemaic era.

NUBIA
Territory which extended from the First to the Fourth Cataracts. It was divided into Lower Nubia, located between the First and Second Cataracts (known to the Egyptians as Uauat) and Upper Nubia, known as Kush.

OSIRIS
Mummified deity and the ruler of the Underworld. The husband of Isis, he generated their son Horus after he was murdered by his brother Seth. He is depicted wearing an atef, or crown, and holding a scepter and scourge.

OSTRACON
A shard of a terra-cotta jar or fragment of stone, used as a writing surface in place of papyrus.

PALETTE
Lance-shaped stone object, originally utilized as a surface for grinding dyes or cosmetics, but which as early as the Predynastic period assumed a special ritual significance. The scenes which decorated the palettes commemorated details in the reign of the pharaoh. The same name was used to indicate the small wooden board used for the scribes' quills and inks.

PRONAOS
The vestibule of a temple or tomb.

PSCHENT
Double crown symbolizing dominion over Upper and Lower Egypt, formed of a white crown inserted into a red one (see White Crown and Red Crown).

PTAH
Creator god of Memphis, the husband of the lioness goddess Sekhmet; he was depicted as a mummiform man holding a was scepter. He was later identified with the original god of Memphis, Sokari, and was worshipped in the syncretistic form of Ptah-Sokari.

PYRAMIDION
Pyramid-shaped monolith which constituted the summit of a pyramid or the apex of an obelisk.

PYRAMID TEXTS
Collection of magical formulae and invocationswhich were inscribed in the pyramid burial apartments, beginning in the reign of the pharaoh Unas.

RA
Ancient sun god who was originally worshipped primarily in Heliopolis. Ra is depicted as having the head of a hawk, surmounted by the solar disk, or with a ram's head during his nocturnal navigation. Starting in the Fourth Dynasty, the kings of Egypt began to use the name 'son of Ra.'

REGISTER
Horizontal subdivision of wall decorations in tombs and temples and in objects such as funerary stelae.

RESERVE HEADS
Sculptures typical of the Old Kingdom which very realistically depicted the features of and became true substitutes for the deceased.

ROYAL JUBILEE
The royal jubilee, also known as the Sed festival or the Heb-Sed, was a ceremony that generally took place during the thirtieth year of the pharaoh's reign and was intended to regenerate royal power.

ROYAL NAMES (or titles)
A group of names used by the king which, beginning in the Middle Kingdom, was expanded upon until there was a total of five names: the name of Horus, the name of the Two Goddesses, the name of golden Horus, the name of the King of Upper and Lower Egypt (or prenomen) and the name of the son of Ra (or nomen), commonly used to indicate the pharaoh. Only the Horus name was used during the first five dynasties.

SEREKH
Stylized depiction of a palace facade from the Early Dynastic period, surmounted by a hawk, the symbol of the god Horus, with a rectangular open space in which the name of the king was inscribed. The serekh was used during the Early Dynastic period until the end of the Third Dynasty. Starting during the time of Huni, the last pharaoh of this dynasty, the serekh was replaced by the cartouche.

SOLAR BARGE
The boat on which the Sun King navigated the heavens: by day he moved from east to west and by night from west to east.

SPHINX
Lion with human head, the incarnation of royal power and protector of the temple gates.

STELA
Slab of stone or wood in various forms ('false door,' rectangular, curved, etc.), bearing decorations and inscriptions of a funerary nature, or, more rarely, used as votive offerings or for political propaganda by the pharaoh ('royal stelae' and large boundary stelae).

URAEUS
Cobra symbolizing light and royalty. Depicted in a rearing position, it can be seen on the foreheads of most deities and pharaohs. It was sacred to the goddess Wadjet and the sun god, whose eye it was believed to be.

VIZIER
Title held by the person who wielded executive power in ancient Egypt; he acted on behalf of the pharaoh in all aspects of the country's administration.

WADJET (UTO)
Goddess depicted as the uraeus, worshipped in Buto on the Nile Delta and the protector of Lower Egypt.

WAS
Scepter characteristic of male deities.

THE WEST
Represented the realm of the dead (the souls of the deceased go to where the sun sets).

ESSENTIAL BIBLIOGRAPHY

GENERAL TITLES

Baines J., Malek J., *Atlante dell'Antico Egitto*, Novara, 1985

Clayton P.A., *Chronicle of the Pharaohs*, London, 1994

Edwards I.E.S., *The Pyramids of Egypt*, London 1972.

Fakhry A., *The Pyramids,* Chicago and London, 1969

Lauer J.-Ph., *Histoire monumentale des pyramides d'Egypte*, Cairo 1962

Lauer J.-Ph., *Le mystère des pyramides*, Paris 1988

Maragioglio V, Rinaldi C., *Architettura delle piramidi menfite*, Torino and Rapallo, 1963–75

Porter B. and R.L.B. Moss, *Topographical Bibliography of Ancient Egyptian Hieroglyphic Texts, Reliefs and Paintings* , Oxford 1927–52, 1960

Siliotti A. , *Egitto, Templi Uomini e Dei*, Vercelli 1994

Stadelmann R. , *Die Ägyptischen Pyramiden, – Vom Ziegelbau zum Weltwunder*, Mainz am Rhein 1991

Vandier J., *Manuel d'Archéologie Egyptienne*, Paris, 1952–69

EXCAVATIONS, TRAVELS, DISCOVERIES
Belzoni G.B., *Viaggi in Egitto e in Nubia*, critical edition by A. Siliotti, Florence 1988.

Siliotti A. (edited by), *Belluno e l'Egitto*, Verona 1986.

Siliotti A. (edited by), *Padova e l'Egitto*, Florence 1987.

Siliotti A. (edited by), *Viaggiatori Veneti alla scoperta dell'Egitto*, Venice 1985.

ARCHAEOLOGICAL SITES

ABUSIR

Borchardt L., *Das Gradbenkmal des Königs Sa-hu-re*, I–II, Leipzig 1910–13.

Edel E., Wenig S., *Die Jahreszeitenreliefs aus dem Sonnenheiligtum des Königs Ne-user-Re*, Berlin 1974.

Ricke H. et al., *Das Sonnenheiligtum Des Königs Userkaf*, I–II, Cairo 1965.

DAHSHUR

De Morgan J., *Fouilles à Dahchour*, I–II, Wien 1895–1903.

Fakhry A., *The Monuments of Snefru at Dahshur*, I–II, Cairo 1959–61.

El-LAHUN

Petrie W.M.F., *Kahun, Gurob and Hawara*, London 1890.

Petrie W.M.F., *Illahun, Kahun and Gurob 1889–90*, London 1891.

EL-LISHT

Arnold D., *The South Cemeteries of Lisht* I, II, III, New York, 1988–92.

GIZA

Curto S., *Gli scavi italiani a El Ghiza*, Rome 1962.

Dunham D., Simpson W.K., *The Mastaba of Queen Mersyankh III*, Boston 1974.

Junker H., *Giza*, I–XII, Wien/Leipzig 1929–55.

Perring J.E. , *The Pyramids of Gizeh, etc*, London 1839–42.

Petrie W.M.F., *The Pyramids and Temples of Gizeh*, London 1883.

Reisner G.A., *Mycerinus. The Temple of the Third Pyramid at Giza*, Cambridge 1931.

Reisner G.A., *A History of the Giza Necropolis*, I–II, Cambridge 1942–55.

Simpson W.K., *The Mastabas of Kawab, Khafkhufu I and II*, Boston 1978.

MEIDUM

Petrie W.M.F., *Medum*, London 1892.

SAQQARA

Duell P. et al., *The Mastaba of Mereruka*, I–II, Chicago (Ill.) 1938.

Ghoneim M.Z., *Horus Sekhem-khet. The Unfinished Step Pyramid at Saqqara*, I, Cairo 1957.

Lauer J.-Ph., *Saqqara. The Royal Cemetery of Memphis*, London 1979.

*168 Aerial view of
the site of the
pyramid of Khufu.*

ILLUSTRATION CREDITS